PUBLIC REASON AND APPLIED ETHICS

Law, Ethics and Economics

Series Editors:
Christoph Luetge, University of Munich, Germany
Itaru Shimazu, Chiba University, Japan

Law, Ethics and Economics brings together interdisciplinary books which deal with at least two of the three constituents. Among other subjects, this series covers issues in ethics and economics, law and economics, as well as constitutional issues in law, economics, philosophy and social theory. The focus is on theoretical analysis that goes beyond purely normative considerations, thus aiming at a synthesis of the desirable and the feasible.

Also in the Series:

Globalisation and Business Ethics
Edited by Karl Homann, Peter Koslowski and Christoph Luetge
ISBN 978 0 7546 4817 8

Deliberation and Decision
Economics, Constitutional Theory and Deliberative Democracy
Edited by Anne van Aaken, Christian List and Christoph Luetge
ISBN 978 0 7546 2358 8

Public Reason and Applied Ethics

The Ways of Practical Reason in a Pluralist Society

Edited by

ADELA CORTINA
University of Valencia, Spain

DOMINGO GARCÍA-MARZÁ
University of Castellón, Spain

JESÚS CONILL
University of Valencia, Spain

Routledge
Taylor & Francis Group
LONDON AND NEW YORK

First published 2008 by Ashgate Publishing

2 Park Square, Milton Park, Abingdon, Oxon OX14 4RN
711 Third Avenue, New York, NY 10017, USA

Routledge is an imprint of the Taylor & Francis Group, an informa business

First issued in paperback 2016

British Library Cataloguing in Publication Data
Public reason and applied ethics : the ways of practical reason in a pluralist society. - (Law, ethics and economics)
1. Applied ethics 2. Multiculturism
I. Cortina Orts, Adela II. García Marzá, Domingo
III. Conill Sancho, Jesús, 1952-
170

Library of Congress Cataloging in Publication Data
Cortina Orts, Adela.
Public reason and applied ethics : the ways of practical reason in a pluralist society / by Adela Cortina, Domingo García-Marzí, and Jesús Conill.
p. cm. -- (Law, ethics and economics)
Includes index.
ISBN 978-0-7546-7287-6
1. Applied ethics. 2. Multiculturalism. I. Garíma Marzá, Domingo. II. Conill Sancho, Jesús, 1952- III. Title.

BJ1031.C68 2008
170--dc22

2008005039

ISBN 13: 978-0-7546-7287-6 (hbk)
ISBN 13: 978-1-138-26629-2 (pbk)

Contents

Introduction

Applied ethics – or rather, the whole *range* of applied ethics – has become an essential part of practical knowledge in pluralist societies at the start of the third millennium: it is an essential part of that practical knowledge which has since ancient times been attempting to guide human beings' behaviour. If theoretical knowledge has been said to seek to *contemplate* and *know*, and technical knowledge means *knowing how*, practical knowledge constitutes *knowing how to act*, though not only at a specific time, but in one's personal and social life as a whole. It is the sort of knowledge which guides the human world of freedom, the human world of choices.

Since the 1970s that practical knowledge has included *applied ethics*, that is, bioethics, genEthics, economic and business ethics, development ethics, the ethics of the media, ecoethics and infoethics, professional ethics (referring to health, teaching, engineering, architecture, law, psychology and the many other professions) and a wide range of ethical reflections on phenomena which are central to human life, like sports or consumption.

To say that this type of practical reflection is only new insofar as it responds to new, hitherto unseen problems, means one is failing to understand what is happening to us in the early 21st century, for applied ethics unquestionably constitutes a *new form of knowledge*, that is not satisfied with applying already known models to new problems, a *new form of reflecting* on moral problems and proposing recommendations for action.

It is morally pluralist societies which have called for the birth and implementation of these ethics. These societies are the ones needing this interdisciplinary form of knowledge, and it is these that require its active presence in public life. Exercising public reason is vital in the open debate on problems that affect all human beings, on the platform for citizens' participation which the world of public opinion ought to be. In order to supply this public opinion with information, reflection and guidance, the active presence of applied ethics is a basic necessity.

The relevance of this matter, not only for pluralist societies, but also for a globalised world, was precisely what led a research group made up of professors from Valencia and Castellón Universities to undertake for several years different research projects financed by the Ministry of Science and Technology and by ERDF funds,[1] also with the economic support of ÉTNOR ('Foundation for the Ethics of Business and Organisations'). We would here and now like to express our thanks to both of these.

1 The references of the projects mentioned are as follows: PB1997-1419-C02, BFF2001-3185-C02, HUM 2004-06633-C02, HUM 2007-CO2-02/ FISO.

As conceived in the initial project, we have been holding seminar sessions with professors from other Spanish and foreign universities. This book contains the main results of this debate and extends it through a selection of significant contributions. It examines the very status of this new knowledge – the field of applied ethics – vital for a pluralist and democratic society to tackle moral problems from the position of its own conscience. Discourse ethics is the thread running through this reflection in most chapters in the book; however, precisely because discourse ethics is now a widely debated issue, other proposals and critical voices have also been incorporated into the discussion.

The book is divided into four parts. The first of these presents a framework for debate on what the status of applied ethics might be (Cortina); the second part considers the nature of this status, both from a constructive position (Bayertz, Conill), and from a critical point of view (MacIntyre, Hortal); the third part approaches the question of the role of applied ethics in a global world (Apel), taking into account that applied ethics faces undeniable dilemmas (Kettner) and makes the creation of trust possible (García-Marzá); and the fourth and final part considers two case types of application, politics (Pettit) and economy (Luetge).

Turning in greater depth to each of the chapters in this anthology, in the first chapter of part one, 'The Public Task of Applied Ethics: Transnational Civic Ethics', Adela Cortina sets out to establish the general framework for discussion. She starts from the basic fact that applied ethics has arisen from a requirement in society, in other words, out of a demand by social reality, what she terms 'the imperative of social reality'. Due to the diversity of the spheres of reality, the various applied ethics will also vary, each with its own history and literatures. However, a common thread can be seen to run through all of them, as they make up a type of knowledge with a shared structure and characteristics. Cortina proposes an understanding of this knowledge as a 'critical hermeneutics of different human activities'. It is precisely from the public task of the various applied ethics that we can discover an ethical intersubjectivity of a global nature, a transnational ethics. The chapter analyses the peculiarities of this knowledge known as applied ethics and defends the basic idea that responses can never be constructed from one single ethical perspective. In applied ethics, commitment to a single ethical theory is paralysing. We must therefore always recognise the 'Aristotelian', the strategic and the deontological moments within each one of the applied ethics. The three moments may be integrated from a hermeneutically expanded discourse ethics, and therefore closely linked to application.

The second part deals specifically with the state of applied ethics. The chapter by K. Bayertz, 'Self-enlightenment of Applied Ethics', starts from the importance and current success of these disciplines to carry out self-enlightenment and self-reflection on its status. He begins by arguing that applied ethics is not merely a fashion, but rather a philosophical response to the pressure of social problems, and goes on to define the characteristics of this knowledge: the interdisciplinary cooperation, the trans-academic engagement and the claim to institutionalisation of its responses. Applied ethics is not limited to academic thought on problems, but rather is understood as a moment in their solution. However, a set of problems exists that must be faced if the status of specific knowledge is to be maintained; these issues include: the professionalisation of experts, its philosophical frailty, and finally, its pragmatism. The author seeks solutions to part of these limitations in Rawls's idea of reflective equilibrium, with the constant premise that philosophy does not 'own' the process, but is one voice among many.

In his chapter, A. MacIntyre presents a critical approach to the claim that we are dealing with a specific knowledge. The answer to his question 'Does Applied Ethics Rest on a Mistake?' is affirmative. Furthermore, he argues that it is an error that has a harmful influence on moral reflection and on solving the problems society poses. His thesis is that when ethics and morality are correctly understood, the concept of applied ethics loses all its application. The basis of the error consists of the presumption that we understand, on the one hand, the moral rules, and on the other, their application, as two separate and separable reasonings. Reality does not follow this pattern: no rule is separated from its applications. Both are correlative with perception of good and bad. From this point of view, what is hidden behind the current success of applied ethics is the need to find shared public agreements in areas that are decisive for our social life. But the argumentation of 'ethics itself' suffices for this end. The rubric 'applied ethics' is only a barrier to understanding what is really happening.

A. Hortal's chapter 'Applied Ethics and Moral Knowledge' also expresses reticence about the concept of applied ethics, which he considers to be redundant: specifically, any ethical statement that is not applied directly should be able to be so. If it cannot be, its very theoretical value is called into question. His analysis of the status of this knowledge is undertaken from the reflection on the moral knowledge it uses, focusing on the case of professional ethics. To this end he refers to Aristotelian ethics, which the rise of applied ethics appears to have relocated in its rightful place in current ethical reflection, together with authors such as A. MacIntyre and P. Ricoeur, to demonstrate the unity of moral knowledge and its dependence on the good and the basic goals of human life. Only from this dimension is it possible to combine the relationship between moral principals and their application to particular cases. The principles illuminate reality, the morality lived out brings the normative specifications and necessary experiential contrast. Critical hermeneutics, but now from a position of an ethics of good, from the consideration of a dignified and full life.

The final chapter in this part, J. Conill's 'The Hermeneutical and Deliberative Nature of Applied Ethics', suggests the need for a hermeneutics open to a normative or critical level in order to account for the status of applied ethics. In isolation, casuistry on one hand and principalism on the other lead to unilateralities, inefficiencies and dangers. A critical hermeneutics grounded in experiential reason that does not reject the deliberative moment can respond to the public task of practical reason today. This proposal is based on Aristotle and Gadamer, but also on Habermas and Apel. Anyway, if the discourse ethics of Apel and Habermas does not accept that application cannot be separated from understanding, that version of applied ethics is then insufficient. On the other hand, the conventionalism of pragmatic and casuistic approaches is also clear. Obviously we need a synthesis. One example of this proposal for synthesis can be found in Gutmann and Thompson's model of deliberation. Conill proposes extending this political process model of deliberation to the sphere of applied ethics, while removing the 'politicism' these authors bring into it. 'Middle democracy' is not the right name for moral deliberation in civil society. By attempting to extend deliberation to all spheres of social life, the connection between applied ethics and a deeper democracy is clarified.

The third part examines further the public task of applied ethics in current global, plural contexts. This reflection once again turns on discourse ethics. In 'Three Dilemmas in Applied Ethics', M. Kettner starts with the aspiration of applied ethics to contribute a fresh approach to the rational organisation of social praxis. However, this new public relevance also has its detractors. In the end, there is always a concern that a new class of self-appointed, questionable philosophers 'expert' in moral issues will emerge, now transformed into advisors, committee members, etc. He raises three basic dilemmas in the task of all potential 'appliers'. Firstly, difficulties arise in the relationship between the grounding theory and the corresponding conception of the application, the extreme points of which are autonomy and dependence. Secondly, we face problems of grounding, which shift between the cynicism deriving from the sanctuary of the multiplicity of ethical theories and the relativism of mere empirical consensus. Finally, the ideological dilemma emerges between grandiosity and resignation, between utopianism and conservatism, the choice between the disproportionate optimism resulting from a 'new ethics' and the false self-moderation of remaining as a 'mere interpretation of the world'. According to Kettner, these dilemmas can be dissolved through discourse ethics understood as a critical theory of ethics in society, a theory that defines practical discourse and consensual action as the appropriate place to effectuate moral ideas.

In 'Responsibility for Praxis: Discourse Ethics as Applied Ethics', D. García-Marzá continues to uncover the potentialities that discourse ethics offers applied ethics. These potentialities concern the moral capacities we have as individuals and that enable us to take on, from a common will, responsible commitments to resolve conflicts of action. The author proposes an understanding of these capacities as moral resources and examines the specific case of trust, of the moral reasons that underlie their genesis and development. Applied ethics is understood from the reconstruction and management of these moral resources in the different spheres of civil society. Discourse ethics provides a good base for this task, as long as it goes beyond the narrow limits of the Habermasian approach in two essential aspects. Firstly, in the field of application, discourse ethics must be capable of going beyond complementation of the moral and the legal, and through its reflection, reaching all action coordination mechanisms that are not measured in judicial terms. Secondly, the definition of the concept of civil society, as the appropriate sphere for these resources, should be expanded to include all spheres in which power is in fact produced and reproduced, for example the economy and its institutions. Here too, commitments and negotiations occur that demand moral validity. If the boundaries of discourse ethics are not extended in this way, we lose any critical perspective on the various spheres of civil society.

K.-O. Apel's chapter, 'Globalisation and the Need for Universal Ethics', starts from the premise that the new challenges in the age of globalisation demand a post-conventional and post-traditional response from moral philosophy. Thus, a call for the need for a universal ethics would be a call for the mobilisation of moral responsibility on a global scale. Discourse ethics constitutes a procedural frame for possible agreement about any material proposals that can be made with regard to common duties and responsibilities in this global framework. In discussing the ideas of other authors such as Küng or Walzer, Apel defends the need for a transcendental-pragmatic foundation which goes beyond the search for shared moral minimums, and does not fall into the fallacy of confusing the genesis and the validity of moral principles. This autonomous, self-sufficient and rational justification also affects what the author terms part B of ethics, charged with complementing the ideal principle with a principle of responsibility for the necessary changes in social institutions. It is part B that can provide a regulative principle for the various spheres of applied ethics, since it enables the principle of discourse to be applied to the different spheres of daily life.

Applied ethics can constitute a specific structuration of civil society if, and only if, our institutional framework allows and strengthens its development. This institutional point of view is the subject of the last two chapters comprising the fourth part of the anthology. In 'The Domination Complaint', P. Pettit shows how the complaint about domination is placed at the centre of political interests and how, therefore, the ideal of non-domination becomes the basic issue of political reflection because of its characteristics of feasibility and desirability. It is a complaint of the first order that must primarily be attended to through the state, by questioning the political framework, the design of political arrangements in which, as far as possible, the state really is forced to follow up all the interests that citizens recognise as common to all. But the task of preventing the situation in which one cannot do anything without others' permission does not only fall to the state, but is also the task of civil society. Although we cannot rely on the spontaneous measures of the economy and civil society, since they also constitute clear spheres of domination and therefore need a political form, firm support is also needed for civic virtue and commitment in order that state can intervene as an efficient agent to act against domination.

In the second chapter in this part, 'Public Reason and Order Ethics: A Critical Assessment', C. Luetge examines the rational motivation of moral action in the implementation of moral norms and designs an alternative Habermas' response. In modern, systemically differentiated societies, the question of 'how we can ensure that norms are fulfilled' is becoming more urgent and demands, in Luetge's opinion, an ethics that speaks of advantages and incentives, that explain the moral surplus necessary for social cooperation. In sum, it requires an ethics of social order. His argument lies in affirming that individuals cannot fulfil moral norms in conditions of competition if by doing so, they have to bear greater costs that place them at a disadvantage *vis-à-vis* their competitors. The final result can be no other than the erosion of the fulfilment of moral norms. An ethics is needed that is not grounded in altruism, but in self-interest, yet within an institutional framework that establishes the necessary conditions for the use of this morality, based on the long-term calculation of the benefits to each individual. An institutional ethics, therefore, based on the expectation of greater benefits within a series of actions and that allows the development of mechanisms of trust and justice.

The conviction that ethics is an investment in all spheres of social life, and therefore, that applied ethics constitutes a true 'investment' in morally pluralist societies is precisely what has impelled the editors to bring out this collection.

PART 1
The Public Task of Applied Ethics

Chapter 1

The Public Task of Applied Ethics: Transnational Civic Ethics

Adela Cortina[1]

The Birth of Applied Ethics

The imperative of social reality

In countries with a western tradition the 1960s and '70s saw the emergence of both general 'applied ethics' and what in time became known as specific 'applied ethics'. The three turns (linguistic, hermeneutic and pragmatic) taken by last century's philosophy were thus met by a fourth, the 'applied turn', implemented in this case in one of the spheres of philosophy, specifically that of ethics or moral philosophy. At that time the problem of the foundation of morality continued to be the major theme of ethics, but along with this importance was starting to be given to the need to apply what had been gained in the foundation process to everyday life, the need to design ethics applied to the different areas of social life, which would give rise to the different 'applied ethics' (Cortina 1993; 1996; 2007).

Curiously, a large number of writers on philosophy took applied ethics with some scepticism. Used as they were to repeating what the great thinkers had said and to taking as problems what such scholars had taken as problems, the new potential objects of philosophy coming forward proved rather awkward for them, whether these involved biotechnologies, the different scales of business organisations, economic activity, peoples' development, exercising professions, the consequences of new technologies, the structure of the media, the information technology revolution or the construction of peace in the new context. There were similarly so many other questions *from everyday life* calling at the door of philosophical reflection with a view to being allowed in for discussion, but also standing at the door of medicine, biology, economics and business, the professions, information technology, ecology or peace studies, because they needed answers rather than recipes; answers thought out in an interdisciplinary way for a social reality which, as Jesús Conill says in this same publication, is stubbornly interdisciplinary.

It is such a pity that universities divide their campuses into polytechnic and literary universities, and then the latter in turn split into 'Humanities', 'Natural Sciences' and 'Social Sciences', precisely when reality is clamouring for replies

1 University of Valencia.

demanding multi-disciplinary, cooperative work! The point is, as has already been said, reality has problems, universities have departments.

Applied ethics thus emerged, rather than through any 'philosophical imperative', through the *imperative of a social reality which needed them in morally pluralist societies*.

Indeed, in the last quarter of the 20th century western societies become clearly aware that they are morally pluralist, that they cannot take up moral questions from a single moral code, because different codes, different 'ethics of maxima' coexist within them. When it comes to tackling moral questions they cannot therefore take it for granted that there are basic agreements, but have instead to discover these, if they exist, or construct them, if there is any will to do so. And then the inevitable question comes up: what authority is legitimated to tackle moral matters and from what ethics can this be done, bearing in mind that such matters are unavoidable?

This is because everyday life flows on, and does not wait for there to be moral agreements before bringing up situations which demand justice, cases which require solidarity, circumstances which endanger the respect for human dignity. Not only does this pose 'moral dilemmas' (may a doctor conceal the truth about a fearful patient's imminent death, or should the doctor be open about this so as not to breach the rule of truthfulness?), not even does it bring up only 'moral problems' (how should the communication media present news about terrorism?), but demands that activities, institutions and organisations should be gone through from shared values, to be able to say that we really live together, and not merely coexist.

Life does not give any respite to allow members of pluralist societies to come to agreement as regards the values that may enable them to construct their existence together. It continues to bring up questions and problems and in the last third of the 20th century pluralist societies realised that they had to respond and did not know from what standpoint. Not from some sort of 'ethical parliament', because ethical parliaments do not exist. Ethical representatives cannot be elected, but every individual instead has to form their own judgements on moral questions and be the protagonist of their own lives. Not from 'ethical churches', which do not exist either, because churches, synagogues or mosques have authority for their believers, and their statements in the public opinion are doubtlessly something that citizens count on for forming their own moral judgements, but they are not the only authorities involved in this.

In fact, the responses began to come *from diverse social enclaves*, from which applied ethics started to be devised even without setting out to do so expressly.

Polyarchic ethics

Governments, first in the United States, then in Europe and later on elsewhere, formed ethics commissions of different kinds, distinct from legal commissions. A changing reality cannot wait through the long legal processes by means of which a code is approved, and neither are 'legal laws' appropriate for tackling moral problems. Local and national *ad hoc* commissions thus came about to handle biomedical questions, problems brought up by the development of technologies, matters referring to proper government of companies, firms' corporate responsibility, acts of communication media or the behaviour of politicians and public administrations. Their task consisted – and still consists – in preparing documents containing ethical recommendations and guidelines, not in designing legal norms. International bodies understood that people's development or ecological problems are international problems and made specific efforts towards solving these morally through directives of the UN, UNESCO, UNDP or the FAO.

The formation of commissions is a central factor in the development of applied ethics, their composition constituting a major problem, since a good deal of what is materialised as civic ethics depends on their work. The usual procedure is for governments to invite experts from the different fields directly or through other institutions, bearing in mind the multidisciplinary approach: along with professionals from the relevant sphere a number of ethicists, jurists and theologians tend to be members of the commissions. This is why the greatest onus is on those who designate the members of the committees not to do this through party or economic interests but for their ability in the field of ethics and in the subjects of the different disciplines. *Ethical decisions must not be political decisions*.

Now, from our vantage point in the 21st century, we can affirm that a lot of what has been gained in applied ethics is due to the work done by the experts on these commissions and that the theoretical reflections that have been made by ethicists have acted, as Hegel said, like Minerva's owl: from their theoretically-learned background of ethical knowledge, the ethicists who take part in relevant commissions attempt in their reflections to express in concepts what they learned in the sessions and while preparing the documents. This is thus ethics learned in the circus arena and not only on the spectator seats of the university office. It is no surprise that Jonsen and Toulmin should recognise having learned the value of casuistry through their work on the National Commission for the Protection of Human Subjects of Biomedical and Behavior Research, nor that others of us working on the Comisión Nacional de Reproducción humana asistida and on the Comité Ético Asesor para la Investigación Científica y Tecnológica have understood how shared values of civic ethics can be discovered and how this is being built as a transnational civic ethics.

A *second social instance* from which applied ethics is demanded and which cooperates in its preparation is that of the *experts* in different social spheres. On one hand, because they are faced with problems for which there are no straightforward solutions and they need to reflect on these with others. But also because professionals with a vocation often need to refresh their professional activity and wish to exercise this with dignity.

If exercising professional activity demands excellence, and it is not enough just to avoid negligence, then law is insufficient: we need to fashion the *êthos*, the character of the activity, which is formed with values, principles and virtues, not merely following laws. This wish is what leads to committees at hospitals, companies, diverse professional spheres, the concern of certain professional associations with complementing the deontological code with an ethical policy, the preparation of ethical codes, the request for ethical audits.

The point is not to elude any legal obligations by means of corporativist ethical codes, but to draw up a non-corporativist self-regulation scheme, from the experience of experts and also taking into account views of ethicists and representatives of those affected by the professional work involved: with *lay members*.

Public opinion is another of the instances that demands and at the same time draws up ethical responses for current questions. Citizens, increasingly aware of their rights, demand that these should be respected in the different fields, that the different activities are at their service, since they are what give any meaning to the existence of the community. But also they sometimes realise that it is not enough to claim rights, but that responsibilities also need to be assumed with direct participation, either in the different spheres, as laymen in the matter, but as protagonists, insofar as they are affected parties, either at *citizens' conferences* or through public opinion, which is one of the bodies through which 'moral republicanism' is expressed.

Public opinion has historically been, and still is today, one of the central areas in which moral problems are debated and proposals are presented and discussed. The way debate in public opinion is undertaken is essential for determining the moral standard of a society, though quite obviously not so much as the way people live. In the last section of this chapter we will attempt to explain what the role of experts in applied ethics is in public opinion, to prevent 'social moral conscience' from being identified with 'political correctness'.

Lastly, some *moral philosophers* have also understood the commitment with applied ethics in general and with particular applied ethics as part of philosophy's responsibility with its age and with the future. Precisely in pluralist societies, in which there is no single voice authorised for declaring what is morally right and wrong, what has been learned in the different ethical traditions (both as regards the content and the form of knowing) is an important asset for finding the answers which we have been talking about: not the only one, but indeed an essential one. Cooperating with the other fields of knowledge in a republican way, along with experts, jurists, theologians, citizens and governments, is a moral obligation.

At the start of the Third Millennium it can be said that applied ethics constitutes an irrevocable form of knowledge and action, the only possibility for changes in these being to more and to better – precisely because they have not been formed at the request of a single instance, but at the call of citizens, politicians, experts and ethicists. From this fourfold demand came forth pioneering applied ethics (bioethics, genEthics, economic and business ethics, development ethics) and also information technology ethics, media ethics, ecoethics, the diverse branches of professional ethics (engineering, architecture, law, psychology, education, etc.) and a whole broad range of ethical reflections on central phenomena in human life, such as sports or consumption.

But what is more, through having been born through the demands of social reality, these are nowadays not only philosophical disciplines, nor even just interdisciplinary forms of knowledge, but *also form part of the social reality*, and have become incorporated in this *institutionally* with no possible turning back: their efforts are already materialised in institutions, organisations and instruments both in national States and in transnational communities and in the global order, apart from having a more than deserved presence in public opinion. Hegel's dream of incorporating morality in institutions has been fulfilled, at least verbally.

Taifa kingdoms?

Nevertheless, the undeniable current significance of applied ethics does not appear to be on a par with sufficient clarity as regards its status and role. *From the outset*, because each of these ethics has its own date of birth, its own particular history and its own authorised bibliography, meaning that a beholder of this panorama may well see something like the myriad of taifa kingdoms. As for bibliographies, the names of the classic philosophical thinkers are repeated in many of them, obviously, but today's classics are completely different from one bibliography to the next, which is understandable enough, since each of the spheres of applied ethics embodies morality in its own way. Still, precisely because the social spheres are different, few authors are concerned about the birth, status, evolution and future tasks of that particular knowledge which is crystallised in applied ethics as such.

On the other hand, this type of knowledge is anything but static and definitive; it is being fashioned by the imperative of reality and implemented in the evolution of reality, as we gradually discover what this consists of and what its tasks are in a global world. Tasks which are vital – a question of life or death – for the future of humanity. Why?

In view of the path that is being taken by the globalisation process, authorised voices demand that this should be guided from ethics. But 'ethics' as a singular concept does not exist and there are diverse moralities in everyday life (Christian, Islamic, Jewish moralities, moralities connected with different versions of Hinduism, Buddhism, Confucianism, personal and social projects of diverse kinds) and different lines of moral philosophy (eudemonism, utilitarianism, pragmatism, Kantianism, personalism, dialogical ethics, oriental ethics). None of these is hegemonic, none of them is *the* morality or *the* ethics accepted by all humanity.

Hence, to save themselves the trouble of thinking it over, those who avail themselves of idle reason agree that moral questions are highly subjective, that there is no intersubjective, publishable morality acceptable for all human beings, which, if true, is highly unfortunate, above all for the Earth's poorest inhabitants, because we could not talk of any more or less ethical operation of the economy and of businesses, nor of more nor less humanizing biotechnological research, nor of more nor less fair distribution of the goods of the Earth.

But fortunately, it is not true that we lack any shared morality, even though this may not be identified with any of the moralities of everyday life and with any of the ethical philosophies; it is from social realities like the existence and progress of applied ethics, amongst others, from which *it becomes obvious that such moral intersubjectivity does exist*, that we are gradually discovering this, in the sense of the word 'discovery' referring to human things, which consists in uncovering what forms us, partly because we have created this.

The *thesis* of this chapter has a dual nature. It consists in asserting that the nature of applied ethics is that of a *critical hermeneutics of different human activities* and that it is *from the work of applied ethics*, which has been done openly for at least three decades, *that there has been a discovery of that ethical intersubjectivity*, which was first thought to be national, but which in the course of its work is proving to be a *transnational civic ethics*, being formed *velis nolis* into a global ethics. This transnational civic ethics, stemming from the exercise of applied ethics, which is already forging ahead, ought to be added to the range of different routes which are being offered to trace out a global ethics as one of the most promising ones.

Accompanying applied ethics in their birth and development, reading in their development what their status and what their tasks are, attempting to anticipate from this point what they should do in the near future, is the purpose of this chapter.

The Status of Applied Ethics

Why not talk simply of morality or ethics?

The expression 'applied ethics' often feels awkward for at least two reasons. Firstly, because people fail to understand why it should seem important to use it, when its content could similarly be expressed through such creditworthy terms as 'morality' or 'ethics', which have always had, built-in, the need to apply their proposals to everyday life, either directly, or indirectly. A new expression is justified when it provides new contents.

Apart from this, the adjective 'applied' would seem to imply that this is a matter of taking moral or ethical principles with clear content, already shared by all social groups and deductively applying these to specific cases to form moral judgements on these, which is what Arras calls '*casuistry 1*'. We would thus be admitting that there are already shared, clearly specified moral or ethical principles, which is a highly moot point in pluralist societies and would also be modifying the standpoint of Aristotle, who was so reluctant to admit the existence of a 'practical syllogism'. According to Aristotle, one does not proceed deductively from principles to apodictic conclusions in moral questions, but moral judgement instead comes through experience, even by direct perception, and only generates probability.

Since the term 'applied ethics' is the central theme in this book, we shall attempt to reply to these two objections in this section and the following one.

Indeed '*morality*' and '*ethics*' are two expressions which are not distinguished either for their etymological meaning or for the use made of these in everyday life. Nevertheless, *from a philosophical standpoint* they ought to be differentiated because they refer to *two levels of reflection and language*: the level of everyday life, on which human beings have lived since ancient times with moral references, and on the level of ethics or moral philosophy, which reflects on morality as experienced in everyday life. One of the tasks of ethics consists in attempting to explain what morality *consists of*, attempting to *ground this*, meaning enquiring into the reasons for which there is a morality or recognising that there are none, and attempting to *apply* the ethical principles discovered to everyday life (Cortina 1986; 1993; 2003).

Through the enumeration of these three tasks of ethics it can be seen that moralities have 'qualifiers' from everyday life (Christian, Islamic, Jewish, Buddhist moralities) while ethics have philosophical qualifiers (Kantian, communitarian, utilitarian, pragmatist ethics) because they attempt to reflect on the phenomenon of morality as a whole, using the methods and language proper to philosophical traditions for this purpose.

There is doubtlessly a close connection between both levels, because philosophers cannot but reflect on experienced morality and because their reflections flow back as an influence on everyday moral tasks. But the distinction between morality and moral philosophy or ethics becomes necessary, in spite of it all, because morality forms part of human beings' living experience, whether they are experts in ethics or not, while the latter requires a specialised learning process and language. Only from this specific type of reflection can ethics venture to give guidelines for everyday life, and this is why its applied part cannot immediately prescribe actions in specific cases, but only guide them mediately, by providing a reflective framework of principles, values and procedures for specific decision-making. Obviously decisions will always be personal, because everyone is the owner of their own judgement and there are no moral representatives.

What is thus the peculiarity of the new 'applied ethics' as opposed to traditional morality and ethical theories? In order to clear this matter up we should look at four traits, as I see it:

(1) Unlike the different moralities of everyday life, applied ethics expressly resorts to philosophical reflection and language as a fundamental aspect. Precisely because it involves philosophical reflection, it is not everyday morality, but applying what has been gained in the ethical grounding processes to everyday problems. For this reason, the tool that it uses to understand and debate the questions is the one proper to Kantianism, utilitarianism or Aristotelianism.

And in fact, the task which philosophers are entrusted with in applied ethics consists in developing the triple capacity of carrying out practical reasoning, applying a body of knowledge proceeding from philosophical traditions and assuming a commitment to using this dual qualification to value the strength or weakness of arguments and moral positions. Ethicists do not provide a sort of 'moral truth' in Plato's wake, but instead an *argumentative style* and a *background of ethical knowledge* (Dare 1998, 185–6).

(2) Applied ethics limits its sphere of prescription to the exigencies of a *civic ethics* and does not get involved in personal projects of a good life. This means that it does not go beyond the right, aware that it is rationally legitimate to provide moral norms in the field of justice, not in that of happiness. It could thus be said to be the expression of civic ethics in the different spheres of social life.

(3) Traditional ethical theories undoubtedly contain a dimension of application, that we have just mentioned. Not only do Aristotelians, utilitarians and pragmatists give examples of specific cases, not only does Kant himself provide four famous examples in *The Foundations of the Metaphysics of Morals*, but Kant's *Metaphysics of Morals* contains six sections on 'Matters of Casuistry' (Kant 1968 a, 423–7).

There is however an *essential difference* between the applied part of a philosophical theory such as the ones that we have just mentioned and today's applied ethics, as born in the last third of the 20th century. And this is the reason why a specific name is required for them, although the one that they actually have may perhaps not be the most fortunate choice.

Applied ethics are not created by philosophers alone, but mostly by experts in different fields, along with ethicists, jurists, theologians and parties affected, who bring their own convictions and interests into debate. Sometimes, the 'place of discovery' may be academic meetings, but the usual place is committees, commissions and summit conferences. The results of debates are given in academic publications, but also and above all in official documents, which have normative capacity for those who participate in a particular activity or for members of a professional body. If such a capacity is coercive, through sanctions, it is one of the questions of the debate to distinguish moral norms from legal ones, but in any case ethical documents claim to have prescriptive force.

Hence the life of applied ethics does not always follow the usual academic sequence of 'preparation of a text by an author or a group – publication for possible interested parties', but often that of 'interdisciplinary debate – preparation of the text – base publication for legal legislation or itself containing regulatory force'. The way applied ethics is elaborated is thus different from the way the applied part of a traditional philosophical theory is written, and its results, often institutional, are also different from the traditional ones.

(4) For this reason applied ethics *should not be constructed from a single ethical theory*. All those who work on them agree that different problems require the presence of different theories to solve these; not for reasons of eclecticism, but because reality is multilateral and each theory nevertheless tends to focus its attention on one or several of reality's dimensions, and be quite a lot less successful at tackling others.

It is thus important for the ethicist working on applied ethics to have a thorough knowledge of the different ethical theories and have sufficient discernment to be able to explain in each case which of these proves most rewarding to help make decisions. For example, in bioethical matters such as research with embryos, ethics such as that of discourse are little help, and in fact Habermas explicitly refuses to go into that field, while he does indeed tackle that of the ethical self-understanding of the human species (Habermas 2001). Nevertheless, discursive ethics is extremely useful for matters such as informed consent, advanced directives, living wills, or designing the ethics of a company, based on the theory of *stakeholders*. Utilitarianism has problems clearing up who should decide what is useful and in what conditions they should do so. Ethical 'monism' – commitment to a single ethical theory – is paralysing in applied ethics; ethical 'pluralism', resorting to the ethical theories that reality demands, is on the other hand extremely fruitful (Cortina 1993, Ch. 11; Dare 1998, 188).

Now that the idiosyncrasy of general applied ethics has been outlined, let us go on to look at their structure.

Possible, but insufficient models

As we have already pointed out, the expression 'applied ethics' proves misleading, as it prompts a sensation of having a set of principles with a clear and differentiated content and that it is only a matter of applying these to concrete cases. It would thus work in a deductive way, drawing conclusions from axioms for concrete situations. This approach coincides with the traditional model of applying ethics, which John D. Arras has given the name of 'casuistry 1'. Is this the structure proper to applied ethics?

Casuistry 1 – The deductive ideal

Casuistry 1 can be characterised as the 'art of applying any type of moral principles at hand to concrete cases' (Arras 1990, 35), as it considers concrete cases as being a particularisation of general principles (Arras 1990, 35; Gracia 1991, 98–101). This model of application stresses the value of theory, deduction and the search for moral certainty. Historically, its origins lie in Plato's philosophy and the notion of theoretical syllogism of Aristotle and Thomas of Aquinas, pursued later by such thinkers as Spinoza. Its concept is the one proper to a supposed practical syllogism which would have two levels: a universal moment, consisting of universal and axiomatic principles, and a particular moment in which concrete reasons would come into play, and in which prudence proves essential as *recta ratio agibilium*.

In my view, casuistry 1 is impracticable as a method for applied ethics, above all for three reasons:

(1) First, from a historical point of view, Aristotle himself understands that practical reasoning proceeds in a very different way to its theoretical side. In moral questions we proceed more inductively from concrete cases than deductively, and we reach conclusions that may demand probability, not certainty. Comparing cases, exercising prudence in these, stockpiling experiences to resort to these in similar cases is the way to generate practical wisdom, unlike theoretical, scientific wisdom, which proceeds deductively from universal principles to certain conclusions.

(2) Apart from this, to resort to such a model for application one would need to have clear universal material principles, which cannot be supplied by any ethics today, because ethical principles are either universal and thus are formal or procedural, or, if they are material, forfeit universality.

Rawlsian principles of justice, for example, are substantive, but as Rawls himself acknowledges, cannot in theory claim any further validity than for western societies with liberal democracy, because they have been discovered through the method of reflective equilibrium between considered judgements on the justice of western societies with liberal democracy, the original position and principles themselves. As soon as we attempt to form an overlapping consensus which includes non-liberal societies, the content has soon to be cut right back. Michael Walzer expressly affirms that any attempt at universal ethics would lead to such a thin morality that this would be expressed in negative norms, as in the tradition of the second Sinai Tablet, and mark the bounds of what is tolerable, but from that thin morality we are not legitimated to criticise other thick moralities, but only to criticise within our own thick morality and at most, to repudiate the most brutal and offensive injustices (Walzer 1987). On the other side, the utilitarian principle of the greatest pleasure for the greatest number is, as Charles Taylor points out, procedural (Taylor 1989), and the principle of the discourse ethics is universal and openly procedural.

Special consideration should be given to the matter of human rights, which is doubtlessly a key component in a transnational civic ethics. The point is that not only are human rights not universally accepted, but above all these are not principles which have to be applied deductively, but moral demands that have to be interpreted from different contexts of action and from different traditions. The task of critical hermeneutics is thus essential, not that of deduction.

(3) Applied ethics have stemmed more from the 'republican' demands of different areas of social life than from the 'monarchy' of principles with a content having to be imposed on social reality. Concrete situations are not simple particularisations of universal principles but a venue for discovery of principles, moral values and virtues proper to the relevant sphere.

Discarding casuistry 1 from the candidacy as a method of applied ethics leads us to ask about the possibilities of other methods.

Casuistry 2 – An inductive proposal

The term 'casuistry' would seem to have been used for the first time in the Middle Ages, to refer to the form of reasoning or research based on cases rather than theory. Cases are grouped together by types, according to their characteristics ('morphology'); similar cases lead to probability and paradigms can be linked to others until a moral taxonomy of cases is attained. Casuistry was discredited as a method because it was identified with sophistry, and some confessors found alibis for their patrons by casuistic reasoning to morally authorise their desires. The abuse of casuistry led to its discrediting (Jonsen and Toulmin 1988).

Nevertheless, in 1980 a fresh impetus was given to casuistry above all when Jonsen attempted to reply to the question: 'can an ethicist be a consultant?'. Jonsen's reply is affirmative, on condition that the ethicist is a casuist (Jonsen 1980; 1991; Kucewski 1998, 423–5). Indeed, as has already been mentioned, Toulmin and Jonsen recognise that they re-energised casuistry when starting work on the 'National Commission', which had to give guidelines for research with human beings. The commission's work materialised in the famous *Belmont Report*, which designs certain duties of the researcher as to the subject – respect, beneficence and justice – which later became principles of bioethics. Cases are also discussed making use of other medium-range principles, such as impartiality and telling the truth. But what matters is that neither of these were used deductively, but as the *common language with which cases are discussed.*

Indeed, those who defend *casuistry 2* as a form of proceeding in bioethics only wish to explicitly assume the method for reaching rational decisions that bioethics has already taken. That is, they only seek to reflect on their own experiences and formulate these as a method, because they realised that, even though it is impossible for them to reach agreements with other specialists in the field of *ethical principles*, the need to make joint decisions has shown that they can come to an agreement as regards certain maxims to act as guidelines in specific cases. If maxims, obtained by convergence, are enough for rational decision-making, what else need bioethics do other than draw the rationality out of these experiences and give form to this methodically?

Casuistry, specifically what Arras characterises as '*casuistry 2*', has been successful in the sphere of current bioethics, through works such as those of Albert R. Jonsen, Carson Strong or Baruch Brody (Kucewski 1998, 425–9). It is a rhetorical and practical kind of application method, understanding rhetoric to mean the art of making probable judgements on individual and concrete situations. In this type of judgements, which attain probability and not certainty, the solution of conflicts is not reached by the application of axioms formed *a priori*, but by the convergent criterion of all men, or at least that of the most prudent and wise of these, expressed in the form of maxims for action (Gracia 1991, 97–8). Would it not be possible to discover principles proper to each of these in the other fields of applied ethics? Would it not be more useful to attempt to detect the maxims which the wisest and most prudent have been coming to in each of these?

The advantage of *casuistry 2* is that it reflects the steps of a method which already works with excellent results. Nevertheless, it is not true that commissions do not have any ethical principle acting as a legitimatory framework for those of bioethics and any maxims and values that may be discovered in the different spheres of applied ethics. It is just that this principle is not material, as *casuistry 1* would have it; and neither does it proceed from a 'pure' reason as a strict Kantianism would prefer, but from an 'impure', historically generated reason (Conill 1991; 2006). This principle constitutes the ethical background of a democratic and pluralist social and political culture and is modulated in a different way in the different fields of social life (Cortina 1993, Ch. 10).

It is impossible to go into the procedure for seeking that principle here, and for this reason I will simply draw the conclusions from what has been dealt with at length elsewhere (Cortina 1986; 1993; 2000; 2003; 2007). That principle expresses the moral consciousness proper to Kohlberg's post-conventional level in the development of social moral consciousness, and has two facets: one strictly Kantian, which is formulated through the categorical imperative of the End in Itself and the Kingdom of Ends, and another which constitutes putting the Kantian principle into dialogue, and is expressed through the principle of discourse ethics (Cortina 1986; 1993; 2007; Muguerza 1990; Conill 1991; 2006; García-Marzá 1992; 2004). Habermas nevertheless insists that there is no applied ethics, and the form of application that Apel proposes proves unsatisfactory in my opinion. For this reason I will first make some remarks on Apel's proposal and on what I consider to be its shortcomings, and then give my own proposal.

The procedural principle of discourse ethics

The ethics of discourse discovers a *foundation of the moral sphere* which dialogically transforms the Kantian formal principle of autonomy of will into the procedural principle of discourse ethics. This principle may be expressed as follows: 'All beings that are capable of linguistic communication must be recognised as persons, since they are virtual interlocutors in all their acts and expressions, and the unlimited justification of thought cannot relinquish any interlocutor and any of their virtual contributions to discussion' (Apel 1973, 400).

In this text Apel reconstructs from a dialogic perspective two concepts that are already classic in western ethics: the concepts of *person* and *equality*. The person now comes forward as a *valid interlocutor*, who as such must be recognised by anyone belonging to the community of speakers; the idea of equality now becomes communicative, insofar as no-one, no valid interlocutor, can be excluded *a priori* from argumentation when this deals with norms that affect them and their interests must be dialogically taken into account. Or, to put this in Habermas' words: 'Only the rules of action which all those possibly affected could agree with, as participants in a practical discourse, are valid' (1983, 103).

It is clear that this principle proves extremely useful for designing the ethical traits of the processes of dialogue and deliberation intended to discover the validity of ethical norms and to take right decisions, both on committees and in public opinion. However, to apply the principle to social spheres, Apel distinguishes between part A of ethics, which is concerned with the rational grounding of the correctness of norms, and part B, dealing with designing the rational framework of principles which allow the principle discovered in part A to be applied in everyday life. What is the specific aspect of part B?

According to Apel, just as part A is guided by the idea of grounding, part B is led by that of *responsibility*. Because it is one thing to discover the ideal ethical principle, and quite another to apply it to specific contexts, in which the application is always conditioned by the context and the consequences. If the discourse ethics were totally Kantian it would have to demand that its ethical principle should be fulfilled at any time and place. In this case the principle would be formulated as Anne Marie Pieper suggests: '(Always) act as if you were a member of an ideal communication community!' (Apel and Kettner 1992, 36).

Nevertheless, morally demanding that one should always act according to the principle of discourse ethics is an irresponsibility. For this reason one should pay heed to Weber's advice and opt for an ethics of responsibility but – I would add – for an ethics of *convinced responsibility* or *responsible conviction*, because it is not a matter of relinquishing convictions, but of being responsible for the consequences that may lead us to a goal whose value we are persuaded of. In the case of discourse ethics this means, according to Apel, that the application of the principle has to involve the use of *strategic rationality*, on condition that two goals are sought by this: (1) preserving the speaking subject and those who depend on him; (2) laying the material and cultural foundations for it to be possible one day to act communicatively without one's own and others' preservation being endangered. The new dialogical ethical imperative would thus state: 'Always act in such a way that your act leads towards laying the foundations for an ideal community of communication (insofar as this is possible)!'

Indeed, the concern with designing a framework for mediation of the ethical principle by strategic rationality gives discursive ethics a 'realism' which makes it applicable in spheres such as the political, economic domain or the world of violence.

Nevertheless, as opposed to the model of application proposed by Apel, I would like to bring up at least three points:

(1) The necessary use of strategies is an important factor in certain spheres of applied ethics, such as those of business or politics, but not so much in others, such as that of bioethics or ecoethics. The characteristic framework of the application cannot consist in the need to resort to strategies.

(2) In the fields in which this is an important factor, it is not the only one. For a business, for example, being able and having the duty to make use of strategies still says nothing about what the values that should guide the company ought to be (co-responsibility, quality, equity, etc.). That is, it says nothing as to how the recognition of those affected as valid interlocutors gives rise to specific values of that world in that social sphere (Cortina et al. 1994; Conill 2004; García-Marzá 2004; Lozano 2004).

(3) Distinguishing levels (A and B) gives the sensation that we are discovering a principle and have to design a framework to apply this to specific cases, when in the real process of forming applied ethics it is a matter of discovering this in the different spheres and finding out how it should be modulated in each of these. If the 'application' of the principle is understood in this way then it proves useful even in such non-'anthropocentric' fields as ecology.

Applied Ethics as Critical Hermeneutics

Critical hermeneutics

As I have stated in detail elsewhere (Cortina 1993; 1996; 2007), applied ethics have the circular structure proper to *critical hermeneutics*: they do not set out from initial principles with content to apply these, because in pluralist societies there are no common principles with content; neither do they only discover medium-range principles from everyday practice, because in any applied ethics there is a certain claim for unconditionality surpassing all concrete contexts. What these actually do, in the different spheres of social life, is to hermeneutically detect ethical principles and values that come forward in a different manner in each sphere: the ethical principles and values which form civic ethics common to all spheres, which have as background the dual ethical principle already mentioned, the Kantian one of the End in itself and the Kingdom of Ends, and that of acknowledging each person as a valid interlocutor, with its different adaptation for each particular sphere in which we find ourselves.

This dual formal principle is a background guideline, which means that we need to have other ethical traditions to structure the application model. The different traditions have gradually been observed to be unilateral, meaning that there has to be complementarity between them. The classic ethical dichotomies – teleological/deontological ethics, ethics of conviction/of responsibility, proceduralist/substantialist ethics – have to be surpassed in a 'third' ethic which constitutes the truth of both. Nevertheless, what is already obvious today in any attempt to ground morality, proves crystal clear in applied ethics: a single model of ethics is powerless to guide the decisions of the political and economic, medical or ecological realms or simply even daily coexistence.

This is the reason why we are forced to take into account the different models at the appropriate point, although the coordinating item will be the ethics of discourse, because this is rooted in communicative action and in the subsequent arguments, which constitute the *means of coordination* – although not the substance – of other human activities. The idea of the subject as an end in itself and as valid interlocutor forms the common background to all spheres, as in all of these it is the person affected who is ultimately legitimated to expound their interests and only norms which satisfy universalisable interests may be deemed legitimate.

From this standpoint, applied ethics has the structure explained below.

Ethics of social activities (the 'Aristotelian' moment)

As Benjamin Barber affirms, referring in this case to politics, in social life it is necessary to deal with activities first and then with the institutions which sustain them. Otherwise, we run a risk of moulding the activity to the institution, and not vice-versa, when human life, is *vita activa*, to say this in the Aristotelian tradition. What is the moral structure of a social activity?

In my opinion, to undertake an activity morally in a modern society at least five points of reference have to be taken into account: (1) the social goals through which it takes on its meaning; (2) the appropriate mechanisms to attain these in a modern society; (3) the *legal-political structure* of the society in question, as expressed in the constitution and complementary legislation in force; (4) the *demands of civic morality* attained by that society, and (5) the demands for a *critical morality* posed by the principle of discourse ethics (Cortina 1995).

First of all, to analyse what a social activity is I will use an Aristotelian model, specifically, of the concept of 'practice' as MacIntyre reconstructs this in *After Virtue*. Practice is a cooperative activity, which takes on its meaning – its specific rationality – from pursuing certain internal goods, which demands the development of certain habits by those participating in this. These habits will be given the name of 'virtues' precisely because they are the ones that allow us to attain the goods.

By transposing this characterisation to social activities, we could say that the internal good of the health system is the patient's good; that of the company the satisfaction of human needs with quality; that of politics, the common good of citizens, that of education, passing down culture and forming critical persons; that of biotechnologies, research for a freer and happier humanity. Those who take part in one of these activities cannot set themselves just any goal, but the one that it has already been given and which gives its action meaning and social legitimacy.

This implies that inside that sphere 'we deliberate on the means', as Aristotle affirms, not on the ends or ultimate goods, because these are already assigned. And our task consists in explaining what medium-range principles, what values and what specific virtues have to be assumed to achieve those ends.

The different activities are thus characterised by the goods that are only achieved through these, by the medium-range principles, by the values that are discovered in the pursuit of these ends, and by the virtues whose cultivation these require. The different applied ethics have in my opinion the task of discovering what principles, values and virtues allow the internal goods to be attained in sphere of social life.

The contributions of communitarianism, the ethics of virtues and contextualism are essential in this moment in applied ethics.

The strategic moment

To come to the internal goods of each activity the specific mechanisms of that society must be identified – in our case, the mechanisms proper to modern societies. And here the need to resort to *strategies* often comes into play, as is required by an ethics of responsibility.

For example, business activity, in the economic context, pursues an internal good – the satisfaction of human needs – but to achieve this it has to have mechanisms, such as the market, competition and the search for profit, and performing particular values such as the search for quality, the ability to make use of resources, in particular human resources, etc.

Indeed, the fact of having to resort to means such as the search for profit or competitiveness to attain its ends arouses the suspicion that this is an intrinsically immoral activity. Nevertheless, this is not the case, as the good through which it takes on its meaning and social legitimacy cannot be attained in a modern society if this is not through those mechanisms. It is quite a different thing for the means to become an end; in this case the activity is immoral, or rather this is 'demoralised'.

The legal framework

Apart from this, the legitimacy of any social activity demands respecting current legislation, which marks the rules of the game of any institutions and activities which have social goals and effects and thus require legitimacy. In a democratic society the constitutional framework and complementary legislation in force must be abided by.

Nevertheless, complying with legal-political legislation is not enough, because legality does not exhaust morality. And not only because the legal framework might have gaps and shortcomings, but because a democratic constitution is dynamic and has to be reinterpreted historically, and because the sphere of what has to be done will never be wholly reflected in law, and neither would this be advisable. So what are the moral authorities which have to be taken into consideration?

The deontological framework (the 'Kantian' moment)

The *first* of these is the civic moral consciousness attained in a society, that is its civil ethics, if we take 'civil ethics' to mean the set of values that the citizens of a pluralist society already share, whatever their concepts of a good life are. The fact of these already being shared enables them to jointly build part of their common life.

For example, in the present times a company must respect the rights of its employees and those of consumers and suppliers, and cannot infringe these claiming that its goal is to make an economic profit, as expressed in the profit and loss account. Indeed, to satisfy human needs with quality an economic profit has to be made, but not at the expense of the staff's rights, those of consumers or suppliers, and neither can the benefit of the company's shareholders go before the consumers' rights. To obtain social legitimacy an activity must manage at the same time to produce the goods expected of this and respect the rights acknowledged by that society and the values that such a society already shares. For this reason there is an interaction between the values arising from the relevant activity and those of society, between the ethics of that activity and civil ethics, it not being possible to do without either of the two poles without being discredited.

However, this level of morality must be sufficiently explained, unless spurious interests lead this to being deformed in an unwanted sense. If this is the civic ethics of countries which have attained the post-conventional level in the development of the moral consciousness, precisely the fact that this ethics recognises that human beings are valid interlocutors, with an internal value, is what provides a criterion to value the consequences of decisions. This means that any activity or institution which claims to be legitimate has to recognise that those affected by the norms of that area are valid interlocutors and this requires considering that such norms will be just only if they could be accepted by all after a rational dialogue. It therefore obliges those affected to be treated as beings endowed with a set of rights and capacities, which will be specifically adapted in each field.

Consequentialism and deontologism are not opposed, but the special dignity or value of a type of beings (deontological moment) is what gives meaning to the question about the consequences of the decisions *for those beings*, what allows them to be appraised. The unconditional, the value of human beings, in spite of any Rorty style contextualist pragmatism, is essential for the moral world. But this value, as well as the ethical principles of a different level, is discovered in the different spheres, as moral responses are gradually invented.

This is why applied ethics can be said to constitute the phenomenisation of a civic ethics which is gradually fashioned from the different areas of social life, in commissions, committees, codes, audits and in the sphere of public opinion; to constitute the phenomenisation of moral intersubjectivity which is discovered through reflection and action (Cortina 2006).

The different applied ethics thus stem from public reflection, their task consists in solving public matters, and they have an essential role to play in public deliberation. Through their work they are forging a *global ethics* which seems to be irreversible.

The Public Role of Applied Ethics

Need for public deliberation

Insidious reality has gradually pushed experts in different fields, politicians and those affected into taking moral decisions as regards the new problems. How can one come up with answers that are respectful with all the ethics of maxima if this is not done from a civic ethics that all can share? And how can one give such answers intelligently, if these fail to take into account the solutions being found by other countries sharing a similar civic ethics? And how are global replies to be found if this is not by proposing ethical principles that encounter support at businesses, hospitals or research centres, whatever their ideology might be?

This is actually how ethical intersubjectivity is becoming vital to provide a shared response to shared problems from the different ethics of each of the spheres of social life. Experts, politicians and parties affected are being forced to make decisions about new problems from the new situation of pluralist societies, and materialise their moral agreements in documents of different kinds. To draw these up they have documents of morally proximate countries, moral positions expressed through public opinion, and their own personal convictions. This explains why ethical intersubjectivity is being implemented from the bottom, and not from the top, why it is being handled in a republican, not a monarchical or aristocratic manner.

As I see it, the only possible procedure consists in undertaking deliberation processes in the public sphere, to gradually discover together the values and principles of a civic ethics common to different groups. In morally republican societies the deliberation process in the public sphere is essential for coming to joint decisions as to what is fair and what is unfair, what is right and what is wrong. It is therefore a pressing matter to analyse what the process of public deliberation should be and find out what role applied ethics should have in this.

This public deliberation process should be carried out in the domain of public opinion, which is a vital institution in the civil society of a pluralist political community. Nevertheless, it is not easy to make out what the traits of public opinion should be for it to be able to decide in the most appropriate way about what is fair and what unfair. As this is a subject that I have dealt with in depth elsewhere, I will now briefly sum up its content relevant to the matter now concerning us, which is the public role of applied ethics (Cortina 1995; 2006).

Public opinion is an institution of liberal societies, which has a long history (Habermas 1962). In our times different models are available, and I would like to propose one that I consider to be extremely realistic. This is a model which has its starting point in the 18th century liberal republican tradition, specifically in Kant's practical philosophy and which today has two essential, but insufficient patterns, the model of Political Liberalism and the Theory of Discourse (Kant 1968b; 1968c; 1968d; Rawls 1993; Habermas 1992). From the standpoint that I am putting forward, not only the enlightened wise (Kant), or citizens (Rawls), not only those persons who are guided by universalisable interests (Habermas) should participate in public deliberation, but *all those affected* by the decisions. In questions of ecoethics, biotechnologies and development this will often mean all human beings, including future generations and also nature, which obviously requires 'representatives' of its own 'interests'. However, if admittance to the process of public deliberation cannot be refused to any person affected by the decisions, how can such a process of public deliberation be implemented without falling into a 'Babel' of unconnected moral opinions, or actually leaving the decisions to those with greatest strength in the 'fight for recognition'?

The reply to this is in my opinion as follows: precisely because the sphere of freedom is greater, the *responsibility* for participating in public debate is also greater for all those with sufficient information in each of the spheres of social life who pursue satisfaction of universalisable interests in these, aware that ethical norms have to take into account all those affected by these, with no exclusions.

The public role of civic ethics: transnational civic ethics

At this point the role of applied ethics becomes decisive. Applied ethics and public opinion are closely linked and it is important for them to continue to be so in order to be able to give 'high moral-content' responses to moral problems. Indeed, in morally pluralist societies citizens are forced to fashion their moral judgement through reflection and taking public opinion into account. This is why it is so important in this public sphere to pay heed to the opinion of those who work in the different domains thoroughly and professionally and are concerned for the work done in these to take into account the standard of civic ethics attained by that society. This is the task that has been and is still being carried out by different applied ethics: in fact these are new references that citizens can make use of to form their judgement in moral questions.

Discovering these shared values and seeking responsible answers from these is precisely the commitment of National and International Commissions and Associations and the ethics committees of public institutions, which discover as they work how a minimum of moral agreements goes beyond frontiers and gradually fashions a *Transnational civic ethics*.

One example of this form of procedure that could be mentioned is that of the National Bioethics Commissions in different countries, to illustrate what the contribution of applied ethics to the transnational public dimension is and what this can be, so that these commissions are really those which are building a global ethics. Apart from the directions being proposed today, and that have been considered in detail elsewhere (Cortina 2003, Ch. 10), the hermeneutic-coherential approach (Rawls), the hermeneutics of social criticism (Walzer) and Trascendental Pragmatics (Apel), we will thus need to add this fourth approach of a transnational civic ethics, which is implemented from applied ethics and which is constructing genuine global ethics.

In fact, any National Commission which attempts to reflect on Bioethics problems will take into account the documents prepared by commissions from other countries. Such agreements do indeed explicitly respect national legislations, in virtue of the respect for the sovereignty of States. But one should remember that the fact of pluralism is not something existing between states, but instead in each one of these, as these are 'transversal' and the minimum ethics is increasingly shared by all.

This is why *bioethics commissions* increasingly constitute a '*phenomenisation*' of a '*civic morality*, a morality that joins *citizens from different States*, creating a transnational civic bioethics. Discovering these minimums makes them put into play the 'public use of reason' through a deliberative process.

As has already been mentioned, bringing out the minima shared by people and gradually extending the sphere of agreement is specifically essential in the field of Bioethics, because it is these people that are affected by the decisions made in these domains, and it is immoral to decide on such questions without bearing in mind 'what everyone might want'. This can only be done through an always dynamic deliberation process, whose solutions are always open to review. This is above all the case in the realms in which scientific-technical progress constantly provides new data, problems and situations which raise doubts about the previous solutions.

Bioethics thus has to play a role in the public sphere which could be characterised in five ways:

(a) First of all it should develop, in interdisciplinary deliberation processes, its own field which may be useful as a model for public deliberation.

For example, to ethically value any particular practice a bioethics commission has to take at least the following steps: (1) Describing the different aspects in depth from the scientific standpoint. (2) Trying to bring to light and formulate the ethical values that the different social groups already share in respect of this. (3) Revealing the ethical principles which guide such values. (4) Examining in the orientation of the specific action to what extent the agreement is already real and where the disagreements start. (5) Opening up a wide-ranging debate on the points on which there is disagreement. (6) Attempting to reach at least the point at which all the positions seem morally respectable. (7) Offering recommendations for the specific question from the majority position, but obviously making a statement of any discrepancies, which in these cases must be of convictions, not of interests, since 'moral pluralism' does not consist of a diversity of interests that have to be balanced, but of a plurality of ultimate convictions which nevertheless find points of agreement.

Through this gradual discovery of shared ethical values and principles from which to judge what type of practices are humanising and which are not, an increasingly dense civic Bioethics enables an already existing *ethical intersubjectivity*, as opposed to relativism and subjectivism, to be brought to light.

(b) Spreading its information and moral convictions to the public opinion, through disclosures and statements, to foster a 'reasoning public opinion' and to avoid any ideologisation stemming from political or economic interests, thus converting deliberation into a cooperative search for what is most just for human beings.

(c) Gradually constructing a transnational civic Bioethics, already essential, because doing good, respecting autonomy and doing justice – the principles of Bioethics – are principles which can only be followed internationally in a world society. The effects of decisions in Bioethics often affect not only a particular *polis* but a *cosmo-polis*.

(d) Cooperating in shaping the 'ethical ethos' of societies. Codes, committees, audits constitute in my opinion a phenomenisation of the moral consciousness of societies, the tangible expression that moral consciousness takes form in the different spheres of social life.

(e) Cooperating in shaping the fair and wise ethos of biotechnological research and public health practice, thus producing a '*public good*'.

These traits are already common in many cases to the different applied ethics and their public role, and in this respect all of them product public goods. A 'Public good' is a commodity whose use is non-competitive. Those who produce this obtain a benefit through it, but at the same time produce a good which is enjoyed by the whole of society with no need to compete for this. In the case of Bioethics such a society, which enjoys the fair and wise ethos of biotechnological research and public health practice, is already cosmopolitan. As Amartya Sen put it, referring to companies, a firm that operates morally is a public good because its morality is contagious, even though this is a company financed with private capital. As far as we are concerned we could say that embodying the ethical principles mentioned above in the different spheres of social life would be the greatest of public goods.

The 'public role' of applied ethics does not only consist in participating in public deliberations and fostering the public use of reason, but also in embodying its convictions in everyday life, generating a 'public good'.

It could thus be affirmed that this public role of realities like the operation of Bioethics Commissions should be assumed by all the different applied ethics. This is leading to the formation of a global ethics that could make the Kantian dream of a *cosmopolitan ethical community*, governed by *common moral laws*, finally come true.

References

Abernethy, V. (ed.) (1980), *Frontiers in Medical Ethics* (Cambridge, MA: Ballinger).
Apel, K.-O. (1973), *Transformation der Philosophie*, Vol. 2 (Frankfurt: Suhrkamp).
— (1988), *Diskurs und Verantwortung* (Frankfurt: Suhrkamp).
— and Kettner, M. (Hg.) (1992), *Zur Anwendung der Diskursethik in Politik, Recht und Wissenschaft* (Frankfurt: Suhrkamp).
Aranguren, J.L. (1958), *Ética* (Madrid: Revista de Occidente).
Arras, J.D. (1990), 'Common Law Morality', in *Hastings Center Report* 20:4, 35–7.
Bayertz, K. (Hg.) (1991), *Praktische Philosophie. Grundorientierungen angewandter Ethik* (Hamburg: Rowohlt).
Beauchamp, T. (1984), 'On Eliminating the Distinction between Applied Ethics and Ethical Theory', in *Monist* 67, 514–31.
The Belmont Report: Ethical Principles and Guidelines for the Protection of Human Subjects of Research (1978) (Bethesda, Maryland: The National Commission for the Protection of Human Subjects of Biomedical and Behavioral Research).
Conill, J. (1991), *El enigma del animal fantástico* (Madrid: Tecnos).
— (2004), *Horizontes de economía ética* (Madrid: Tecnos).
— (2006), *Ética hermenéutica* (Madrid: Tecnos).
Cortina, A. (1986), *Ética mínima* (Madrid: Tecnos).
— (1993), *Ética aplicada y democracia radical* (Madrid: Tecnos).
— (1995), 'The General Public as the Locus of Ethics in Modern Society', in Ulrich, P. and Sarasin, C. (eds.), pp. 43–58.
— (1997), *Ciudadanos del mundo* (Madrid: Alianza).
— (2000), 'Civil Ethics and the Validity of Law', *Ethical Theory and Moral Practice* 3:1, 39–55.
— (2002), *Por una ética del consumo* (Madrid: Taurus).
— (2003), *Covenant and Contract* (Leuven: Peeters).

—— (2006), 'The Public Role of Bioethics and the Role of the Public', in Rehmann-Sutter, C. et al. (eds), pp. 165–74.
—— (2007), *Ética de la razón cordial* (Oviedo: Nobel).
Chadwick, R. (ed.) (1998), *Encyclopedia of Applied Ethics*, 4 vols. (San Diego: Academic Press).
Dare, T. (1998), 'Challenges to Applied Ethics', in Chadwick, R. (ed.), pp. 183–90.
García-Marzá, D. (1992), *Ética de la justicia* (Madrid: Tecnos).
—— (2004), *Ética empresarial* (Madrid: Trotta).
Gracia, D. (1988), *Fundamentos de bioética* (Madrid: EUDEMA).
—— (1991), *Procedimientos de decisión en ética clínica* (Madrid: EUDEMA).
Habermas, J. (1962), *Strukturwandel der Öffentlichkeit* (Darmstadt: Hermann Luchterhand).
—— (1983), *Moralbewusstsein und kommunikatives Handeln* (Frankfurt: Suhrkamp).
—— (1992), *Faktizität und Geltung* (Frankfurt: Suhrkamp).
—— (2001), *Die Zukunft der menschlichen Natur* (Frankfurt: Suhrkamp).
Jonsen, A.R. (1980), 'Can an Ethicist be a Consultant?', in Abernethy, V. (ed.), pp. 157–71.
—— (1991), 'Casuistry as Methodology in Clinical Ethics', *Theoretical Medicine* 12:4, 295–307.
—— and Toulmin, S. (1988), *The Abuse of Casuistry. A History of Moral Reasoning* (Berkeley: University of California Press).
Kant, I. (1968a), *Grundlegung zur Metaphysik der Sitten*, Vol. 4 (Berlin: Walter de Gruyter), pp. 385–464.
—— (1968b), *Beantwortung der Frage: Was ist Aufklärung?*, Vol. 8 (Berlin: Walter de Gruyter), pp. 33–42.
—— (1968c), *Zum ewigen Frieden*, Vol. 8 (Berlin: Walter de Gruyter), pp. 341–86.
—— (1968d), *Die Metaphysik der Sitten* (Berlin: Walter de Gruyter), pp. 203–494.
Kettner, M. (Hg.) (2000), *Angewandte Ethik als Politikum* (Frankfurt: Suhrkamp), pp. 21–50.
Kucewski, M. (1998), 'Casuistry', in Chadwik, R. (ed.), Vol. 1, pp. 423–32.
Lenoir, F. (1991), *Le temps de la responsabilité* (Paris: Fayard).
Lipovetsky, G. (1992), *Le crepúscule du devoir* (Paris: Gallimard).
Lozano, J.F. (2004), *Códigos de ética empresarial* (Madrid: Trotta).
MacIntyre, A. (1981), *After Virtue* (London: Duckworth).
Martínez Navarro, E. (2000), *Ética para el desarrollo de los pueblos* (Madrid: Trotta).
Muguerza, J. (1990), *Desde la perplejidad* (Madrid: F.C.E.).
Nida-Rümelin, J. (Hg.) (1996), *Angewandte Ethik. Die Bereichsethiken und ihre theoretische Fundierung* (Stuttgart, Kröner).
Noble, C. (1982), 'Ethics and Experts', *Hastings Centre Report* 12, 7–15.
Oakley, J. and Cocking, D. (2001), *Virtue Ethics and Professional Roles* (Cambridge: Cambridge University Press).
Putnam, R.D. (1993), *Making Democracy Work* (Princeton: Princeton University Press).
Rawls, J. (1993), *Political Liberalism. Lecture VI* (Columbia: Columbia University Press).
Rehmann-Sutter, C. et al. (eds.) (2006), *Bioethics in Cultural Contexts. Interdisciplinary Approaches* (Dordrecht: Springer).

Rosenthal, D. and Shehadi, F. (eds) (1988), *Applied Ethics and Ethical Theory* (Salt Lake City: University of Utah Press).
Sosoe, L.K. (1998), *La vie des normes et l'esprit des lois* (Paris: L'Harmattan).
Taylor, C. (1989), *Sources of the Self* (Cambridge, MA: Harvard University Press).
Ulrich, P.R. and Sarasin, C. (eds) (1995), *Facing Public Interest* (Dordrecht: Kluwer Academic Publishers).
Walzer, M. (1987), *Interpretation and Social Criticism* (Cambridge, MA: Harvard University Press).
Winkler, E. and Coombs, G. (eds) (1993), *Applied Ethics: A Reader* (Oxford: Blackwell Publishing).

PART 2
The Status of Applied Ethics

Chapter 2

Self-enlightenment of Applied Ethics

Kurt Bayertz[1]

In a remarkably short period, applied ethics has established itself as a sub-discipline of moral philosophy in both academic teaching and research. The number and variety of specialist publications expands as rapidly as the number of journals and conferences. At the same time, it has become apparent that (a) applied ethics is increasingly being integrated into the training procedures of various professions and that (b) the field is being called upon on different levels of practical decision-making, for instance, in ethics commissions or parliamentary advisory committees. Thereby, it has expanded beyond the realms of academic moral philosophy into a *public role.* Applied ethics has an impact not only in the form of books and essays but also in the form of practical decisions and thus action. This impact is not occasional or coincidental, but rather regular and systematical.

Applied ethicists have noted this success with satisfaction, but not perceived it as an opportunity for self-reflection. One question, especially, has rarely been raised: What are the consequences of the institutionalisation of applied ethics for the function and structure of moral thought? The essential self-reference which has always characterised philosophy seems to have fully reverted to problem-reference in the case of applied ethics. The political success of applied ethics and the *responsibility* stemming from its new public role could have provided a good opening for self-reflection and self-enlightenment. I take the thoughts developed in this article as a step in this direction. First I would like to delineate what is currently perceived as the purpose and definition of 'applied ethics' and what can be regarded as its social function. Then, I will outline some changes in the social status of morality that are linked with the project of applied ethics. I will conclude with a few observations on the types of thought and argumentation found in applied ethics.

I

Appropriately, the self-reflection of applied ethics should start with an account of the social context in which it developed and its function within the context. Present-day societies are characterised by a tremendous acceleration of social change. This change leads to various 'redundancies' which are made public by the ever-present media

1 University of Münster. Copyright © 1999 Taylor & Francis Group. Source: P. Kampits and A. Weiberg (eds), *Angewandte Ethik/Applied Ethics*, Wien: Verlag Hölde-Pichler-Tempsky, 1999, pp. 73–89. Translated by Doris Schroed and Garrath Williams.

and perceived as problems worth discussing. In democratic systems, it is difficult to enforce solutions 'from above'. Power and authority are not the only elements within public discourse; arguments are relevant too. Formulated more generally: Modern societies are reflective societies; nearly everything in them can become the object of communication and reflection. In a first approximation, applied ethics can be understood as one part of this communication and reflection process which tries to apply philosophical methods to a growing number of problems. Although ethics has always reacted to social problems (as has philosophy in general), this reaction was mostly abstract and indirect. The difference between traditional and applied ethics lies in the latter's direct approach to social problems.

Seen from this perspective, the amazing success of applied ethics loses its appearance as merely fashionable and instead fits into broader tendencies within history and society. In addition, its often mocked categorisation into various sub-disciplines (bio-, business-, environmental, computer-, even museums- and bankruptcy-ethics)[2] becomes more comprehensible. If ethical reflection is seen as part of society's self-reflection and if society is divided into various sub-subsystems and institutions. this differentiation must be reflected in a similar differentiation of ethics. It is therefore unreasonable to hope or fear that applied ethics will disappear without trace as have other philosophical fashions. The field will continue to grow as society encounters new problems.

Which types of problem does this apply to? Problems for applied ethics are, above all characterised by four features. (a) They are, evidently, of a normative nature, resulting from a loss of orientation and a growing uncertainty about right actions. (b) Another distinctive feature is that they are – so to speak – thrown into being by life itself (Bayertz 1994, 22). The field does not deal with hypothetical problems used by philosophers to illuminate their thought or to illustrate their teachings. Instead, applied ethics deals with 'real' problems that are perceived as such by non-philosophers and that require a solution. (c) Even though these problems are normative, they are in a non-trivial and often complex way linked to empirical questions. In order to find solutions it is often necessary to have detailed knowledge of factual connections; in many cases, interdisciplinary co-operation is inevitable. (d) The direct connection with reality implies that often small and very specific problems have to be dealt with. Applied ethics does not investigate the 'problem of death in a technological society' but the 'legitimacy of therapy abatement in terminally ill patients'. And it does not ask about the 'nature of women and their relationship to men' but about the 'legitimacy of affirmative action in the public sector'.

An additional feature of applied ethics is its aim to go beyond theoretical reflection and offer practical solutions or, at least, contribute to solutions. When Martin Heidegger studies the area of reproductive biology and medicine, his perspective differs fundamentally from reflections within applied ethics that deal with in-vitro-fertilisation and similar techniques. For Heidegger 'artificial impregnation' (1954, 91)

---

2 This is not a joke as Kilpi's book (1998) shows. The advertising material of the publisher innocently says: 'The fundamental ethical problem in bankruptcy is that insolvents have promised to pay their debts but cannot keep their promise. *The Ethics of Bankruptcy* examines the morality of bankruptcy.'

is a sign of the 'void of the being-desolation of the self-centred human for whom the consumption of being for the making of technology, including culture, is the only way to rescue subjectivity into the state of superhuman-dom' (1954, 87). Heidegger takes the project of artificially creating human beings as an opportunity to illustrate his philosophical diagnosis of decay. It represents a 'topic' of his reflections, but not a 'problem' to whose solution they might contribute. However, this is exactly the demand which characterises applied ethics and this is of significant importance because it steers the field beyond the limits of academic 'philosophy'. For obvious reasons, the probability of helping salve the sort of social problems sketched above is higher if applied ethicists are engaged in ethics commissions and political consultancy rather than restricting their work to university seminars, journals and conferences. The 'trans-academic' engagement of applied philosophy is a consequence of its practical demands.

The tendency towards engagement beyond the Academy not only results from shifting interests of applied ethicists. The increased institutional employment of applied ethicists shows that this engagement is being welcomed by society and accepted by its various subsystems. If it is correct modern societies are characterised by increasingly intense self-observation and self-reflection and if it is true applied ethics can be understood as part of this process. It is not surprising that the search for orientation is no longer restricted to the private initiative of passionate thinkers, and instead is finding a more permanent foundation. Modern societies have developed *special organs* for self-observation, particularly the sciences and the media – and most recently applied ethics.

The increasing institutionalisation of applied ethics is most pronounced in the bio-sciences and medicine. Various forms of ethics committee have long been established in OS hospitals, laboratories and other health institutions. Now, several European countries have started to form similar committees. Specialist institutionalised activities are evident at four levels: (a) ethics committees of single hospitals or research institutions at *local* level; (b) *national* ethics commissions, for example, within the German Bundersitz Kammer (National Chamber of Physicians) or the ministry of health; (c) several working groups of the EU and the European Council at the *translational* level; (d) and specialist committees of UNESCO at the *global* level. In short: bioethics is the most advanced institutionalised sub-discipline of applied ethics.

The above institutional activities do not, of course, represent the whole spectrum of applied ethics which remains a sub-discipline of the academic field of philosophy with its traditional activities of research and teaching. As a sub-discipline, it cannot be separated from theoretical ethics and general philosophical reflection. However, it must be stressed that applied ethics has an inherent tendency to go beyond the limits of philosophical reflection and engage within institutions. My article focuses on this striving for direct practical effectiveness, of which the institutionalised form of applied ethics is the purest example. This leads to my first claim:

> The institutionalised role of applied ethics points to a changed purpose for ethical reflection within modern societies. I would call this change a process of "politicisation". Applied ethics does not only reflect problems of modern societies in a theoretical manner;

> but understands itself as a part of society's problem-solving process. Due to this direct practical involvement, the field relinquishes its distanced position from social reality. It leaves philosophical departments and allows itself to become involved in practical institutionalised processes of problem-solving.

Evidently, the context and the 'form' of ethical reflection changes significantly with this institutionalisation. Without claiming comprehensiveness, I would like to stress five aspects of this change. (1) The paradigmatic *subject* of applied ethics is no Socrates who incites interested citizens on the marketplace to engage in shared reflection; no scholar who – on his or her own initiative – starts to reflect on a problem; and no populist[3] who rebels against authority. Instead, the subject is a professor (that is, a civil servant) appointed to a commission that has to fulfil a specific task. (2) In most cases, the *aim* of commission work is not the advancement of knowledge or the deepening of understanding *per se,* but a practically useful recommendation, directive or decision. (3) The *process* of work and reflection does not take place in unconstrained solitude but rather within the framework of a committee alongside representatives from other professions and within a certain set of roles; philosophy does not govern the proceedings but represents only one voice amongst many. (4) The *end-product* of this process is not a text written according to the roles and traditions of scientific publishing but rather a protocol, a report, a recommendation or a directive. This end-product must achieve more than just truthfulness (for example, practical relevance, feasibility, legal acceptability and so on). (5) The *addressees* of the product are not academic colleagues but a non-academic audience that is not interested in exploring knowledge but practical use.

I would like to stress one aspect of this development here. Philosophers are being appointed to committees and councils because it is assumed that they can competently answer normative questions due to their education and experience. In other words: because people are confident that philosophers have a particularly marked ability for moral reflection and judgement. It must be assumed that they believe in this ability themselves, otherwise they would not accept the responsibilities. This, however, means that philosophers take on the role of *experts* in questions of morality,[4] a role which, in the history of moral thought, has mostly been rejected. In the famous myth that Protagoras narrates all political and moral virtues are being declared common

---

3 In a recent interview Paul Ricoeur remarked upon the changing times and the resulting shift for philosophical tasks: 'The modern or postmodern philosopher, whatever you prefer to call him, can never be a populist such as Sartre again. He is rather somebody who works in a team with people from other fields – natural scientists, lawyers, physicians. economists and politicians. Our contribution as intellectuals are arguments and rationally justified moral convictions.'

4 I will open the understanding that commissions and councils as a whole take on this role. Such commissions and councils usually include representatives from different professions and disciplines. Hence, philosophers only represent one perspective amongst many. On the other hand, it is philosophers (possibly in conjunction with theologians) who emphasise the moral and normative perspective, whereas natural and social scientists concentrate on empirical issues. It is true, however, that roles are not always distributed so clearly. In any case, in this article I focus on the role of philosophy and philosophers.

property of humankind (*Protagoras* 322a–23a). Kant also believed that 'common reason' can have the same hope to hit the right moral judgement as a philosopher (1785, 404). Theories and positions that give decisive powers in questions of morality to specified elites were always an exception.[5] It is, hence, not surprising that expertise in morality as it is institutionalised in committees and councils of the above type would meet with scepticism and reservations.

It is beyond the scope of this article to discuss the arguments brought forward *against* the professionalisation of moral (not ethical) discourse be they metaethical or political. On the other hand, it is difficult to ignore the argument that topics relevant in applied ethics are very complex, both in their normative and their empirical aspects, and that common sense *on its own* cannot provide decisions. A solution requires lengthy reflection and a solid training; in other words: competent experts. If my interpretation of the context within which applied ethics developed and became institutionalised is correct, this is an inevitable, social process. Certainly, *public discourse* will not be made redundant by this development. However, for a variety of practical reasons, public discourses are not well suited to make the necessary decisions, if only because these discourses are in principle open-ended. As in the case of politics, which in a democratic society cannot be removed from public debate but can neither dispense with professional experts, it is necessary to find possibilities for meaningful co-operation on moral questions between public discourse and moral expertise.[6]

II

The institutionalisation of applied ethics is a feature which distinguishes the field markedly from traditional ethics but which has nevertheless not received much attention from moral philosophers. The reason is probably that this

---

5 Plato belongs to the exceptions because he developed the infamous model of philosopher king rule in the *Republic* (47Ic–4b). The same is true for Nietzsche who tried to enthrone philosophers as 'Legislators of Value Estimations' (1882–85, 258f.).

6 How delicate this question is can be deduced from the rather convoluted comment of an otherwise clear and concise ethicist like Bernard Gert. On the one hand, he strictly rejects the idea of 'moral experts'. On the other hand, he has to admit that the quality of moral decision-making depends upon competence which cannot be presumed in every citizen alike.

> Of course some people are better at dealing with moral problems than others, partly due to their training and experience, and partly due to their intelligence and good judgement. But skill in making moral decisions is not an academic speciality, and no one can legitimately claim to be a moral expert. Unfortunately, some people, including some philosophers, have taken the title of 'ethicist' as if they were experts concerning moral decisions in fields such as business or medicine in the same way that chemists are experts in chemistry. The primary task of philosophers, including moral philosophers, is to clarify. They can also sometimes show whether a commonly held view is justified. Moral philosophers clarify the nature of morality and try to show that it is justified, but those who have a better knowledge of the relevant facts and more experience in the relevant field are more likely to make better moral decisions in that field (Gert 1998, 11).

institutionalisation is regarded as a mere surface feature which might be interesting to moral sociologists but which is insignificant for moral philosophers. Such a distinction between (sociological) form and (ethical) content is rash and superficial. The institutionalisation has, as I will show, implications from a philosophical point of view. We saw that the object of applied ethics presents itself mostly in the form of 'real' problems and that these problems are normative. A considerable proportion of them are being raised as the consequence of scientific-technological progress. This process constantly produces new possibilities for action for which existing moral norms and values do not offer adequate evaluation criteria. It is sufficient to just name the numerous techniques with which human beings can be created (or produced?) either now or in the near future: artificial insemination, in-vitro-fertilisation, embryo transfer, surrogate motherhood, cloning, to evoke a series of impressive examples for such direct problems. But not *every* technical innovation creates problems of this type. Microwaves, for instance, represent without any doubt a revolutionary, new procedure to heat water-containing substances. Nevertheless, the development and implementation of this technique neither provoked controversial public debates nor significant efforts from applied ethicists. The reason for this is simple: Although this procedure might be revolutionary in its technical aspects it is completely harmless from an ethical point of view. It is not evident how the use of a microwave could clash with moral norms. However, what would happen if a technical innovation were to stand in *obvious* and *serious* opposition to moral norms and values within our society? Let us think of a computer module which would allow us to kill any Internet user at any place in the world, at any time without being able to trace the sender of the command. Such a 'module of gyges' would probably not achieve a better mobilisation of applied ethics than the microwave. The evil of such a module would be too obvious; it would be a problem for the police not for applied ethics.

This draws our attention to one characteristic feature of problems for applied ethics that has not been mentioned before. Normally, alternatives for actions present a 'problem' if they can neither unambiguously nor without doubt be declared 'morally permissible' or 'morally reprehensible'. Their normative content lies in the fact that they can be discussed using terms such as 'on the one hand – on the other hand', without an obvious leaning to either side *at the beginning*. There are good arguments for both sides. (This does not exclude the possibility that some individuals or groups have made up their mind in favour of 'on the one hand' at the start and for whom it is *a priori* clear that the specified option for action is permissible or reprehensible. If there is nevertheless a 'problem' in the described meaning of the word, it is because simultaneously *other* individuals and groups exist who decided at the start in favour of 'on the other hand'.) Applied ethics, therefore, grows in a sphere of moral in-between. Its area is an evaluative and normative *clair-obscur*, where light and shadow need to be separated. More directly: It presumes the existence of *unresolved moral* problems and suggests that a solution ought to be found.

But what does '*finding* a solution' mean in this context? This formulation can imply that the solution does exist but is unknown to us. A second interpretation which interprets 'finding' [*finden*] as 'inventing' [*er-finden*] is, however, more convincing and more appropriate than the platonic assumption of pre-existing solutions. An adequate solution is, hence, being *constructed* by using specific 'instruments' (moral principles, values, intuitions etc.) rather than being found. However, the concept of 'construction' has in recent times been inflated and used indifferently. Therefore, I hesitate to use this fashionable term here. But as the available alternatives are incriminated to nearly the same extent, 'construction' appeared to be the smaller of two evils, particularly since the term, on second sight, graphically illustrates some of the most important elements. It is necessary to be aware what 'construction' means in a technical context. The following are some important components of its meaning: (1) Constructions are finite, they are subject to serious constraints given by nature. (2) These constraints do, however, allow room for alternative solutions. (3) The decision for one particular solution is based on non-technical criteria. (4) Construction requires care and expertise.

I would like to look at two further components that are particularly relevant in our discussion. (5) Something that already exists cannot be 'constructed', only 'reconstructed', Construction aims at something new, be it a solution to a new problem, or a new solution to an old problem. Applied ethics deals with the latter case where new solutions are to be found for new (and sometimes old) problems. As these problems are moral problems, applied ethics aims at something that could be called *new morality.* This aim is inherent in the above constellation that led to the evolution of applied ethics. If existing morality does not provide sufficient criteria for the direction or evaluation of actions, it must be adapted to new conditions. Existing morality is a historically evolved entity that can be overtaken by the development of new possibilities for action and that can, therefore, be in need of revision and adjustment. This hypothesis is the starting point of applied ethics. The other starting point is the confidence that such inadequacies can be corrected by ethical reflection and that it is not only necessary but also possible to create a 'new morality'.

Before returning to this point, some reservations must be made. Talk of a 'new morality' is exaggerated if it is interpreted to mean a complete revision of the old morality. Applied ethics certainly does not want to replace the 'old' by a 'new' morality but only aims to make precise, local corrections or extensions of the existing system. This becomes obvious when the analogy to technical construction is being taken seriously and when a further component of this term is being taken into account. (6) Every technical construction is 'conservative' in parts because existing materials are being used and 'old' solutions are being considered. The new construction does not impinge on the majority of other constructions that form 'the technology'. This is also the case with regard to the new solutions of applied ethicists. They are never 'revolutionary' in the sense that the totality of 'old' moral opinions ceases to be in force. The new solutions are developed by applying gene rally accepted norms and values. They look for generally accepted moral orientations and they leave the majority of moral convictions untouched. Particularly the core of morality (the ban on harm) is not open for reconsideration. That innovations within applied ethics can never overthrow philosophical foundations is partly because the field is situated in a 'midway-realm'. Issues that are obviously wrong do not normally develop into problems for applied ethics.

In spite of this reservation, it remains a fact that applied ethics has a 'revisionist' element. Established moral beliefs are no longer sacrosanct, a development which explains deep-rooted disquiet about the field. Obviously, revisions can be regarded as very drastic, even if they are limited in scope and do not comprehend 'the whole' of morality. The most apparent example being public reactions (in German speaking countries) to the belief of some authors that euthanasia of newborns can be legitimate under certain circumstances. The author's intention to partially reform morality was interpreted by parts of the public as its abolition or at least as the peak of an iceberg of efforts to adapt morality to technical possibilities and economic profit-making. This controversy is certainly an extreme case which, however, indicates that the 'construction' of morality is always a problem and sometimes a provocation. Public reservations towards applied ethics can mostly be explained by its 'revisionist' element. They are read by the apprehension that 'all will be allowed' in the end if humans start to 'make' morality.

This brings me to my second hypothesis. The project of applied ethics does not only reveal the changing function of ethical reflection within modern societies, but also a change of function and status of morality itself. Morality can no longer be perceived as an independent element which (seemingly at least) exists outside society's actions and serves as a timeless standard for the evaluation of these actions. Morality becomes the object of modifying reflection and thereby a changeable institution. As applied ethics becomes the instrument of direct problem solving, morality is being made positive, that is it results from human settings and 'construction'.

But is the claim that applied ethics has a constructive aspect so remarkable? Or is it as dismaying as some contemporaries believe? Has morality been left unchanged since the beginnings of humankind? And if today's morality differs from Stone Age morality (as we hope!), who has induced this change? Obviously, it would have been humans who changed morality in the passing of time. But then, the 'making' of morality would be historically normal. Besides, even the insight into the construct-character of morality is not new. Two and a half thousand years ago, the sophists declared that moral norms and values do not exist 'in nature' but only exist because of human conventions (Plato, *Gorgias*, 482e/483d). In his influential book *Ethics. Inventing Right and Wrong*, John Mackie claims that morality is not discovered but made and that 'good' and 'evil' are 'inventions'.

> Morality is not there to be discovered but to develop and to be worked on: We have to decide, which moral rules we want to accept and which standpoint we want to take … We need to decide what we ought to do, what we approve of and what we condemn, which principles we want to accept and support as a guide for our and other people's actions (1983, 132).

And finally: not only the construction-claim is old but also its critique, Plato's dismissal of the sophists being the best known but not the only example. And, criticism did not only come from philosophers in the past. 'Radical' philosophical ideas (or those which were perceived to be radical) have frequently provoked strong reactions from those in power and/or the public. It is sufficient to remember the execution of Socrates (or the pietists' driving away Christian Wolff from Halle). The alleged endangering of religion and morality by philosophical reflection is hardly a new phenomenon.

In response to these reservations, we have to emphasise three points.

(1) It is right that moral thinking is being influenced by historical change, just as any other form of thinking. The unchangeability of morality is an illusion which is partly caused by a longing for stability, partly by not keeping enough distance from history. And if we disregard God as a source for change, only one conclusion is possible: human beings changed their morality. The 'making' of morality is therefore the norm and not the exception. Nevertheless, we must not overlook the following. (a) In the past, moral change was often experienced over long periods of time. Today, however, the change is quick enough to be perceived by individuals within a lifetime, which causes uncertainties. (b) In the past, such change usually occurred as a non-intended consequence of human action, i.e. it happened behind people's backs. Today, this sort of change happens spontaneously; it is consciously aimed at and even institutionalised. This implies that moral change, as a conscious and intended process, links with responsibilities. Applied ethics creates the question of a 'meta responsibility', a responsibility not only for the consequences of our actions but also for the consequences of our constructed morality.

(2) It is true that the human origin of morality was remarked upon early on in the history of ethical thought. But we must not forget that the sophists did not represent the mainstream of ethical thinking and that Mackie's claims are strongly disputed. Within the mainstream of ethics, morality was a given fact which needed interpretation, systemisation and, most of all, justification. Construction or revision was not part of the work of ethicists.[7]

The only practical demand that ethics made in more recent times dealt with questions of moral education. In other words: Only the improvement of individuals was a practical aim for ethics not the improvement of morality itself.

(3) Finally applied ethics needs to be distinguished from the sophists' approach in two ways. When the sophists emphasised the conventional or constructed character of morality, they formulated (a) a meta-ethical and (b) a sceptical position! But this is not the case for applied ethics. Applied ethics does not *claim* that moral norms are constructs, but instead it 'constructs' moral norms. The field *does* what sophists and Mackie only announced for meta-ethical reasons. However, the second point is even more important. The sophists interpreted the construct-character of morality as an argument for its relativity and subjectivity. They were 'first order' sceptics who supported the following position: As there are no objective values, it is legitimate for

7 Kant made this very clear with a famous note in his preliminaries to the *Critique of Practical Reason*. 'Who would want to introduce a new principle of morality and invent it at the same time? As if the world had not known what duty was, either out of ignorance or consistent error, before he came' (1788, 8). Following on from Kant, Jürgen Habermas argues: 'Trivially, subjects must allow those maxims that they want to judge in the light of categorical imperatives to be given to them. In the same way, I understand practical discourse as a procedure that does not serve the creation of justified norms but rather the evaluation of the validity of existing norms which became problematic or the evaluation of the validity of hypothetically considered norms' (1984: 220f.).

everybody to do whatever they feel is right.[8] Applied ethics is *not* bound to this position and the majority of protagonists definitely do not support the view that morality is relative and subjective. On the contrary: The project of applied ethics relies on the assumption that moral problems can be solved adequately and objectively. This claim of objectivity can give way to many interpretations within meta-ethics. But applied ethics cannot forego a weak claim on adequacy and objectivity (in the sense of impartiality and fairness) because it would otherwise question its own existence. A relativistic or subjective identity of applied ethics would remove all authority from its problem-solving suggestions and thereby reduce itself to *mere* politics.

III

It is a widely held perception which partly stems from the name 'applied ethics' that the field applies general moral norms and principles to special cases or case groups to arrive at conclusions. 'Applied ethics' does therefore not deal with the justification of norms but takes their existence for granted and only applies them. This over-simplified and misleading perception has been criticised by several authors on the following bases: (a) applied ethics does not aim at the justification of norms but must be understood as an innovative enterprise and (b) the argumentation and reasoning within applied ethics does not move on a one-way street which leads from general principles to concrete cases and case groups.[9] Indeed, the results which applied ethics achieves are rarely based on higher order normative principles but more frequently on precedence, broadly accepted particular judgements ('intuitions') and background theories which can be partly descriptive and partly normative. Hence, justification does not only come 'from above' but also from a horizontal direction and 'from below'. The preferred justification strategy of applied ethics comes very close to what John Rawls (1979, 38f. and 68ff.) calls 'reflective equilibrium', a technique which Norman Daniels has sought to make fruitful for applied ethics. 'The key idea behind the technique of reflective equilibrium is that we "test" various parts of our system of moral beliefs against other beliefs we hold, seeking coherence among the widest set of moral and non-moral beliefs by revising and refining them at all levels' (Daniels 1996, 2). The starting point for this method is the renunciation of *privileging* a specific type of moral convictions. This stands in marked contrast to the perception of applied ethics as a process which deduces specific conclusions from general principles, where these general principles are supposed to have a privileged standing. When we ask for the motives for this preference towards a coherence-orientated justification strategy we will uncover two arguments. On the one hand, efforts to identify a 'foundation' for ethics within modern philosophy have not led to results equally acceptable for everybody. As it is unlikely that such a foundation

8 For the difference between scepticism of a first or a second order see Mackie 1983, 14f.

9 See Bayertz 1994, 34ff., as well as the newly available collected works of N. Daniels, from which I quote: 'Nearly all disputants agree that the term "applied ethics" is terribly misleading. It suggests that there is a supply of ready-at-hand general moral theories or principles and that the task of finding out what to do in particular cases consists of specifying the "facts" that would connect the general principles to a specific case' (Daniels 1996, 344).

will be identified in the near future, applied ethics must look for alternatives to theoretical foundationalism. Justification on the basis of 'reflective equilibrium' means: the creation of a possibly broad weave of convictions that support each other without admitting a privileged position to any particular type of conviction. This model opens a way towards the justification of morality under the constraint that a generally accepted foundation is not available.

Apart from this philosophical argument, the method of 'reflective equilibrium' also presents 'strategic' advantage for applied ethics, the importance of which should not be underestimated. Applied ethics does not only want to construct ethical theories but provide solutions for real and relevant normative problems. In this sense, the field has much more *practical* goals than standard ethics. To realise these practical goals, the first priority for proposed solutions is not philosophical acceptance but rather convincing the relevant public or the relevant institutions (as it is their actions that are meant to be directed). The solutions applied ethics provides will be more convincing to the public the closer they come to convictions held. In other words: The chances of applied ethics becoming practically effective strongly rely on the *connectedness* of its suggestions for solutions.[10] This connectedness is facilitated by reference to generally accepted norms, be it moral roles or principles or be it morally relevant legal norms, particularly basic rights and human rights, as well as the principle of human dignity. In addition it relies on reference to generally accepted values (for example, health) and interests. Although these generally accepted norms, values and interests do not play the role of a *fundamentum inconcussum* of applied ethics, they do have priority for the process of strategic justification.

Applied ethics is sometimes charged with a lack of philosophical depth, the source of which is, in fact, the goal of connectedness. But other points of reference – be they extremely deep and pleasing – are mostly out of the question for applied ethics. This becomes clear when we look at approaches to applied ethics that do *not* follow this anti-foundationalist style of thought and argumentation. This can be particularly pronounced in environmental ethics. An author who pursues the programme of revalidating non-human nature and who demands the recognition of its inherent value faces two problems. First, he needs to rely on presuppositions that are non-consensual and that, therefore, cannot justify generally binding guidance for action. This does not mean that the approach must necessarily be ineffective in all respects. It can influence consciousness at the level of society and thereby (at least in the long-term) foster a new consensus. But this would be an indirect effect of the type we know from the history of philosophy; it would not be a *direct* contribution to problem solving, as is normally aimed at by applied ethics. Second, his position is *too* foundationalist to derive practical guidance for action from it. Agreeing with Hans Jonas that there is a 'metaphysical reason for ought' (1979, 93) and that nature has its own ethical [*sittlich*] right, one is still not in a good position to find ethically convincing and practically feasible answers for specific questions, such as the structure of an ecological tax reform or appropriate limits for environmental pollution. The immediate, practical relevance which applied ethics aims at has to

10 This is another limit for 'revisionism'.

be achieved by foregoing involvement in profound philosophical issues and by concentrating on a 'pragmatic' approach to thought and argumentation.

Another constraint characterises the dominant type of thought and argumentation in applied ethics, the significance of which is hardly taken seriously. This is the existence of a plurality of diverging moral convictions. In today's society, that is under the condition of radically reduced dependence on religious attachments, a rapid change of living conditions, and a net of multicultural links, it is only possible to achieve a unified and morally substantive value and norm system by using oppression and violence (and even that would be difficult to achieve in the long-term). This is why Rawls talks of a 'Fact of Pluralism', in analogy to Kant's 'Fact of Reason'.

> This is not a passing historical phenomenon but, as I see it, a permanent feature of the political culture within modern democracies. By protecting basic rights and liberties, the political and historical conditions of democracy have secured the plurality of positions and will possibly enable their expansion. A public and practical agreement about one single, general and comprehensive moral system could only be upheld by the use of repressive state power (Rawls 1987, 299).

When constructing general ethical theories, it is easy to evade the fact of pluralism and to concentrate on justifying the relevant evaluative or normative conceptions with regard to competing conceptions. Whether such an approach is sensible or whether it should be described as an ostrich-type-approach need not be decided here. Certainly, this approach is not open to applied ethics. The field can only disregard the fact of existing plurality in evaluative and normative convictions at the price of being practically irrelevant. The prospect of recognition and practicability is reserved for those solutions acceptable from a variety of perspectives. Hence, the type of thought and argumentation that is prevalent in applied ethics tries to consider a variety of competing evaluations and principles when looking at specific problems and tries to find solutions that as many people as possible 'can live' with. Particularly *procedural solutions* present themselves for coping with situations of moral conflict under these conditions. Such solutions avoid commitments to particular convictions and leave the decision in specific cases to the individual and his or her voluntary agreement. (An example of this strategy is the discussion about 'passive euthanasia', which is mostly restricted to the framework under which doctors can legitimately arrive at a decision to stop the treatment of terminally ill patients. The core of this framework is the announced or the assumed will of the particular patient.) Where such procedural solutions are not possible, it is necessary to weigh several possibilities carefully with the aim of preserving as far as possible the interests of the people affected by an action and to keep unavoidable damage of these interests to a minimum as well as distributing unavoidable harm as justly as possible.

This leads to my third thesis. The aim of applied ethics to achieve immediate practical relevance leads to a preference for 'pragmatic' types of thought and argumentation. The place of last foundations – God's will, the nature of things, the nature of human beings, the laws of reason – is being filled by links to current consensus and reference to human interests, including their legitimate plurality. Moral thinking loses its categorical character and becomes a medium for harmonising several interests: the 'truth' or validity of results is measured by the 'appropriateness', the 'practicability' or the 'reasonableness of demands'.

Applied ethics pays a price for gains in practical relevance which should not be overlooked but which has not, so far, been widely acknowledged in the field. Although there are good reasons to accept this price, it should not come as a surprise that some view it as a sell-out of philosophy or (even worse) a sell-out of morality. The disquiet is directed both against the tendency towards 'pragmatic' solutions on the level of material decisions and against foundational strategies that are no longer relying on unshakeable foundations but on existing consensus and interests.

It is obvious that procedural roles and the weighing of goods lead to solutions which – from the point of view of strong convictions – can only have the character of compromise. If one starts from the ideal of a 'moral philosophy of life' which includes a universally binding value system and minimises the scope for divergent narrative judgements and decisions, then one can only take the 'Fact of Pluralism' as a contingent matter which is regrettable and even a sign of moral decline. The (pejoratively understood) 'pragmatism' or 'utilitarianism' of applied ethics, its preference for procedural solutions or weighing goods appears to be a sign of capitulation before the *Zeitgeist*, which does not leave any room for 'real morality'. However, ibis evaluation is not the only possible one, as moral pluralism is neither a mere, contingent fact nor the expression of a general retreat from strong values. It should instead be viewed as the result of strong evaluations, an evaluation – incidentally – which has been made possible by long political struggles across generations. This pluralism is the result of acknowledging the moral autonomy of individuals and their legal and political safety within liberal democracies. It is, hence, a fundamental error to view the preference of procedural solutions exclusively as capitulation or compromise and not as a moral and political *achievement.*

The mistrust that accompanies the change in justification strategies is just as deep. If it is true that morality becomes a social institution capable of being deliberately shaped and that moral thinking approaches political thinking – 'political' not in the sense of party politics or everyday politics, but in the sense of pragmatically moulding given conditions towards the most comprehensive satisfaction of human interests – then, this is surely important for the reliability and safety of results achieved under this framework. If there are no more solid foundations for moral thinking and if the best we can do is a coherent and self-supporting system of normative and factual convictions, how can we ever be sure of anything? If the morally right is not given anymore but must be 'constructed' with regard to human interests, what guarantees are left that not 'everything will be allowed' in the end?

It will be difficult to remove the worries that are expressed in this question, but I would nonetheless like to mention two arguments. (1) It was previously stressed that the 'construction' of morality should not be equated with arbitrariness and that applied ethics retains the claim that results are objective, a claim which is not being made in politics to the same extent. A total 'politicisation' of morality does therefore not take place. In some respects, applied ethics is more like *law* than politics. Even legal norms cannot rely on unshakeable foundations without thereby giving up the idea that 'true right' and arbitrary right can be distinguished. (2) It should not be forgotten that references to unshakeable foundations have only ever given apparent certainty and that 'guarantees' of moral truth have never existed. The conscious renunciation of foundations and guarantees is not an innovation of applied ethics but expresses a tendency which goes back to the beginning of modern ethics. At the start stood a theory (Hobbes' social contract) which replaced metaphysical strategies of foundationalism with reference to human interests. Obviously, it does make a difference whether the 'construction' of morality is only a hypothetical procedure (to justify a theory) or whether it is 'real' (with material consequences).

Applied ethics is in the situation described by Otto Neurath (1932–3, 206) half a century ago: The ship of our morality is at high sea. If we are faced with problems that require repairs or alterations to the ship, we cannot put in at a safe port and use a dry dock. We have to do the work at high sea. This situation may appear uncomfortable and possibly dangerous, but we obviously do not have an alternative. Giving the ship up or jumping into the water would be even more dangerous while looking for an authoritarian captain or ship builder would be worse still.

References

Bayertz, K. (1994), 'Praktische Philosophie als angewandte Ethik', in Bayertz, K. (Hg.), pp. 7–47.

— (Hg.) (1994), *Praktische Philosophie. Grundorientierungen angewandter Ethik*, 2nd Edition (Reinbek: Rowohlt).

Colli, G. and Montinari, M. (Hg.) (1980), *Sämtliche Werke. Kritische Studienausgabe in 15 Bänden* (Munich and Berlin: Deutscher Taschenbuchverlag and de Gruyter).

Daniels, N. (1996), *Justice and Justification. Reflective Equilibrium in Theory and Practice* (Cambridge: Cambridge University Press).

Gert, D. (1998), *Morality. Its Nature and Justification* (New York: Oxford University Press).

Habermas, J. (1984), 'Über Moralität und Sittlichkeit – Was macht eine Lebensform "rational"?', in Schnadelbach, H. (Hg.), pp. 218–35.

Heidegger, M. (1954), 'Überwindung der Metaphysik', in *Vorträge und Aufsätze* (Pfullingen: Neske), pp. 67–95.

Hinsch, W. (Hg.) (1992), *Die Idee des Politischen Liberalismus* (Frankfurt: Suhrkamp).

Jonas, H. (1979), *Das Prinzip Verantwortung. Versuch einer Ethik für die technologische Zivilisation* (Frankfurt: Insel).

Kant, I. (1785), 'Grundlegung zur Metaphysik der Sitten', in *Akademie Textausgabe*, Vol. 4 (Berlin: de Gruyter, 1968).

— (1788), 'Kritik der praktischen Vernunft', in *Akademie Textausgabe*, Vol. 5 (Berlin: de Gruyter, 1968).

Kilpi, J. (1998), *The Ethics of Bankruptcy* (London: Routledge).

Mackie, J. (1983), *Ethik, Auf der Suche nach dem Richtigen und Falschen* (Stuttgart: Reclam).

Neurath, O. (1932–33), 'Protokollsätze', *Erkenntnis* 3, 204–14.
Nietzsche, F. (1882–85), 'Nachgelassene Fragmente. Juli 1882 bis Herbst 1885', in Colli, G. and Montinari, M. (Hg.), Vol. 11.
Platon, *Gorgias.*
—— *Protagoras.*
—— *Politeia.*
Rawls, J. (1979), *Eine Theorie der Gerechtigkeit* (Frankfurt: Suhrkamp).
—— (1987), 'The Idea of an Overlapping Consensus', in German, in Hinsch, W. (Hg.), pp. 293–32.
Ricoeur, P. (1998), 'Die Geschichte ist kein Friedhof', Interview in *Die Zeit* 42 (8 October 1998), pp. 68–9.
Schnadelbach, H. (Hg.), *Rationalitat. Philosophische Beiträge* (Frankfurt, Suhrkamp).

Chapter 3

Does Applied Ethics Rest on a Mistake?

Alasdair MacIntyre[1]

'Applied ethics', as that expression is now used, is a single rubric for a large range of different theoretical and practical activities. Such rubrics function partly as a protective device both within the academic community and outside it; a name of this kind suggests not just a discipline, but a particular type of discipline. In the case of 'applied ethics' the suggestive power of the name derives from a particular conception of the relationship of ethics to what goes on under the rubric of 'applied ethics'. Not everyone who conducts activities under that rubric owes allegiance to this conception and there are doubtless some who would repudiate it as strongly as I do. But it is that dominant conception from which most work in this area derives or aspires to derive its philosophical legitimacy. What is that conception?

Ethics as such, on this dominant view, has as its subject-matter *morality as such.* Morality as such imposes requirements upon human individuals *qua* human individuals. It has the function of regulating the relationships of anyone whatsoever with anyone else. It thus moves at a level of abstraction and generality which detaches its concerns and its formulations from all social particularity. Being concerned with persons *qua* persons its formulations make no reference to particular social roles or institutional forms. It is not however without explicit social content. Society is understood as an arena of rival and competing interests and what morality supplies are rules which from a neutral and impartial point of view set constraints upon how these interests may be pursued. The rules are neutral and impartial in that they are such that any rational person who had detached him or herself from the distorting causal influence of his or her interests would assent to them. It follows that in the formulation of such rules only concepts available to rational persons as such may be employed: either concepts whose application is involved in any evaluation whatsoever of discourse as rational-concepts such as those of consistency, truth, universality, necessity and the like-or concepts which specify either universal or near universal features of desired states of affairs ('being found pleasant' is one frequent candidate for this status) or universal or near universal objects of desire ('liberty to get what one wants' might be claimed to be such a concept).

Morality as such thus concerns what is true of everyone and anyone in their capacity as rational persons. The requirement of agreement by rational persons removes from the realm of morality one area that has been sometimes thought to

---

1 University of Notre Dame. Copyright © 1984, *THE MONIST: An International Quarterly Journal of General Philosophical Inquiry*, Peru, Illinois, U.S.A. 61354. Translated and published by permission.

be central to it. Our social order is not only an arena for competing interests; it is also one for competing views, religious and nonreligious, as to the best way for human beings to live. On the dominant view it is held that either because rational agreement on the nature of the good life for human beings cannot be reached or just because as a matter of fact it has not been reached or because it is a key part of the freedom of each individual to choose whatever he or she takes to be the best life for him or herself, the rules that constitute morality must be neutral between alternative and conflicting views of the good for human beings. Pluralism about the good is to coexist with rational agreement on the rules of morality.

There are of course many versions of this dominant view of morality: Kantian, utilitarian, contractarian, Kantian-cum-utilitarian, Kantian-cum-contractarian and so on. But the adherents of all such views agree in attempting to specify universally binding principles or rules whose universality has the scope of humanity itself. Detachment from and disinterestedness towards all social particularity and positivity is thus a defining mark of morality. It follows that morality can be formulated and understood in-dependently of any considerations which arise from highly specific forms of social structure. Ignorance of sociology and history will not be a defect in the student of morality as such. But what then of those areas of human life in which the regulation of conduct requires the framing of rules which specify how institutionalised relationships are to be conducted? Examples are the contemporary and shifting relationships of physician, nurse and patient, of lawyer, client and judge, of elected public officials to civil servants and to the public. The answer, according to the dominant standpoint, is that the rules of morality as such have to be *applied* to this kind of socially and institutionally specific subject-matter to yield socially and institutionally specific rules. The academic discipline of *ethics as* such, which enquires into the nature of morality as such, has to be supplemented by the discipline of *applied ethics*. Applied ethics derives its conclusions from sets of premises in which conclusions drawn from ethics are conjoined to factual finding about some specific social and intellectual area. Its rational claims upon our attention depend first then upon the justifiability of the account of morality which it presupposes; secondly, upon the warranted character of its account of the structures of medical or legal or political or military or business institutional and social relationships; and thirdly, upon its ability to derive its conclusions rationally from its premises. It is upon the first and third of these that I shall focus attention.

I

The central requirement of the dominant conception of ethics is then that the rules of morality are such as any rational agent would agree to. But it is an equally notable fact about the moral philosophers who share this conception of ethics that they are in fact unable to agree either upon the precise content of the rules of morality or upon the appropriate way in which such rules are to be rationally justified. Kantians or post-Kantians, utilitarians of different schools, contractarians and the various mixtures of these remain intractably at odds with one another. And in the extent of both ranges of disagreement they mirror the dominant trends of that liberal culture of which they are the articulate spokesmen.

Of course in the culture at large the range of disagreements on both counts is even wider, for all the dissenters from the dominant point of view, theological and non-theological, also have to be counted in. If then, in spite of the dominant requirement of rational agreement, disagreement on what the rules of morality actually are is rampant and in the foreseeable future unresolvable *and* if applied ethics is in fact an application to cases falling within particular social spheres of what are taken to be the rules of morality, then we should expect to find that the disagreements over moral rules reproduce themselves within applied ethics. Doubtless to some extent and on some issues they do: for example, in many debates over abortion. But in an interestingly high proportion of examples either large disagreement on what the rules of morality are turns out to be compatible with large agreement on issues within the domain of applied ethics or, where there is disagreement within that domain between contending parties, it does not reproduce the disagreements between them on the fundamental rules of morality.

Since the former type of example is the more striking, let me discuss one particular report of such a combination of disagreements and agreements. Commenting on the work of the National Commission for the Protection of Human Subjects of Biomedical and Behavioural Research, Stephen Toulmin, who was a staff member for that commission, has described how the commissioners found it relatively easy to reach agreement, or in a minority of intractable cases at least local and isolable disagreement, on particular concrete issues raised by specific difficult types of case, but continued to have fundamental and radical disagreements on matters of moral principle, on what the rules of morality actually are, even although each of them individually aspired to justify his or her views on the concrete issues by appeal to his or her principles (Toulmin 1981, 31–2).

This type of situation is recurrent within applied ethics and there are three possible explanations for it. The first is that rival and conflicting moral principles do, when applied within applied ethics, surprisingly and unexpectedly yield the same answers. But were this to be true more than very occasionally, grave doubt would be cast on whether the principles or rules being invoked really were in conflict with each other. And since we do seem to have independently adequate grounds for holding that the principles and rules in question are rival and conflicting, we do have grounds for rejecting this explanation. The discrepancy between the agreements on the issues that fall to applied ethics and the disagreements over the principles and rules which constitute morality is just as radical and disturbing as it appears to be.

The second and third types of explanation agree on one central contention: that in such cases the various parties involved in the disagreements at one level and the agreements at another are not in fact applying the moral principles or rules about which they disagree. One possible explanation, which is, I take it, Toulmin's own in the case of the National Commission, is that a very different type of moral reasoning is at work – one in which the fundamental appeal is not to rules, but to cases. On this view, on occasions on which this explanation holds, the participants are behaving rationally in reaching their agreements within applied ethics, but may misrepresent to themselves the nature of their own moral reasoning. A third possible explanation is of a different order. It is that in some such cases at least – although not necessarily of course in that of the National Commission – there is indeed a misrepresentation by the participants to themselves and to others of how agreement is being reached, but that a central feature of the misrepresentation is that what is in fact a non rational social transaction is being presented as though it were a process of rational argument. I shall want to suggest that in some at least, although certainly not in all of the cases falling under the rubric of 'applied ethics', this third type of explanation needs to be seriously considered.

II

One reason for this last suggestion is that it seems clear that in applied ethics the rules or principles which on the dominant conception constitute morality *cannot* be being applied in the way that is commonly supposed. For the relationship between a rule and its applications cannot be what on the dominant view it is taken to be; that is, it cannot be the case that we can first and independently comprehend the rules of morality as such and then only secondly enquire as to their application in particular specialized social spheres. For, were this to be the case, the rules of morality as such would be effectively contentless. On the dominant view, for example, we are first and independently to frame a rule or rules about truth-telling and honesty in general and then only secondly need to enquire how it is, or they are to be applied in such relationships as those of physician to patient or lawyer in respect of his or her client's affairs and so on. But no rule exists apart from its applications and if as we approach the question of whether a physician on a particular type of occasion ought to answer a question by a patient truthfully or not it must be in the light of previous applications of the rule. But these applications will have been to situations and relationships quite as socially specific as is the physician-patient relationship. It is characteristically and generally in such relations as those between parent and children, teacher and pupils, clergy and congregation that rules of truthfulness are first learnt. And in extending the rule so that it applies to new situations there are only three possibilities. The first is that, although the rule was first learned and formulated in certain socially specific types of situation, it was learned and formulated as applying to persons as such independent of what type of situation and relationship each may be involved in at any given time. But if so, there is no new, secondary task of applying the rule to the physician-patient relationship: what the rule says is already clear. Physician-patient relationships in this case are simply part of the subject-matter of morality as such. There is nothing left for applied ethics to study. A second possibility is that the rule *is* formulated with specific reference to what has been the range of its applications so far, that in its function as a rule of morality as such it does make reference to certain particular socially specific rules and relationships and that in extending it to the physician-patient relationship we are moving beyond the type of case hitherto covered by that rule. But, if so, the task of now reformulating it so that it covers this new class of relationships will be no different in kind from the task already performed of formulating it with reference to those relationships to govern and regulate which was originally brought into being. In this latter type of case the conception of the rules which constitute morality as such differs from that appealed to in the framing of the former type of case, but, just as in the former type of case, the rule that covers the physician-patient relationship turns out to be a rule of morality as such, no different from any other such rule. And once again after we have understood how the rules of morality as such are formulated and function, no task remains over for something called 'applied ethics' to perform.

Both these possibilities are exemplified of course in actual moral practice: the first by strict, practising Kantians and also for example by the kind of pietist Christian believers from whom Kant's parents learned the rule about truthfulness which they taught to Kant; the second in the extension of rules specifically prohibiting, and providing penalties for, the slaying of an identified member of another kinship group, and rules specifically prohibiting the slaying of strangers, to rules prohibiting homicide in early English society. Is there or could there be a third possibility, a third type of case, which would provide tasks specific to applied ethics? Or do the two types of case which I have sketched in outline exhaust the possibilities, so that in essence the case against applied ethics is already complete? These questions could only be adequately answered by a fuller account of what is involved both in rule-following and in the extension of a preexisting rule to some new class of cases.

III

No rule exists apart from some range of applications. But the relationship of a rule to the specification of its applications varies of course with the type of rule. At one end of the scale there are those rules which the conditions of discourse as such enforce upon us, so that we cannot escape the logical consequences of violating them: such is the rule forbidding the assertion of a statement conjoined to the denial of that same statement. The penalties of inconsistency in the statement and bafflement in the understanding of those who hear or read it are inescapable. In these cases there is no such thing as understanding the rule and not knowing how it is to be applied. This is also true at the other end of the scale where the type of rule is such that to understand it involves the identification of particulars and the specification of context. 'Do not enter the greenhouses except by the side doors' as an item in the list of rules governing use of a particular botanical garden is a rule not to be grasped except in terms of particular identifications in a particular context. The rule and its applications are necessarily grasped together.

There are of course crucial differences between these two extreme types of rule: an understanding of some particular rule of the former type can be exhibited quite independently of a knowledge of any formulation of it, whereas understanding and following a rule of the latter type depends upon grasping that there *is* such a rule, something that does require knowledge of its formulation. Moreover, rules of the latter kind are examples of pure positivity. They have their status as rules purely in virtue of the fiat of some authority. Whereas rules of the former kind have no taint of positivity at all; each rational agent must utter them, as it were, to him or herself.

Moral rules – in any useful sense of 'moral' – are and must be of some intermediate type. It is characteristic of moral reflection, as of some other centrally important kinds of thinking, that we move to and fro from the rule to some range of examples of its application and from these particular applications back to the rule; and this movement is an important clue to the nature of moral reflection. For this kind of rule cannot be adequately understood by any individual agent apart from some set of particular exemplary applications. But to grasp some particular rule is nonetheless also to go beyond *any* set of particular applications, for no one has grasped a given rule adequately until he or she has learned how to extrapolate justifiably from the cases in which he or she has understood that rule so far to an indeterminate range of possible future applications of that same rule. The justification for extrapolating in one way rather than another may be a complex matter. It must be partly retrospective, a matter of some tolerably high degree of consistency with past applications of the rule; but it will also be partly prospective, a matter of bringing out crucial or at least relevant resemblances and differences between cases that apart from this kind of application of the rule would have to go unremarked or obscured. And since all rules occur in sets, it is also partly a matter of the implications for other members of the same set-new applications for an expression used in the formulation or reformulation of one rule have to have some kind of consonance with uses of the same expression in other rules. What is crucial is to be able to distinguish between cases in which a rule is extended in its applications but remains one and the same rule from cases in which a rule by the nature of the extension of its applications has had to be to lesser or greater degree reformulated, so that what we have is a new rule, which however is in some strong sense the successor to its predecessor, and both of these in turn from cases in which a rule has simply been abandoned, perhaps being replaced by no rule at all, perhaps by a rule which embodies a quite different standpoint. What are the criteria in virtue of which we are able to make these distinctions?

It may seem trivial to begin by asserting that the same rule is being applied only if it is applied to the same kind of instance of whatever it is, in virtue of those instances possessing the same characteristic or characteristics in virtue of which it was applied to earlier instances. But this is not the same as saying that it is the same rule which is being applied only if the characteristic or characteristics of instances in virtue of which it is being applied to them are being *understood* as identified in the same way that they were understood in those earlier instances. Continuity in the use of some particular rule does not require continuity in the understanding of that use. And sometimes when prospectively the extension of a rule to some apparently new class of instances seems to create grave problems as to whether after application to this new class of instances the rule could possibly be the same, retrospectively it may become clear that what had to be changed was not the use of the rule, but the understanding of its use.

Consider two very different examples. One is that of the proposal, whenever it was first made (perhaps by some Indian anticipator of Bhaskara in the 12th century), to extend the rule of subtraction so that some operation of subtraction, that of -1 perhaps, could be performed upon the number 0. The other is the proposal (made perhaps by some Alexandrian Jew to the local Aristotelians in the second century) to extend to cases of infanticide and abortion a prohibition upon the taking of human life which had hitherto been understood not to exclude these. In each case the appeal made by whomsoever was proposing the extension of the rule would have been *to* that in virtue of which in fact the rule had previously been applied to the instances to which it had been applied and *against* that in virtue of which it had been understood to have been so applied. So in the first example the argument would have been that it was the properties of integers *qua* integers and not their properties as *positive* integers in virtue of which the rule had been applied; in the second example it would have been that it was the property of being an innocent individual member of the human species which brought someone under the prohibition of killing and not, for example, the property of being a potentially useful human individual (by being, say, male rather than female; it was female infants who were most often abandoned to their deaths in the ancient classical world). Thus the justification of the extension of the rule derives from a particular kind of reexamination by the members of the community whose rule it is of their understanding of their own rule, one which characteristically involves *both* an enquiry into how the rule had been applied in the past and the nature of the reasons adduced for applying it *and* an enquiry into what members of the community would have said, had the rule been applied to certain types of case to which it had not in fact been applied. Such an enquiry can of course have a variety of outcomes. Because it involves counterfactual considerations, its outcome may be indecisive; and even if decisive, what it discloses may be that agreement on the understanding of the rule has not in fact been present, or at least has not been present to the degree requisite for an appeal to it. Nonetheless it is clear that the requirements for a justified extension of a particular rule to cover some particular new type of case can be applied with sufficient clarity for us to be able to discriminate cases which clearly are those of justified extension from cases which equally clearly fail to satisfy the requirements and both from cases in which no verdict can be justified.

What then of the second type of case, that in which we are concerned not with a new application of some particular established rule, so that it is still one and the same rule that is being obeyed, but rather with what is a reformulation of the old rule? Here again there are clear and applicable requirements. For some new rule applied to some new class of instances to be accepted as a reformulation of some other rule to which hitherto allegiance had been given, the justification of the new reformulated rule and of its applications must be auxiliary to and parasitic upon the justification of its predecessor. So the movement from the several prohibitions of several distinct types of killing to a single comprehensive prohibition of homicide, a movement actually made in a number of earlier societies, could satisfy the requirements for a justified reformulation if not only could the set of more limited prohibitions embodied in the earlier rules be deduced from the new reformulation, but the reasons which provide the grounds for obedience to the rule in its new reformulation either give a more fundamental insight into the grounds adduced earlier for the several independent prohibitions or pro-vide more adequate grounds for those prohibitions. To speak of a reformulation in this respect is of course to understand the new rule as more and other than a mere conjunction of the earlier prohibitions. Moreover the reformulation need not forfeit its status as a reformulation if in addition to its greater comprehensiveness, it in some small measure has to correct the older prohibitions or injunctions in order to make them deducible from the new formulation. What matters is that those corrections should not be of what was at the core of the older formulation, but should concern only their more marginal aspects; and thus correction is only in place where it is possible to distinguish the central intention of a prohibition or injunction from the details of its embodiment in a particular rule.

As with the cases where one and the same rule is being applied to some new class of instances, so also in the cases where a rule has been replaced by a rule that is clearly a reformulation of *that* rule, the criteria are adequate to enable us to distinguish those cases of rule innovation which clearly do fall under that description from those which equally clearly do not, and both from those cases where difficulties in applying the criteria hinder or prevent any decisive verdict. What is crucial in the cases where the new rule is a justified reformulation of some older rule or rules is that it was possible to appeal in the course of the reformulation to some shared background of evaluative beliefs. What kind of background must this be?

When the issue of extending a rule to cover some new class of instances arises, whether the outcome is that one and the same rule continues to be used, but with a new understanding of its point and purport, or it is that the rule is reformulated or it is that no change whatsoever is made, it must always be because members of that particular community could agree in seeing some substantial good at stake in responding in one way rather than another. The following of rules and the understanding of rules, implicit and explicit, is always correlative to the apprehension of goods and evils and what the rules are is in any given community a partial, although only a partial specification of goods and evils as understood in that community: a specification of, not a derivation from. So it is true that all rules are to be understood as instantiations of *Bonum est faciendum, et prosequendum et malum vitandum* (Aquinas). Notice that we are speaking here of goods generally: what is at stake in moral rules is good generally, not some special kind of good to be called 'moral good'. Notice also that if the making and remaking and extending and amending of rules is to be a rational activity the goods by appeal to which these activities are carried on must themselves be rationally ordered in some hierarchy. A shared theory of goods of some fairly extensive kind is presupposed, and the notion that genuine rules could be neutral between rival theories of the hierarchy of the goods is ruled out.

Rules and goods both generally find their place within some more comprehensive moral scheme, within which goods ordered hierarchically, virtues, duties, obligations and liberties all find a place. It is with reference to their place in such a scheme that changes in the understanding of rules, reformulations of rules, formulations of new rules and the like are or are not rationally justifiable. It follows that at the core of all issues of rational moral justification is the question of whether the scheme as a whole is or is not rationally justified. When I speak of an overall moral scheme of this kind, I do not merely mean a theory, but rather a theory that is actually embodied in the practices and relationships of a specific society, a theory which if and when it is articulated at the level of explicit theorising will have to be able to give an account of its own embodiment, if it is to sustain its claims.

Such moral schemes themselves have histories and part of that history is the dialectical movement between the consideration and apprehension of higher order goods and principles. It is within this movement that the consideration of individual cases find its place, either as exemplifying the application of some existing rule, or as providing an occasion for the reformulation of a rule or a set of rules, or sometimes as proving unamenable to treatment in terms of rules and calling for the exercise of judgement of a different order. For no rule or set of rules can cover every relevant contingency; and the discovery of a case not so covered need not provide and on occasion cannot provide adequate reason for extending or reformulating these particular rules. Nonetheless even such cases are defined in terms of and acquire their significance and their status from the rules in question. Thus the notion that there could be systematic disagreement about moral rules or principles, but agreement about particular cases without some irrationality on someone's part is at the very least highly implausible. But if this is so, the notion of a 'case method in ethics', as championed by Toulmin, makes no sense (Toulmin 1981). There is no method of handling cases except in the context of some large degree of agreement upon rules and, for the reasons already given, on a good deal more than rules.

What makes a rule a specifically *moral* rule? This is a question to which an answer has been presupposed throughout my argument, but never spelled out. The answer is that a rule is a moral rule if and insofar as obedience to it is required in exercising the virtues of character, among which the virtue of justice is preeminent in its rule requirements. It may seem however that the account which I have given of how rules may be extended, reformulated to greater or lesser degree (and even abandoned or replaced) is incompatible with the kind of regard for rules which justice requires. Does not justice require us to regard some rules at least at holding for all human beings throughout time, so that my discussion of changes in the understanding and formulation of rules, let alone any more radical kind of moral change, will be ruled out in advance for *those* rules? This is after all not only the doctrine of some modern liberal thinkers, but also of Aquinas and Scotus, and Aristotle himself was surely committed to some such thesis by his belief in natural, as against conventional, justice.

The relevance of this objection to my central thesis is clear. I first suggested that when ethics and morality are rightly understood, the concept of applied ethics loses all application. This suggestion depended for its force upon what the relationship of a moral rule to its applications is. The investigation of this relationship has so far at least confirmed the original suggestion. Moral rules exist only in and through their range of applications and the history of moral rules in key part is the history of the changes in their applications. The conception of morality articulated in this account of moral rules is one according to which moralities are social phenomena, each of which has its own peculiar history of growth and change, of learning and failing to learn, of victories and defeats. But the conception of morality which both generates and underpins the dominant contemporary conception of applied ethics is one according to which morality, not moralities, provides the subject-matter for ethics and according to which morality has at its core a set of timeless principles or rules. It is indeed just because these principles or rules are ahistorical and independent of social change, that the changing realm of the social and the historical raises problems about their application, problems specific to particular sets of social institutions in particular times and places. And such problems are precisely those that provide modern applied ethics with its domain. Hence it may seem to follow that the case for applied ethics and the case for timeless, ahistorical moral principles or rules stand or fall together.

To this argument I concede at once the following: the argument which I have deployed against the very concept of applied ethics does indeed entail the rejection of any conception of moral principles or rules as timeless and ahistorical. What it does not rule out is the possibility of there being enduring moral principles or rules. An enduring moral principle or rule is one which remains rationally undefeated through time, surviving a wide range of challenges and objections, perhaps undergoing limited reformulations or changes in how it is understood, but retaining its basic identity through the history of its applications. In so surviving and enduring it meets the highest rational standard that can be imposed, and there clearly comes a time in the history of a morality when the possibility of some particular principle or rule being either overthrown or radically emended, although still open in principle – quite new forms of challenge can never be finally ruled out – provides no ground at all for any limitation upon our practical allegiance to that principle or rule. And it is no more and no other than this kind of allegiance to this kind of rule that the exercise of the virtue of justice requires.

The theory of knowledge presupposed by this account of the central principles or rules of justice is that set forth in germ by Plato in the *Gorgias* (509a) where Socrates is represented as saying that he does not *know* what is in fact the case with regard to the matters about which he is speaking, but that no one has so far been able to maintain an incompatible view without manifestly falling into error, and that in consequence he holds that matters are as he takes them to be. The Socrates thus represented by Plato was also represented by him as a moral rigorist. And if moral rigorism required principles that could in the Socratic sense be 'known', Socrates would have been deeply inconsistent; but, as he himself notices in the same passage, what he requires are principles supported by arguments as enduring as 'iron or adamant', enduring, that is, in the face of counter-arguments, counter-examples, rival theories of knowledge and the like. This is the same requirement that the conception of morality which I am defending imposes upon its fundamental principles and rules.

IV

My central claim in this chapter is that applied ethics cannot be the kind of activity that it is so often claimed to be, for there is not and could not be any such kind of activity. But what then does go on under that highly misleading rubric? I shall want to suggest that at least two quite different types of activity are being conducted; but a necessary prologue to making this suggestion is a scrutiny of what the morality of our contemporary liberal individualist, morally pluralist society is. For what applied ethics actually comprises turns out to stand in an illuminating relationship to the condition of contemporary morality. What then is the morality actually embodied in those transactions and relationships which are of central importance to the social order of our modernity?

It cannot be the morality spoken of by contemporary liberal moral philosophers; for that morality is constituted by a set of principles or rules to which any rational agent would assent and, as I pointed out earlier, no such set of rules has as yet been identified. It does not of course follow that this conception of morality is without social influence; and what it tends to provide are a set of standards by means of which each contending party in fundamental moral disputes is able to discredit the rational pretensions of its opponents. And this is one more source of the systematically inconclusive character of debate over fundamental issues in our contemporary moral culture. But the ongoing necessities of social life require that these fundamental rifts and conflicts be kept out of view so far as possible; hence the everyday practical life of our social institutions has to be insulated so far as possible from fundamental debate. The phenomenon, which Toulmin noted in the members of the National Commission, of an ability to combine disagreement on moral issues at theoretically fundamental levels with agreement at the level of immediate practicality is in fact and has to be pervasive in our social lives. One central way in which this is achieved is by conferring a high degree of indeterminacy upon our actual shared moral principles.

By our actual shared moral principles I do not mean a set of principles formulated as persons of any one highly determinate point of view – let alone moral philosophers – would formulate what they regard as their own moral principles. I mean a set of principles which have been rendered indeterminate in order to be adequately shared, adequately shared for the purposes of practical life, that is, with persons of quite different and incompatible standpoints. What those principles then amount to has to be expressed in sentences without any clear ending: 'One ought to tell the truth, but there are a range of occasions on which truth-telling is problematic and then …', or 'One ought to obey the law, but there are a range of situations in which lawabidingness is problematic and then …'. It is of the essence of such principles that although they may list a number of the types of situation in which the application of the principle is not straightforward, such a list will always end with an 'etc.' for the class of possible exceptions to the rule can never be made fully determinate.

If these were genuine moral rules, they would indeed furnish a decisive counter-example to my thesis about such rules, namely that this kind of rule can never be specified apart from the range of its applications. For these principles can indeed be fully specified in all their indeterminacy prior to their applications; and no finite number of applications will remove that indeterminacy. A decision to apply the principle in one way rather than another in one particular situation does not characteristically and generally make it any less problematic how the principle is to be applied the next time a similar situation recurs. Why is this? It is first of all because characteristically and generally what renders the relevant type of situation problematic is the adducing of a number of rival and incompatible considerations and hence in arriving at a decision how to act the idiom of 'a balancing of considerations' is often and appositely used; only – there are no scales – and so the metaphor of balancing, if thought of as a rational process, is a misleading and disguising fiction. And secondly it is because there is no social process of accumulating precedents, of understanding Rules as emerging from a history of successful and unsuccessful attempts at reformulation. Socially made decisions are treated in the vast majority of cases as occurring historically *in vacuo.* We do not bind *our* successors and we are not bound by our predecessors. Nor indeed could we if this account of *our* shared principles and rules is true, for the indeterminacy of our principles or rules is such that they do not in any substantial sense at all bind us. This is why these are *not* genuinely moral principles or rules.

It is crucial to reiterate that I am not here speaking of the principles or rules of those clear-headed adherents of highly determinate moral standpoint who provide our society with its deviant moral subcultures: Catholics or Southern Baptists, pacifist members of the Society of Friends or radical feminists. What I am speaking of are those simulacra of moral principles that are what moral principles are transformed into in the great pluralist mishmash of the shared public life of liberal societies. And if I am to any large degree right about this, it is not difficult to understand why what is named 'applied ethics' should have been called into being. For there are of course centrally important areas in our social life where there has to be shared public agreement and agreement of a kind incompatible with the indeterminacy and imprecision of what function as, or perhaps rather instead of, shared moral principles in our general public social life.

What areas are these? Unsurprisingly they are just those areas in which applied ethics has flourished: medicine, law, the world of such professions as accountancy and engineering, and the military. These are areas in which highly determinate types of action of great moral import have continually to be taken. It is impossible most of the time at least to fudge the question of what one is actually doing. These are also areas in which public confidence in professional activity is required and a necessary condition for such confidence is a high degree of warranted expectation. Such warranted expectation can only be provided by relatively uniform behaviour on the part of those engaged in such professional activities within any one particular profession. And such uniform behaviour requires a high degree of uniformity of moral education and of ways of handling the problematic. Hence the ubiquity in those areas of codes, explicit and implicit; and hence also the unimportance of these codes being in agreement with one another.[2] The scope required of warranted expectation is by and large no greater than the single profession.

Yet for each profession of this kind the task of showing that it is morally credible and morally accountable has to be an important one. Thus the need to affiliate its particular code or procedures to morality in general arises and with it the need for applied ethics. And at once the ideological function of the dominant conception of applied ethics becomes clear. If and insofar as the codes and procedures of particular professions, of physicians or lawyers or corporate executives, actually were the application in their specific sphere of the rules of morality as such, then those codes and procedures would have all the justification that morality can provide. It is small wonder that in a time of relative economic hardship applied ethics should have flourished financially as well as in other ways. But if the conclusion that I have reached in this chapter is correct, applied ethics cannot in fact be achieving what, on the dominant view, it purports to achieve. What actually is going on?

The answer is: at least two quite different kinds of activity. In some areas the ideological function of the dominant conception of applied ethics masks transactions

2 It was in one recent period the case that the professional code of American psychologists prohibited lying to subjects in the course of their research enquiries, while that of American sociologists permitted such lying in certain circumstances and under certain conditions.

in which professional power and authority are being asserted in a way that protect professional autonomy from general moral scrutiny. But in other areas what the dominant conception of applied ethics partially conceals from view is a rediscovery of morality as such, and this is notably so in the case of a great deal of work in medical ethics and among the military in the last decade. Such work has been hampered, although often only marginally, by the need to think of it in terms of applied ethics. When physicians or nurses for instance discuss truth-telling, honesty, trust, and allied subjects it is almost always the case – I speak from experience of such discussions in a number of hospitals – that they are doing nothing other than reopening that general discussion of truth-telling in which Aristotle, Maimonides, Aquinas, Kant and Mill are among their predecessors. Their questions concern what the rules are and whether they need to be extended or reformulated, questions perhaps occasioned for them by peculiarly medical issues and questions peculiarly urgent for physicians and nurses, but not at all peculiarly medical questions.

The rubric of 'applied ethics' is thus in both areas a barrier to understanding what is actually going on. In some instances it protects power from scrutiny, in others it disguises the general moral importance of what is occurring. Applied ethics is not only based upon a mistake, but upon one that has proved to be harmfully influential.

References

Aquinas, *Summa Theologiae*, I–IIae, 94, art. 2.

Toulmin, S. (1981), 'The Tyranny of Principles', *Hastings Center Report* 11:6, 31–9.

Chapter 4

Applied Ethics and Moral Knowledge

Augusto Hortal[1]

> But could it be true that ethics exist in the world that can impose norms of *identical* content on erotic, commercial, family and professional relationships, on relations with the wife, grocer, child, rival, friend or the accused?
>
> (Weber 1969, 160)[2]

Applied Ethics and Ethics

My interest in the different areas of applied ethics and the light they shed on other areas is certainly greater than my liking for the term 'applied ethics' itself. The Spanish dictionary (*Diccionario de la Real Academia Española de la Lengua*) defines 'applied' ('aplicado, aplicada'), past participle of the verb to apply, as the effect or result of using principles or procedures of something to achieve a specific goal.[3] This definition does not seem to me to be an effective way of describing the relationship that exists between ethical 'principles or procedures' and the various fields in which they must be lived and put into practice.

In a certain way the term 'applied ethics' seems tautological. Surely all ethics have to be applied. There is nothing to stop us from talking about ethics in general or theoretical terms, without referring to specific examples of how they are put into practice. But in such instances, it should be made very clear that we are talking about an abstraction, which is a long way from true and complete ethics, and could only be applied on a secondary level to the different areas. Any ethical statement that is not applied directly should be able to be so. If, when you try to put it into practice, it becomes clear that this is not possible, then its theoretical value should also be put into question. For this reason, in my view, it is more accurate to talk about ethics in general on the one hand and ethics with the respective specification for each case

1 University Comillas, Madrid.

2 E. Durkheim states this more categorically: 'Nous avons des devoirs comme professeurs, qui ne sont pas ceux des commerçants; l'industriel en a de tout autres que le soldat, le soldat que le prêtre,… Ces morales ne sont pas seulement distinctes les unes des autres, il en est entre lesquelles il y a une véritable opposition …' (Durkheim 1937, 536ff.).

3 *aplicar* (Del lat. *applicare*, arrimar) tr. Poner una cosa sobre otra o en contacto con otra. 2. fig. *Emplear alguna cosa, o los principios o procedimientos que le son propios*, para mejor conseguir un determinado fin. 3. fig. *Referir a un caso particular lo que se ha dicho en general*, o a un individuo lo que se ha dicho de otro … ' (the last two italics are mine, A.H.).

(economic, political, family, professional, financial, sexual, ecological) on the other. But attempts to prescribe how terms should be used in ordinary language usually have little success. So I resign myself to using the common expression 'applied ethics'.

It is interesting to establish the relationship between ethics and applied ethics. What is common to all ethics and to any particular field of applied ethics? What do ethics always entail by definition and what makes it different and plural by being lived and put into practice in different areas and subject matters? This article aims to concentrate on how ethical knowledge in general is illuminated when approached from the various areas of applied ethics and from morality itself experienced in different areas. As I have suggested in other essays, 'Those who live and create ways of life …, and those who suffer unbearable ways of life, also create visions that extend the ways in which we evaluate shared human life. Lived morality is not just a field of application of previous knowledge, reached through a distancing process and conceptual and social distillation. Knowing how to live, at least knowing how to learn from the lessons of life is necessary, useful and fruitful as far as ethics is concerned', with regard to its plural and singular qualities (Hortal 1999, 87; the aim here is to further the discussion presented in that article).

Within applied ethics we will concentrate on professional ethics, in which aspects mentioned in our ethical discussions are at stake. Plato and Aristotle frequently enquired into the nature of crafts and professions and used arguments based on them in their treatment of philosophical questions. In recent times, a small number of philosophers have elected to examine the area of professions. Instead the biggest contribution to this field has come from the professionals themselves and from sociologists.

Neither the deontological nor the utilitarian ethical approaches are particularly concerned with professional ethics. In utilitarian terms, all the colours of the professional rainbow are grey. Historical traditions, social locations and profiles distinct from any type of role, including professional roles, are treated with distrust as well in the realm of 'final ends'. Participation in communicative dialogue without impositions or asymmetries or fair negotiation of the existing norms for all, necessitates neutralising differences, including occupational differences, which are perceived as particularisms and suspect circumscription into domains.[4]

Communitarian ethics, inspired by Aristotelian thought, place the focus on the social context, on cultural traditions, on the morally qualified agent based on virtues; thereby providing a different approach from *professional ethos* which is always historical and contextual. As moral philosophers have begun to deal with themes of 'applied ethics', Aristotelian ethical theory has begun to find its way into the arena once more. Faced with the importance and complexity of biomedical themes, ethics

4 For example, K.-O. Apel: 'Even today there is a parallel coexistence, rationally influenced, *of morals of roles* or *professions* – for instance, pertaining to a soldier or salesman and even a mafia boss, who is at the same time a devout member of the Church – a parallel coexistence which recalls those archaic situations in which a guest while inside a tent or house was inviolable but as soon as he left the confines of the house and went outside become the subject of bloody revenge also imposed morally' (Apel 1986, 107ff.).

have moved away from psychologising subjectivism and cultural relativism towards interest in comparative case studies (casuistry) approached with circumspection, to focus on the specific duties of professionals and it has opened out new avenues in which to explore this kind of equity which – in contrast with equality – takes into account the differences (Toulmin 1982, 744ff.).

Any profession is undertaken with a view to achieving the goals that form part of the *telos* of a good or virtuous life. These ends are sought and reached according to the opportunities and uses available at any given time in history; they define the standards of excellence in the execution of each profession. The world of the professions is a field where ethics have to cultivate the themes of goodness and virtue. Being a competent and responsible professional does not simply consist of being a rational and free individual as described by universalistic ethics of a deontological nature. A professional is a human being who has undergone a socialisation whereby it is assumed that he has acquired not just skills but also ways of acting. This encompasses a sense of belonging to a professional group and to a tradition centred on the best individualised rendering of a specific type of service, a sense of what it is to be a good professional, what his professional obligations are, how to interpret them today from a traditional or historical perspective – written or otherwise – of professional practice, his best achievements and deviations or bad practice. Professional ethics could counterbalance the homogenisation of moral agents and of the 'moral space' in general. This undoubtedly affects the perception of the unity of ethics and the way in which different elements relate to one another within this.

The Three Levels of Ethics

We understand by ethics a systematic, reflexive and critical understanding which studies moral life in order to guide, justify or question the acts or decisions of moral agents. This guidance, justification and questioning is sought in ethics at three interrelated levels:

a. *the general ethics level* at which everything that ethics entail, demand or recommend is reflected on always and in all circumstances. Let us leave open for the time being the question of whether the aim at this level is solely to support and justify or whether the practical and prescriptive dimension of ethics is also present and operative, be it substantive or simply procedural. In order to clarify my position, I would suggest that general ethics also has a practical and prescriptive dimension, which is internal to ethics at any level. Such practical and prescriptive dimension I would argue is substantive and not simply procedural, however problematic and in need of justification that these statements may be under modern conditions;
b. *the special ethics level*, also called applied ethics: economic ethics, political ethics, medical ethics, legal ethics, professional ethics, business ethics, educational ethics, family ethics … In order to guide, justify or question the acts and decisions of the moral agents in these fields, the general demands, approaches and recommendations of the previous level do not suffice (much

less mere theoretical or exclusively procedural support and justification). At this level it is necessary to take into account of the peculiarities of the different areas of human life, seeking specific guidance applicable to specific acts and decisions;

c. *finally there is the level* of ethics that reflects on, accompanies, seeks to illuminate and guide the process of taking decisions in each individual case.

A. Cortina[5] and M. Kettner (2000), departing from Apelian approaches that they elaborate on and make more flexible, identify three separate parts in ethics:

a. *part A* of ethics is concerned with rational support for moral norms in general (*im Allgemeinen* – in M. Kettner's terms);
b. *part B* concerned with the principles that allow the principle discovered in part A to be applied to the various areas of everyday life (*im Besonderen* – according to M. Kettner);
c. and *part C* of ethics that aims to clarify the decision-making process in each individual case (*im Einzelnen* – in M. Kettner's terms).[6]

Moreover D. Gracia describes what he calls three levels of moral reasoning:

a. the level described as 'formal, purely canonical, which affirms the totals respect of all human beings';
b. the level concerning the 'content of the moral principles deriving from the latter, such as the four principles of bioethics: autonomy, beneficence, non maleficence, and justice'; and
c. the level concerning the 'analysis of the circumstances and the consequences of individual cases' (Gracia 1997, 37).

At the risk of introducing a slightly different terminology than that shown above, it could enrich our discussion of the statute of applied ethics to mention a recent article by P. Ricoeur entitled 'De la morale à l'éthique et aux éthiques' (VV.AA. 2000, pp. 103–20). The author claims that this article represents a rewriting rather than a retractation of the chapters dedicated to ethics in his book Soi-même comme un autre (1990). Ricoeur believes it is necessary to use two terms, moral and ethics, to reflect the complexity of the moral phenomenon, which he compares to a river at different stages of its course. Morality is located halfway through; what he calls 'anterior' ethics are upstream ('amont') and 'posterior' or applied ethics are

5 (Cortina 1993, Ch. 10, pp. 161–77; see also Cortina 1996).

6 Adela Cortina does not seem to identify part C with the casuistical tradition in either of her two versions: *Casuistry 1* or 'the art of applying any type of moral principles at hand to specific cases' and *Casuistry 2* or 'the art of making probable judgements on individual and punctual situations' (rhetoric). For her prudence 'virtue pertaining to the application of rules and principles in specific situations' only makes sense in traditional ethics; in modern times '*Casuistry 1* stopped making sense and lost legitimacy as regards shared morality' and *Casuistry* 2 only has a place in American pragmaticism, of the 'American way of thought that inevitably accompanies the American way of life'. See Cortina 1993, 167–72.

downstream ('aval'). Morality refers to the regions of norms and sense of obligation: the feeling of being obliged by the norms. Immersed in the midst of the stream of the moral experience, Ricoeur suggests going back upstream (amont) towards the source which what he dubs anterior ethics or going downstream (aval)[7] where we find what he calls the support for the norms or posterior ethics and which usually corresponds to what we call applied ethics.

Ricoeur underscores the need for a dispersed or split concept of ethics covering both anterior ethics and posterior ethics. He makes and comments on two fundamental assertions in this text: (1) Anterior ethics seeks to root itself in the norms of life and in desire; posterior ethics seeks to insert norms in specific situations; and (2) The only way of reaching what precedes the norms (which is what anterior ethics proposes) is to reveal its contents at the level of practical wisdom, which is none other than posterior ethics (104). The only way of disclosing the primordial depths of ethics is to project this at the post-moral level of applied ethics (114).

Similarities can be observed in the presentation of the three parts or levels of ethics, but differences can also be perceived in the way in which each part is described and its relationship with the other two. Below I aim to examine the issue of the statute of applied ethics departing from the question of moral knowledge. Ethics referring to specific fields, or applied ethics, can be placed in the middle ground between general ethics and decision-taking in singular situations. On some occasions, they will be closer to general ethics and the formulation of principles, norms and criteria in universal terms albeit circumscribed to a specific field of application. On others, the emphasis will fall on application, putting into practice and obviously any application or putting into practice means that specific decisions have to be taken in each situation.

The moral knowledge appropriate to applied ethics has to combine two items:

1. The first question raises the subject of the relationship between universal norms and principles on the one hand and individual cases, punctual situations and decisions on the other. In other words, as M. Kettner puts it, how the universal (both the generic and the specific) relate to the individual.[8]
2. The second question concerns how the particularisms or specificities of the various areas of applied ethics are related to the unity of ethics of a human life. What type of complex unity might be involved in ethics which must be applied at home and at work, in politics and the economy, in classrooms and the law courts, in engineering and in journalism, etc.?

7 The French term 'aval' means 'downstream' as well 'support or guarantee'. This word play is untranslatable into English.

8 It is important to draw a clear distinction here between 'universal' (as opposed to 'singular' or individual) and 'general' or 'generic' (as opposed to the 'specific') in the terms used by Hare (1963, 38ff.). On occasions, 'particular' is contrasted with universal and on others with singular, which serves to complicate the terminology. Applied ethics are specific ethics or particular ethics which, like general ethics, are formulated in universal terms and are always practised, like the former, in particular and individual situations.

We will start by exploring the theme of the putting into practice or application of the universal norms and principles to individual cases, decisions and actions in punctual situations.

From Principles to Contexts: From Contexts to Principles

Any action or any decision subject to an ethical judgement has to take place in an individual situation and a particular context. Norms and principles can only to put into practice ('applied') through singular actions and decisions in singular situations. The theme of the relationship between the universal and the individual – the eternal problem of universals which here concerns us from a practical standpoint – is common to both general ethics and special or sectorial ethics. Each action or 'application' is always singular and individual; principles, both the generic or general principles of ethics and the specific principles of applied ethics (and any moral norm) are universal. In other words principles are valid for a range of elements that the corresponding principle (or norm) refers to in more or less detail or degree of generalness. It is just as universal to say 'all human beings are born free and equal in dignity' (general principle) as 'doctors should act with the informed consent of their patients' (specific principle of medical ethics) or 'doctors shall respect the privacy or intimacy of their patients during medical examinations'. Reserving the term universal for principles of maximum generality that concern all human beings is obviously inaccurate and in turn presents specific principles as mere 'application' of generic ones or as unacceptable particularisms.

Applied moral knowledge aims to guide the responsible action of persons in situations where they have to act and take decisions. For this purpose they need to move at different levels that could and should combine together to say and justify what it is right to do and what we should avoid in said situations. To start with this involves (a) knowing the situations and circumstances; (b) perceiving the possibilities they entail; (c) the various courses of action that emerge. In order to grasp what is at stake in each individual situation we tend to have recourse to (d) typologies that show us what is similar and what is different in each situation to other comparable situations and other courses of actions we are already familiar with, either because we have lived through them or experienced them ourselves or because they are part of a common culture, rich in stories, proverbs, etc. This enables us to measure what is at stake in these situations and in these different courses of action. Moreover this necessitates (e) good judgement to see which typologies this situation is subsumed under and the appropriate courses of action, (f) which principles need to be called on, (g) how any potential conflicts between such principles can be approached and possibly resolved, (h) how a hierarchy can be justified among them and (i) whether this order is stable or changing depending on the circumstances.[9]

---

9 Jonsen and Toulmin (1984) call taxonomy a typology, which they compare with the description of symptoms and illnesses of the condition which the doctor bases himself on to make a clinical diagnostic of a case he has before him. The discussion between casuistry and principalism presented by US bioethics undoubtedly has a bearing on our subject matter. See DuGose, Hamel and O'Connel (eds) and Gert, Culver and Clouser (1997).

It is evident that moral knowledge is much more than a simple deductive application of a single principle or a rigid hierarchy of principles. Nor is it simply a descriptive knowledge of situations, circumstances, actions and consequences. In moral knowledge descriptions of facts, gathering possibilities and normative evaluations are inextricably linked but not blurred. The best way of approaching this complex issue is to enter the hermeneutic circle in which the situations illuminate, confirm or call into question the applicability of the principles and the principles illuminate, make intelligible and make demands on the actions we carry out in the situations. '*The structure of applied ethics*, Adela Cortina writes, *is not deductive or inductive*, instead it enjoys the circularity pertaining to a critical hermeneutic ...' (Cortina 1993, 174). It is implemented by 'impure experimental reason' (Conill 1998; see also Conill 1997).

I am happy to jump on the bandwagon of a critical hermeneutic of human activities. Principles need to adapt to situations in order to be practical and to be taken into account. In order to understand what is at stake in situations and decisions they need to be described and narrated in terms that presents them as subsumed or subsumable, at least in part, under principles. Only constant mediation between the principle and situations in which we have to act sheds light on, in a reciprocal way, the specific morality lived and the ethics conceived in universal terms, regardless of whether these are generic or specific. Is it possible to access principles from singular decisions in each singular context. The contexts and decisions in turn are illuminated by the principles that are at stake therein.

Compliance with a norm and putting a principle into practice is never, or seldom, simply an application of an individual case of a universal principle or norm. Only the stereotypical examples from de-contextualised discussions would make us think otherwise, but at the expense of the complex reality of the specific and changing situations in which we have to act. Moreover, in order to understand what is at stake in the situations and decisions as far as moral life is concerned, they should be seen, described and narrated in terms that present them as subsumed or subsumable (at least in part) under norms and principles. On occasions, it is worth interpreting the situation and decision in the light of different and contrastive norms or principles that are difficult to harmonise. In such situations and decisions with their contexts, host of factors, unrepeatable opportunities, unavoidable conflicts, foreseeable consequences, there will also be aspects that are difficult to catalogue. This means they cannot be fully understood if they are classified as just another case of a particular type regulated by universal norms, laws and principles.

Although a reaction against formalist or procedural universalism of deontological ethics guides us in our endeavour, we do not intend to go to the other extreme, namely to fall into casuistry or situationist 'nominalism'. The alternative we seek draws a fine but distinctive line somewhere between rationalist deductivism and abuse of casuistry. Every time we act we perform a totally singular act at a given time and in singular circumstances. But the words we use to refer to this act and these circumstances could equally be used to refer to other similar acts and circumstances that we may have already experienced or that other people have experienced or might experience. We act in significant contexts and circumstances, perhaps within a particular institutional framework in which we play a particular role, within a cultural tradition with which we identify or with which we have a distinct and conflictive relationship. The ethical judgement that two similar actions merit in similar circumstances must be the same, unless significant differences can be identified between one action and another, between certain circumstances and others; those predicated by time and place and the change of one subject for another are not sufficient criteria to discriminate between an ethical judgement for one action and that of another similar action, *caeteris paribus*.

Aristotle states that 'reasoning based on first principles differs from that which leads to principles' (EN 1095a 31ss). Principles, by associating with the ineluctable aims of human life, provide the situations and actions in which they must be put in practice ('apply them') with guidance through which it is possible to bestow moral unity and coherence on the moral trajectory of the person performing the act. In absence of principles shared to a lesser or greater extent by the persons living and living together, there will not be any coherence between what some people do and what others do, nor will there be any social cohesion, justice, nor ethical criteria beyond arbitrary preferences or changing opinions of each individual at any given time.

On the other hand, ethics that only adhere to principles becomes rigid,[10] as it fails to take into account the peculiarity of the different areas or the changing circumstances. This ends up modifying the specific judgement that the actions merit in different contexts. Adhering to the same principles in situations that are not the same could lead to potential injustices by applying identical criteria to circumstances that are not identical. Morality lived through singular actions brings normative specification and experiential contrast to principles. Thus enabling us to call into question the knowledge and guidance that principles provide in situations that hitherto seemed comparable.

We adhere to principles when we do not wish to enter into the complexities and peculiarities of the fields in which we act, when we are not willing to yield to circumstantial considerations that could relativise what these principles seek to protect, safeguard, guarantee and what we believe should be protected, safeguarded and guaranteed. We have recourse to casuistry and contexts when we would like principles to be negotiable, at least as far as their applications and the attention to circumstances that concur in a specific situation are concerned.[11]

What are Principles? What Role Do They Play in Action?

Before entering into an epistemological consideration of principles it is worth clarifying the contribution they make to the intelligibility of an action and what is at stake by acting in one way or another in different situations.

10 Tyranny as described in Toulmin (1981). But to use J. Conill's expression, a 'tyranny of contexts' could also exist and should be avoided.

11 Engelhardt (1995) refers to the book by Jonsen and Toulmin (1984) and argues that any recourse to casuistry is misguided, only appropriate in crisis situations when different moral visions coexist.

According to the linguistic analysis of R.M. Hare moral principles and norms are universal imperatives that prescribe or prohibit, recommend or advise against something. In strictly logical terms, it is acceptable to describe principles as comparable to imperatives, providing that we bear in mind the way in which the universal nature of principles bestow the terms 'imperative', 'prescribe' and 'prohibit' with a meaning that is metaphorical or derived to a certain extent. Principles, separated from situations, and speaking in general terms, rather than prescribing, ordering or prohibiting an action (as a speaker can do to an interlocutor through an imperative expressed in an individual situation) propose an evaluative perspective that should be taken into account when performing and evaluating specific actions. An imperative as such prescribes an action to the person who has to perform it in a punctual situation; the principle formulates a binding reason to act in a particular sense. A principle does not say whether exceptions are allowed due to special circumstances nor does it mention the ways in which it could come into conflict with other principles that could be invoked and prevail, notwithstanding the binding and valid nature of the first principle formulated.

From the point of view of the theory of action, principles formulate and highlight elements that an agent or group of agents feel especially bound by, to give their actions direction and personal and social coherence and prevent them from becoming merely occasional, opportunist or arbitrary. The principles that an agent adopts in his actions enable him to maintain personal and group commitments linked to the ultimate goals of human life through different episodes and contexts.

For Onora O'Neill (1989) maxims are underlying principles that make sense of the various specific intentions of an agent. This notion is likely to be misunderstood by thinking of them in terms of adopting norms that prescribe or proscribe specific actions. Maxims and principles are indeterminate directives that can only be put into practice when they are complemented with more specific intentions.

For instance, if I wish to give a friend a good reception I prepare a cup of tea, I warm the teapot, I offer him sugar ... What guides and gives meaning to these specific subordinate intentions is the underlying principle of giving a friend a good reception. If I held the opposite principle (bad reception) I would do other things. If I held the same principle in another culture I would carry out other acts. The same underlying principle in different cultural situations is expressed through different specific intentions, such as offering wine instead of tea, conversation, etc. It is possible that the specific intentions that put into practice an underlying principle in an appropriate way in a context, serve to carry out another different principle in another context. Today the maxim that commands us 'not to deceive others' can be translated into not signing cheques that will bounce, not being a spy, not manipulating public opinion ... In the days when there were no cheques, spies or public opinion these actions would be incomprehensible. In other contexts, deception could refer to not carrying weapons hidden on our person.

Actions become intelligible in the context of practices and institutions. Such contexts have their own history without which the different intentions of the agent become unintelligible. By adopting maxims of an appropriate moral type rather than adopting a set of moral norms we are adopting certain directives for life: to live a particular type of life and be a particular type of person.

Morality, according to this author, consists not so much of having appropriate principles, but of shaping one's actions to specific norms and criteria. By adopting the maxims or principles of a certain type of morality rather than adopting a set of norms we are adopting certain general directives for life, for a particular type of life and to be a particular type of person.

This fits well with the consideration of principles as ends, as we find in MacIntyre. In any shared moral culture the universal principles always have a material content and they articulate in the form of a principle what they take as given, the goals of human activity of individuals and groups. In practical life the *telos* provides the principle.[12] The various areas of application of ethics are built around particular goals that are more or less determinate: recovery or healthcare in medicine, generation and distribution of wealth in the economy, extending knowledge in research, etc. The goals that make up the principles in each of these fields are not totally clear; just as the search for the good life consists of striving to ascertain what the good life consists of for man, being a doctor consists of striving to ascertain what health is and how it is looked after or restored and the same is true in other professions and fields pertaining to special or applied ethics.

The content of moral principles, when applicability is intended, will invariably bear the imprint of the situations in which they are usually invoked. While society does not change either objectively (the situations are recurrent) or subjectively (the goals and aspirations are the same) the moral principle maintains its content, imprint and applicability. Should the circumstances, goals and aspirations of the moral agents change, the principles become (at least in part) problematic. They can be and usually continue to be maintained but one clause or another is either added or taken away to deal with the new objective situations or subjective aspirations.

The problematic nature of principles may reside in the fact that are not valid in themselves or that the formulation they have been presented in has proved incorrect. Mostly principles become problematic not because they are not valid in themselves or because they were never valid, but usually because the formulation they have been presented in has become problematic due to a change in the pragmatic grounds associated with its usual formulation. They need to be reinterpreted, that is to say, a hermeneutic approach needs to be adopted.

In situations of social and cultural stability, principles acquire an intuitive proof and they enjoy stability in their applications in recurring situations. When circumstances change, they become problematic both subjectively and socially. Principles with normative contents are not there, nor do they enjoy immediate and unquestionable proof on the fringes of the stability or instability of the social situations in which they are invoked. The principles are adduced to justify or forswear specific actions and acts. And before they are adduced they are invoked. Which moral and intellectual guarantees are offered? How can a principle be justified? Based on what? Or on what basis?

12 '*Archê*/*principium* and *telos*/*finis*, so it must seem, stand or fall together' (MacIntyre 1999, 7).

How are Principles Justified?

At an epistemological level, principles are axiomatic propositions which serve as the point of departure for a demonstration. In the field of ethics, principles are universal principles which makes fulfilment thereof morally necessary, at least until they come into conflict with other principles that are not compatible with the first (*prima facie*, as described by D. Ross). They are called upon to justify or authenticate specific types of evaluations or specific types of actions involving them. And this begs the question on what cognitive basis these principles can be asserted and justified.

In *Nicomachean Ethics* (1098b, 3–5) Aristotle suggests that principles can be known through intuition (*aisthesis*), abstraction (*aphairesis*), experience contrasted with individual cases that allow us to engage in the elaboration of rules and drawing of general conclusions (*epagogé*, also called induction) or, finally, through habit or custom (*ethismos*). Each of these forms of knowledge contributes in part to the moral knowledge that principles enclose.

For centuries 'intuition' has been understood as immediate proof of first principles with normative content. For Aristotle the sensitive experience (*aisthesis*) was passive and immediate, hence there was no room for error. This characteristic of being unquestionable immediate proof is later claimed by the *prima facie* duties in intuitionism. Before this the propositions of the natural law of stoicism or scholasticism, as well as those of pre-Kantian modern rationalism considered that the first principles of morality enjoyed an unquestionable proof rooted in the rational human nature. From these first proofs it is worth deriving, at a secondary level, the contingent and circumstantial 'applications'. Later the intuitionism of D. Ross takes the first principles ('*prima facie duties*' as he calls them) as primary unquestionable data present in all intellectually and morally healthy minds. They are not demonstrable, but they can be 'shown', hence no rational foundation is sought for them other than that which is in accordance with the intuitive immediacy with which they are associated.

Critics of intuitionism, a group I include myself in, usually point out that such appeal to intuition takes away the principles appealed to, and to an even greater extent the terms and contents with which they are associated, from the rational debate. Measurements become impossible in the midst of intuitive proofs. There is a core of truth in intuitionism. Only beings capable of moral experience can feel connected by ethical principles; but what these are and, above all, which normative contents they are associated with, which specific actions violate them and which fulfil them, is to a large extent linked to common judgements and uses of the moral culture in which such principles are invoked and in which those invoking them have been socialised. It is legitimate to appeal to the specific moral experience and therefore also to the sensitive experience of each individual. Whenever we exhort, encourage, question another in moral terms we are appealing to his conscience and moral sense. Notwithstanding, any attempt to base the intersubjective validity of normative contents on this subjective instance is similar to confusing the stage in a theatre with the play being put on there.

The normative contents of our shared intuitions, unless proved otherwise, coincide as they emerge from customary ways of assessing our culture. Such customary ways possess a very deep subjective proof and are reflected and reinforced constantly through language as they have been internalised in the first socialisation. Nonetheless, this does not make them any less questionable.

Although they are not unquestionable or unchangeable, moral principles are backed by the guarantee of an accumulated experience of the habits and customs of a way of life that has been or is being lived by a human group. This form of knowledge regarding principles can be associated with what Aristotle calls knowing principles through habit or custom (*ethismos*). Moral knowledge has a social and cultural basis that is condensed in a number of principles in which many different evaluations and guidelines converge and are integrated in a broad range of contexts. The fact of being broadly adduced and applied by a group that takes them as a guide does not confer on them indisputable authority. Nonetheless they are supported by rich experience contrasted through recurring situations, which in synthetic terms, they make available to new agents. This knowledge stems from experience and is usually transmitted through language; but this alone does not support an ultimate foundation, nor can it be supported by this. Principles with normative content cannot offer or claim a definite justification if they are only based on accumulated cultural experience. But the latter contributes essential knowledge as regards detailing, specifying and comparing the normative content of ethical principles.[13]

Discussion concerning intuitions or contrasted customs cannot be resolved by appealing to the immediate experience of each subject nor at the level of shared experiences in a specific culture or tradition. The other two methods, namely comparative consideration (*epagogé*) and abstraction (*aphairesis*) set forth by Aristotle take us a step further. Principles can be understood as sensible generalisations in which the moral experience acquired by individuals or groups up to that point in time is accumulated and formed. Experience acquired through action provides guidance on what we wish to encourage or avoid in the future; this moral experience sheds light on any recurring situation reminiscent of the one already lived. The richer that experience is, because it has been compared with other situations and perspectives, the richer the content of the knowledge of the principles will be and we will know how to apply it better to changing situations. Situations that do not belong to one's own tradition or culture should also be approached from the same hermeneutic perspective, in an attempt to understand. The problems are twofold here: either they stem from a rejection from the outset of the experience of others as it does not tally with what one knows from one's own experience or from trying too hard to understand and ending up not understanding anything at all.

Comparative considerations bring a rich variety of cases to moral knowledge. Abstraction, in view of the myriad of situations and cultures that exist, seeks universality. It is feasible to abstract universal contents? Which formula allows us to appeal to principles as valid in all the situations in which they are invoked? Through abstraction we reach formulations of first principles that are more or less formal or tautological: 'Avoid evil and do good', 'Live an honest life, do no harm to anyone;

13 'All ideas of importance do not discover what they are worth or how they can be polished, in divine and human terms, unless they are put into practice and experienced, shared and refined by many people over a significant period of time' (Tornos 1995, 11).

give to each his just reward'... It has often been pointed out that moral principles are either vacuous tautologies or their normative content is problematic, as made manifest in the divergent and even contradictory views that authors have attempted to justify, based on natural law or reason over the centuries. The tautological vacuity of these principles considered in isolation is filled as soon as they serve to name important aspects at stake in contextualised decisions and to encourage specific courses of action and argue against others in situations that without these principles offer us a blinding richness.

Kant replaces the intuition of principles with normative intentional content with the rational need through which the moral agent wishes to act rationally and independently. First principles, or in other words the only categorical imperative, bereft of any empirical content, constitute the supreme and sole law governing moral will. Practical reason is that which must be assumed to make possible and give meaning to any moral experience and any ethical approach. Principles are understood as *a priori* propositions that have to be assumed so that any moral experience and any ethical approach is possible or has meaning. This goes a step beyond abstraction; it offers an *a priori* rational criterion (a formal one) enabling any normative content to be subjected to a test and excluding any contents that do not meet the formal requisites set forth in said test.

Hermeneutic criticism of human activities, to reach an understanding of moral experience in all its facets, needs to take into consideration sensitive experience (J. Conill refers to 'experiential reason'), the rational structures without which all understanding lacks consistency and stable intelligibility, as well as taking into account social or cultural experience (*ethismos*) and the sensible way of gradually clarifying what the social and personal experience accumulated can give us in terms of practical wisdom. It is also worth asking about what cannot be and the conditions of possibility of rational moral knowledge; thus the *a priori* dimension will be revealed which, in order to be applied, must be measured and reinterpreted in the light of the situations, contexts, experiences and wisdom accumulated and tested by comparative appreciation.

From a teleological perspective principles are anchored to the *telos* of human life, whether this is understood as the basic aspirations that structure and authenticate a culture's way of life or as the *telos* with anchorage in human nature or rationality. When seeking to justify practical principles we need to turn to what we achieve through them and examine to what extent they derive from goals that cannot be overlooked in human life. This does not mean that dignity has to be diluted simply in search of happiness. The *telos* of human life has the dimension of an end in itself and it has a dimension of *telos* anchored in and enriched by the cultural experience of different traditions.

MacIntyre (1999) argues that in today's world we see a principle as an affirmation or norm that serves as the basis of our arguments. For Aristotle or St. Thomas of Aquinas a principle was also the reality that the principle refers to. They united what our contemporary language divides. First principles only have a place in a universe described in terms of specific fixed and unalterable end. No principle is a first principle in itself today; it is only a first principle from a specific standpoint. The primacy of principles is related to contexts, as well as to individual or social ends.

The supreme principles of human endeavour are nothing more than a normative translation of those ineluctable ends of human life. In practical life the *telos* provides the principle, the first principle of practical reasoning.[14] In the light of this we aim to cover the theme of the unity of ethics.

Unity and Plurality of Ethics

We have been concerned up to now with relating general ethics to special or applied ethics (parts A and B of ethics) to singular actions and decisions that put them into practice (part C). Universal principles, both generic ones belonging to general ethics, and specific principles of applied ethics, are enriched, modulated, specified and contrasted in the light of the 'applications' that put them into practice. Our focus now shifts to our other theme of discussion: how part A is related to part B of ethics, how the generic aspect of ethics is related to the peculiar, particular or specific nature of applied ethics.

Moral life is conducted in different areas, in a host of situations and contexts shaped by different normative structures. To guide, justify or question the decisions and actions of moral agents in the fields of economic ethics, political ethics, medical ethics, business ethics, educational ethics or family ethics, it is not sufficient to establish approaches or requirements or recommendations at generic ethics level. If we aim to find specific guidelines that enable us to take decisions, carry out or question specific actions, the normative structure of each field needs to be examined in turn. Everything that applies to one context does not necessarily apply to another. A doctor's commitment to caring for the health of a patient or a judge's duty to pass sentence in a conflictive lawsuit, or the labours of a researcher, architect or journalist are not subject to the same norms, principles and ethical criteria. In the terms employed by Max Weber in the quotation included at the beginning of this article: those who engage in erotic, commercial, family or professional relationships are not governed by the same norms and no person has the same duties towards a spouse, child, shopkeeper, competitor, friend or the accused.

It is always possible to draw similarities, points of comparison and even basic binding principles in all contexts, simply through abstraction and formalisation. We can always say that an individual should fulfil 'his duties' (father, son, etc.), should respect the other as a person, act justly; 'avoid evil and do good', 'each person should act in accordance with maxims that can be universalised' or 'help to make as many people happy as possible'... The specific points that are eliminated or diffused in the process of abstraction and formalisation need to be recovered when they are put into practice to serve as a guide in specific areas. Therefore, once again what is applicable to certain areas will not be applicable to others.

The plurality of normative fields and the modulation of valid and applicable principles therein present us with the problem of the unity of ethics. How can

14 Aristotle says in passing on one occasion (EN 1144 a 23ss) that 'practical reasoning has a starting point, for example "given that this is the end", or "given that this is the best"...'. In other words the end is the starting point/principle.

we entertain the notion of the unity of ethics of human life when it is inevitably fragmented into family, economic, political, medical ethics, etc. etc.?

Utilitarianism, at first blush, has an easy task before it. Regardless of the kind of action that is done in any context, the only thing that matters is the contribution of those actions to generate pleasure and to avoid pain to the largest number of people possible. But as the modalities of pleasure and the satisfaction of preferences are many and varied, the problem reappears as the unitary calculation of heterogeneous magnitudes becomes impossible. Could pleasures generated by friendship ever be compared to those generated by the professional activity of an archaeologist or an architect who designed a park?

In deontological ethics the unity of moral life rests on a person's (the moral agent) autonomy and dignity. Self-governing reason establishes the formal and procedural principles that underwrite the unity and universality of ethics in a plurality of situations, fields and cultures. The unity of ethics is based on the rational subject being capable of imposing himself (*ipse*) as well as imposing the norms that he feels bound by. This appeal to what Ricoeur calls *anterior* or 'fontal' ethics ('upstream') means that the subject is capable of adhering to his self-governing reason through the changing circumstances and contexts at the heart of the ethical discussion. The multiple actions of moral life only merit being classified as moral inasmuch as they can be attributed to the rational and free subject that carries them out adhering to the supreme law of his rational autonomy. This represents the unit of attribution or 'fontal' unit of ethics in Ricoeur's terms. Without this dimension ethics is degraded and fragmented into an array of accommodating and heteronymous pseudo morals.

This approach guarantees unity but it relegates multiplicity and diversity to second place. Differences are not negated but they are blurred, especially in 'fontal', *anterior* or fundamental ethics, as singular and self-sufficient. Sectorial ethics are thereby reduced to mere fields of 'application' that do not add anything from an ethical point of view, only empirical circumstances, repercussions and consequences so that nothing modifies the most generalised, universal, singular, normative foundation.

The adventure of living humanly, undoubtedly is such because one lives it, projects it, suffers it and talks about it but we believe it also possesses a unity in which a host of facets, contexts and vicissitudes are integrated and which make it and shape it. Being a child must be related in some way to being a parent or a grandparent, being a man must be related to being a woman, being a friend to being a shopkeeper, being a lawyer to being an architect, being a soldier to being a journalist ... In order to gain a thorough idea of both the unity of general ethics and the multiplicity of specific sectorial ethics it is essential to link *anterior* ethics with *posterior* ethics. There can be no river without a source; but a river is always more than just a source. In non-metaphorical terms what we need is hermeneutic criticism of how that unique truth of ethics of autonomy is conveyed in different normative contexts. Ricoeur argues that the three formulas of the Kantian imperative point in three separate directions: the first formula points to maintaining the identity ('*ipseité*') of the individual and obliges the moral agent to act according to the dictates of practical reason in all circumstances; the second formula points to the other person as an end, who must be respected in all circumstances; the third formula points to an egalitarian participation of each person as a citizen in a state of law.

If ethics have to be implemented in different areas of personal, social, professional and political life, it is not sufficient to demand equal respect from all human beings in all contexts. The human being is not just the moral agent, he does not simply deserve respect, he also deserves to be nurtured, helped and encouraged in his search for a good life or the supreme goal which includes, apart from dignity, perfection (at least in one's own) and happiness (at least another's). Ricoeur summarises and articulates the major ethical discussions surrounding the search for a good life for and with others in just institutions. These three major discussions are not independent, they interrelated, but it would be wrong to go as far as to say that they are normatively homogenous. It is not the same to articulate ethics on the care required by another's fragility (ill person, marginalised person, etc.) as ethics on litigation and conflict of interest and rights. It is not the same to concern oneself with promoting a habitable urban space as to concern oneself with promoting fast and secure communications or true, relevant information that respects the privacy and rights of individuals.

The search for a good life contains an undeniable teleological logic and searching for good in each field can be performed and articulated in many ways, albeit many resemble one another. Recent deontological approaches also seek mediation. Some authors attempt to unblock this mediation by appealing to the two sources of Kantian morality (respect and utopia) (Gómez Caffarena 1983) or by trying to convey the convergence between the respect for the dignity of the end which is all men with the fulfilment of those ends that are also duties: perfection (one's own) and happiness (another's) (Bielsa Drotz 1998).

It is possible and legitimate to think of ethics in terms of their pure and rational nature. But 'application', in other words, implementing ethics *more kantiano* has to include at least the empirical and the changeable elements not just of this circumstance or the other or individual desire but also of that particular sector of human activities with its institutionalised ends and uses. This only seems to be less critical than adhering to the area of unmoveable, formal certainties. There is a mode of philosophical criticism that questions not just the conditions of possibility in the *a priori* structure of the subject of knowledge and moral want, but also the material and social conditions that make a decent life possible or impossible, the respect for people and the realm of ends in the different contexts in which the life and dignity of people is at stake: in classrooms and offices, in law courts and companies, in parliaments and hospitals, in the street and in the market, on the beaches and in the jails or simply sitting in front of the television or the computer. This is approached from the deontological area of ethics in one form or another as soon as interest in putting it into practice appears in the different fields of applied ethics.

The Unity of Ethics from a Teleological Perspective

In teleological ethics informed by Aristotelian theory the advantages and disadvantages are inverted. In this instance plurality is guaranteed and the problem is how to access unity from the former. Good or virtue are said in many ways; even in the field of ethical good it is not possible to apply the same criteria in different contexts. The same criteria cannot be adduced to praise or approve in a moral sense a good father, a good husband or a good son, a competent and responsible doctor, a good governor or a good citizen etc. These criteria vary according to the fields and contexts.

Here unity does not come from a single substratum, although this is not disclaimed either, but from the articulation and integration of virtues in the framework of other ends or superior goods, and then the latter in the end or supreme good that integrates them all: a full human life. Nothing is truly good, ethically good, if it is not inscribed in the project of a good life and finds its right place therein. This means that any ethical principle and teleological justification thereof needs to be interpreted in the integrating framework of the global *telos* of human life in general and the life project of a particular culture and biography. Only in this integrating teleological perspective does any partial aspect, any activity, any profession acquire ultimate legitimacy and justification. When justice is the supreme end (*fiat ius pereat mundus*; *summum ius summa iniuria*) it is not even justice. The inhuman element in ethics does not come from dimly identified pre- or para-human backgrounds but from the unilateral emphasis of a human facet which, separated from the whole, is emphasised unilaterally, at the expense of others or all others.

The supreme good is living a good life to the full; this is the end for which everything is done and it is done by itself. From there any activity can be and should be judged insofar as it contributes or harms the realisation of the supreme good. The question of what this supreme good consists of in general or specific terms is permanently open to debate. Discussion about what a good life consists of and the role specific virtues play (generally or specifically) and its more or less integrated contribution which is more or less conflictive with other superior, inferior or parallel goods … is the central theme of the ethical debate and of human life which is only resolved in part through the accumulation of practical knowledge contrasted with experience.

Naturally there are discrepancies and discussions about the degree of authority it is good for a father to have and the mode of exercising that authority; or whether a doctor should favour quicker and more efficient therapies over slower less traumatic ones; where a lawyer should draw the line in deciding which cases he should accept and which cases he should not if he wishes to fulfil his professional duties honestly … We are not talking about incidences that can be eliminated, but about an inherent feature of the ethical predicates associated with the human good and the basic ends of human life. What Aristotle says about *eudaimonia* (there is consensus of opinion that this is the supreme end in which all is sought, but there is a lack of agreement about what this should consist of) could be said of everything that could be considered a constituent good of a virtuous and full life: health, freedom justice, friendship, security, solidarity, love …

A logical analysis of moral language says that 'good' is a predicate that cannot be saturated: in any definition of good in terms of empirical characteristics, any list of criteria of virtue that is draw up, however extensive it may be, the question will always remain as to whether something that fulfils said criteria or possesses all characteristics can indeed be considered as good. This is true of an action to be classed as good, as well as for an ethically good professional, for a moral agent and for different virtues that are subject to such scrutiny.

This inherent lack of determination of the good, which only experience serves to elucidate, leads via typification and habituation of situations, actions and evaluations to sedimentation of experience in rules, regulations and principles. Rules and regulations are usually connected to certain types of actions carried out in specific types of situations giving specific types of evaluations and results. Kant's aim was not simply to distinguish but to separate in a radical sense rules from ability, advice from wisdom and mandates or laws from morality. Here we propose to relate and integrate the technical imperatives and prudential considerations in the framework of practical moral wisdom which is not restricted to fulfilling norms and duties but which puts forward both options and imperatives from the standpoint of aspiring to a decent and full human life. And this type of open *telos*, this type of principle is the human being.

The habituation and typification of situations, actions and evaluations within the framework of social interaction help to avoid having to learn everything first hand. Moreover, this builds the foundation for a fundamental value of human life: reciprocity and equality, inherent values of social life. The same situations resolved by the same type of actions and the same type of social agents merit the same moral judgements. The virtue ethics has been, in principle, clarified and institutionalised to a greater extent in some areas of human activities than in others, and those who live and act (or suffer) in them, know better than others what should be approved or condemned.

We stated that each profession is carried out with a view to fulfilling the goals that form part of the *telos* of a good life and contribute to shaping it. All applied ethics develop in their field a cataloguing of situations, topics, conflicts and ways of approaching them and resolving them that facilitates the typification and collecting of what is at stake in the decision-taking regarding the different courses of action that these situations offer or present. Occasionally new elements will appear or even unprecedented elements that were unknown, had never been named or taken into consideration; but any novelty is seen in the light of the background of known, named and typified elements. And in the end each profession has to decide whether to pose the question about its better or worse contribution not just to the specific ends of its own activity, but to human life as a whole and, what is more, not just in abstract or timeless terms but taking into account the historical, material and social conditions attending such professional activity.

Does Dignity have a Place in a Teleological Approach?

Respect for personal freedom, dignity and rights, of each person as an end in itself forms the basis of deontological ethics striving for universality. Any teleological ethical project carried out in the present day has to accommodate the idea of a person as an end in itself. Dignity, human rights, universality are not just goods, but 'hypergoods' (Taylor) without which no life project is acceptable in our culture. This is the weak point of ethics informed by Aristotelian theory. However they do contain elements and insights that can be developed without having to abandon the ethics of goods, albeit transforming and going beyond this substantially. Below we adumbrate some of the elements that enable us to move forward in this respect.

Aristotelian theory presents the concept of *activities that have an end in themselves* ('*praxeis*'), and the supreme example of this is *eudaimonia* or living a pleasant and virtuous life. The Aristotelian concept of *eudaimonia* in contrast to the medieval concept of beatitude or modern conceptions of happiness, rather than being a state or an end result represents plenitude in action: living well and acting virtuously. In addition, we find the idea that *only by acting virtuously do we become virtuous,* by practising justice do we become just, etc. In other words any goodness ends up contributing to the good or forming part of it (living well and acting virtuously) and this goal in itself once achieved means that those who achieve it necessarily become virtuous too. This suggests to a certain extent a remission of the posterior ethics to the anterior or 'fontal' ethics posited by Ricoeur.

Goods are ethical goods insofar as they are realised by human beings who as the cause of their own actions give them their ethical nature (*ethos*). They are ethical goods inasmuch as they affect, benefit or make those who do them, practise or reach them virtuous. In the Aristotelian notion of *praxis* (activity that has a goal in itself), in his conception of *ethos* or the moral character we become through our actions (only by practising justice do we become just etc.) and in the Aristotelian notion *eudaimonia* (living well and acting virtuously) as the supreme end there is not just an element of what complexive ethics cannot be without but also a germ of what becomes the goal in itself in Kantian ethics.

Ethics inspired by Kantian theory view the person as a goal in itself, personal freedom and dignity, not just as something to be reached but also as a basic assumption without which morality is unthinkable and unliveable. We could say using Aristotelian terminology, although going beyond its literal meaning, that no good can be integrated into the project of a full human life if it fails to respect the condition of goal in itself, both of the person who acts and those affected by his action. The inhuman is not a different reality, instead it is a disfiguration of the human, a way of pursuing goods that do not take due account of the other goods with which they should be combined in order to shape a full human life. Respect for the freedom and dignity of persons will be the main axis, drawing together all other goods, in order to make them goods worthy of man.

Goods are ethical goods because they are personal goods, goods enacted by persons and that affect persons. The person is a goal as such; what happens to said person has an ethical dimension as it affects one or more persons. Each person is the protagonist of his enactment of the good. An ethical good cannot be such if it is imposed on the person. People need to be respected, their dignity, freedom and rights need to be respected even when doing good to them. But the condition of person is not an entelechy or a nucleus that can be isolated from the corporal, social and historical being of each human being; it is not an added characteristic that can be separated from other corporal and social characteristics; it is the way of being what we are through the appropriation of our own possibilities which provide rational knowledge and the free desire that equips us to be, to some extent, authors of our own biography. Fulfilling oneself as a person and respecting people includes the corporal dimension (it requires food, protection, healthcare, respect for physical safety, etc.). Fulfilling oneself as a person includes the social dimension, respect and promotion of human rights, demanding responsibilities in terms of equality, freedom, justice and solidarity. All this must be done in the cultural and historical conditions that shape the possibilities and aspirations but also the inescapable demands of what it is to be a person.

Therefore it is not possible either to confuse or separate the fulfilment of a person from the fulfilment of the different facets of the human in specific historical conditions. If they are separated, respect for the person becomes void of all content and the promotion of the human becomes a mere strategy of desires. If they are confused, one facet and its historical realization are identified with the fulfilment of the person in all his facets and in all historical situations.

The personal dimension of human beings supports the constant prescriptive meaning of the word 'good' (good is always that which is recommended). The corporal, social and historical dimension of persons provides changing criteria of application of what is ethically good in certain, singular circumstances. The meaning of good and the application criteria can neither be separated nor blurred. There is no truly human happiness without dignity, nor dignity without overcoming misery, wrote once Ernst Bloch.

Translated by Clare E. Nimmo

References

Alemany, J.J. and Quinzá, X. (eds) (1999), *Ciudad de los hombres. Ciudad de Dios. Homenaje a Alfonso Alvarez Bolado* (Madrid: Publicaciones de la Universiad Pontificia de Comillas).

Apel, K.-O. (1986), *Estudios éticos* (Barcelona: Alfa).

Bielsa Drotz, A. (1998), 'Las claves teleológicas del Formalismo moral (Los fines morales del hombre y el hombre como fin en sí en la Ética de Kant)', *Convivium* 11, 80–101.

Conill, J. (1997), *El poder de la mentira. Nietzsche y la política de la transvaloración* (Madrid: Tecnos).

— (1998), 'Concepciones de la experiencia', *Diálogo Filosófico* 41, 148–70.

Cortina, A. (1993), *Ética aplicada y democracia radical* (Madrid: Tecnos).

— (1996), 'El estatuto de la ética aplicada. Hermenéutica crítica de las actividades humanas', *Isegoría* 13, 119–34.

DuBose, E.R., Hamel, R. and O'Connel, L. (eds) (1999), *A Matter of Principles. Ferment in U.S. Bioethics* (Valley Forge, PA: Trinity Press International).

Durkheim, E. (1937), 'Morale Professionnelle', *Revue de Métaphysique et de Morale* 44.

Engelhardt, T. (1995), *Los fundamentos de la bioética* (Barcelona: Paidós).

Feito Grande, L. (ed.) (1997), *Estudios de bioética* (Madrid: Universidad Carlos III, Dykinson).

Gert, B., Culver, C.M. and Clouser, K.D. (1997), *Bioethics: A Return to Fundamentals* (New York: Oxford University Press).

Gómez Caffarena, J. (1983), *El teísmo moral de Kant* (Madrid: Cristiandad).
Gracia, D. (1997), 'Cuestión de Principios', in Feito (ed.), pp. 19–42.
Hare, R.M. (1963), *Freedom and Reason* (Oxford: Oxford University Press).
Hortal, A. (1999), 'Sobre lo que viene llamándose ética aplicada', in Alemany and Quinzá (eds), pp. 77–90.
Jonsen, A.R. and Toulmin, S. (1984), *The Abuse of Casuistry. A History of Moral Reasoning* (Berkeley, University of California Press).
Kettner, M. (2000), '¿Qué marco normativo necesita la ética aplicada?', German original in Kettner (ed.), *Angewandte Ethik als Politikum* (Frankfurt: Suhrkamp), pp. 388–407.
MacIntyre, A. (1999), *First Principles, Final Ends and Contemporary Philosophical Issues* (Milwaukee: Marquette University Press).
O'Neill, O. (1989), 'Kant after Virtue', in *Constructions of Reason. Explorations of Kant's Practical Philosophy* (Cambridge, MA: Cambridge University Press), pp. 145–62; also in *Inquiry* 26 (1984), 387–405.
Ricoeur, P. (1990), *Soi-même comme un autre* (Paris: Seuil).
Tornos, A. (1995), *Cuando hoy vivimos la fe* (Madrid: San Pablo).
Toulmin, S. (1981), 'The Tyranny of Principles', *The Hastings Center Report* 11:6, 31–9.
—— (1982), 'How Medicine Saved the Life of Ethics', *Perspectives in Biology and Medicine* 25:4, 736–50.
VV.AA. (2000), *Un siècle de philosophie* (Paris: Gallimard).
Weber, M. (1969), *El político y el científico* (Madrid: Alianza).

Chapter 5

The Hermeneutical and Deliberative Nature of Applied Ethics

Jesús Conill[1]

The aim of this reflection on the standing of different forms of applied ethics is to present the basic methodological framework in which these attempt to solve the problems being dealt with. As I see it, beyond the traditional approaches, there are today two predominant slants which I would venture to call 'pragmatic' and 'hermeneutic' and which ultimately depend on whether the notion of 'application' is taken in a more pragmatic or more hermeneutical sense. In any event, both approaches break the traditional pattern of ethical theory and draw nearer to a contextualist and situational approach. It is precisely this line that has been taken by some contemporary slants, such as that of the new 'casuistry' and that of 'deliberative democracy', which I feel could be extremely useful to guide the work of applied ethics, on condition that these manage to overcome their hermeneutical shortcoming, improve the deliberative processes and own up to their unavoidable presuppositions.

The aim of this work is thus to give an account of the hermeneutical and deliberative nature of applied ethics, in order first of all to help clarify the current notion of 'applied ethics' and then provide a basic philosophical framework – that of a critical hermeneutics – for public exercise of reason through the diverse applied ethics, availing ourselves of the contributions of new casuistic procedures and the novel proposals for developing deliberation in modern social life.

The Notion of 'Applied Ethics'

The term 'applied ethics' has methodological difficulties and connotations that have often given rise to rebuffs and have led to other nomenclatures being proposed. Only if a more appropriate notion is outlined and the use of the terms involved is cleared up will one be able to go on using this with any accuracy in the republic of knowledge. To this end some preliminary observations ought to be made on this matter.

First of all it is hard to see why it would be any better to replace the fundamental ethics/applied ethics duo with that of general ethics/special ethics, as is proposed (though 'with scepticism') by Augusto Hortal (Hortal 1999, 77–90). I feel that this proposal does not provide any better solution for the problem, but simply refers back

1 University of Valencia.

to the distinction between general and regional senses of ontology; but the fact is that applied ethics, as these are being developed, break this pattern of the traditional relationship between the universal and the specific, between unity and differences. They might indeed come closer to the type of relations established by Hegel, including his peculiar way of understanding the relationship of the foundation, even though this is in a new setting, which is not essentially logical-transcendental, but deliberative (whether this is pragmatic or hermeneutic).

Apart from this, applied ethics attempt to make ethical points of view effective in factical reality, in conditions of modern and contemporary life. But this claim does not presuppose the conception of 'two worlds' as Peter Ulrich suggests (Ulrich 2000, 555–67), that is one amoral sphere and one moral sphere which would act as an authority for correcting the previous one. In my opinion, not all conceptions of applied ethics are understood under the premise of two worlds, as Peter Ulrich[2] assumes. This is not the case in a concept of applied ethics such as '*critical hermeneutics*' (Cortina 1993, Ch. 10). Furthermore, not all applied ethics is of a corrective nature, as the corrective nature is assumed by certain versions of applied ethics through the way the relevant field of activity is understood, whether this is more or less open to a self-critical ethical reflection transforming the factical reality in question.

Consequently, neither does the attempt to do without the term 'applied ethics', as seen in Ulrich's case, solve any problems, as all it actually does is to replace the term 'application' with the following periphrasis: 'explanation of the competitive relationship between two normative orientations of the action'. However, this seems above all to ignore the hermeneutical function of the application once more, that is, that this is a constituent part of understanding and thus forms an essential facet of the possible explanation of the orientation of the action. A further point should be added here. A good (better) 'understanding' of the matter itself would reveal that the competition is not essentially between normative orders, that is, between normative logics, but on a more basic level for orientation of the action: experience in a hermeneutical sense and the deliberative processes, which go beyond the 'normative conflict'.

On the other hand, if applied ethics were to understand itself from its hermeneutical background, then it would have to be explicitly acknowledged that *application* is a constituent ingredient of *understanding*, that is, of a better understanding of the real logic of each human activity. This point is decisive for understanding the specificity of applied ethics, unlike traditional approaches, and the reason why one must insist on the hermeneutical and deliberative nature of applied ethics, regardless of the conceptions of man and society (cosmovisions) being brought into play. There is no alternative other than to proceed hermeneutically and deliberatively, if the aim is to implement the project of applied ethics in the diverse spheres of social life.

Thirdly, it must be realised that although the hermeneutical standpoint does not initially provide 'normative presuppositions', it does indeed provide the factical

2 In a spirit of healthy polemics, we should not forget that Ulrich's proposal also makes use of 'two worlds' or two standpoints, which precisely for this reason needs to 'integrate' ('*integrative* Wirtschaftsethik' is what he calls his proposal), thus in this respect one ought also to include Ulrich's proposal within the descriptive term of 'applied ethics'.

properties of the logic of the situation itself. It is therefore useful to 'integrate' the factical structure and the possible normative presuppositions within a broader ethical horizon or context, above all if this is a critical hermeneutics. For example, in economy, the 'principle of gain or profit' can be bettered by a mere 'objective coercion' proper to economic facticity (only avoidable idealistically), if it is illuminated, interpreted and structured in a broader horizon or setting.

Overcoming the Hermeneutical Shortcoming in Applied Ethics

What is perhaps most striking in the approach of applied ethics in both its discursive perspective and in political liberalism consists of the fact that both methodologies have restricted themselves to the formal and procedural moment. The excessive or almost exclusive importance granted to the normative ('normative presuppositions') and the 'formal' (turned into procedural) realms overlooks the equally decisive question of the hermeneutical facticity of deliberative processes in the sphere of applied ethics.

Thus, for example, the concept of communicative reason in Apel and Habermas is excessively formalist. This is why it is important to display the virtualities of a broader notion of reason, a notion of *experiential reason*, which may help to rebuild practical reason from the hermeneutical standpoint (Conill 1991, Ch. 4; 1997, Part II), in order to more appropriately understand each sphere, each human activity, its peculiar rationality and its main facticalities.

One central point is the dominant role of experience in reason, which ties in with the role of the '*world of life*', on whose radical priority from experienced morality Augusto Hortal also insists (Hortal 1999). Another extremely relevant aspect of this approach is the consideration of *time*, as occurs in the transformation of the Kantian imperative by Hans Jonas (Jonas 1979). From this angle time forms a constituent part of hermeneutical practical reason, as otherwise it would hardly extend as far as dealing with consequences (even the unforeseen ones), the growing spectre of (foreseeable and unforeseeable) risks or future generations.

Apart from this, this hermeneutic-experiential approach may help to make universalism more dense and more contextualist. Hermeneutical reason thus not only leads one to understand the conditions of application of ethics – in our case, discursive ethics – (for example, in the situation of the 'poor' [*áporoi*] in the present global jungle or that of the sick in the field of public health), but also constitutes a vehicle for opening up to 'the others' from different cultures, communities and persons.

Hermeneutical reflection shows that when we defend reason we are not only in the realm of form and procedure, but we are fighting for significance, for vital values, for liberty (and the possibilities of liberation) as all this is also involved in the exercise of practical reason.

I thus think that Augusto Hortal's constructive criticism could find in the 'hermeneutics of experiential reason' (as we understand this here) a way to correct the excesses or unilateral facets of applied ethics in certain discursive versions (Hortal 1999, particularly 83–4). The referral to the world of life, to historic and cultural contents, to pragmatic situations and assumptions, to traditions, requires stepping beyond the logical-argumentative level to stand in the historical and vital reality of human communities and persons in their respective horizons and contexts. This has precisely been one of the now classic contributions of the hermeneutical approach in its different modalities (Gadamer 1975).

However, paying more attention to specific historical contexts and life situations in which human activities take place in each case does not mean doing without principles, which is the reason for the need to combine in a critical hermeneutics those two ineluctable sides of practical reason, the universalist claim expressed through principles and attention to the cases and contexts which form the weft of our lives. Is it possible to hermeneutically-critically integrate the first side, defended by the approach known as principlist (principlism), and the second side, cultivated by the casuistic approach (casuistry)?

The New Casuistry[3]

The work done by the *National Commission for the Protection of Human Subjects of Biomedical and Behavioral Sciences* over 1974 to 1978 led to two different and opposing interpretations, which have guided the practice of bioethics and thus of the pioneer in today's applied ethics: the one that formed the 'principle approach' (principlist) and the 'casuistic approach' (casuistry) (Gracia 1991, Chs. 2 and 3).

At first the interpretation proposed by Beauchamp and Childress prevailed (Beauchamp and Childress 1979), with its claim that the matter involves drawing up moral principles that can be applied until common rules for guiding action are obtained, in spite of not coinciding on the ethical theories sustaining these (utilitarian in one case and deontologist in the other). Nevertheless, the difficulties of this principlist approach for coming to agreements and overcoming conflicts, even between the same principles that were being invoked, favoured another interpretation of the National Commission proceedings, which led to the emergence of a new form of casuistry.

The other perspective of the *National Commission* from Jonsen and Toulmin's interpretation comes from their common sensitivity, favourable to exercising a contextualised rationality, either through the influence of Jesuit probabilism (in Jonsen's case) or through Wittgensteinian contextualism (for Toulmin). Both insist on the possibility of coming to relevant agreements on specific questions, aside from moral principles and ethical theories.

According to Jonsen, 'the Commission's success came from its attention to concrete cases, in which the principles were discovered as these were applied' (quoted in Gracia 1991, 39). This formulation, curious at first sight, should be taken note of since, if this is properly looked at, it is only truly intelligible if construed within a framework of hermeneutical rationality, in which the application is a constituent part of understanding (as was stated earlier).

Hence, in spite of the discredit and derogatory usage of the term in many philosophical circles, casuistry has gone from strength to strength since the 1980s,

3 See Gracia 1989; 1991; Kucewski 1998; Feito 1999, Chs. 3 and 8.

particularly in bioethics (and also in business ethics), in the former basically through the work of Albert Jonsen and Stephen Toulmin (Jonsen and Toulmin 1988) who assure that the initial thrust forward for this came at the now famous 'National Commission' and attribute their success to having proceeded 'taxonomically', well away from theoretical commitments. The cases were debated in the light of certain 'principles', though these were not used in a deductive way but as a sort of 'common language'. Here is yet another expression revealing a background and procedure whose best explanation would be the one provided by hermeneutics.

'Casuistry' consists basically in case-based reasoning or in any method of research which is governed more by cases than by theories. In applied ethics casuists hold that ethical theory is of little help in solving particular moral problems but if due attention is on the other hand paid to circumstances and to the details of each case, acceptable resolutions can be achieved.

The casuistic approach turns out to be a sort of diagnosis of the situation, by means of which an attempt is made to develop a moral taxonomy, after taking into account the morphology of the case. The morphology means the general features of the case and consists of a complete description of this. The following step consists in classifying the case by assimilating this in a certain type, thus recognising certain common rules to such a type of cases. After categorising the case, one has to consider both the circumstances within the corresponding social and institutional context and the convictions and ideals of the persons involved in the actions in question. Experience is required to carry out this consideration process and assess the most relevant aspects of the case (Kucewski 1998).

The paradigmatic types acting as a taxonomic guide are formed from non-controversial cases in which virtually everyone agrees. But when it comes to questions in which there is no consensus, defenders of the casuistic procedure may opt for either describing the traits of a case which could be the one most likely to give rise to some agreement, or take a more Aristotelian route and defend that paradigmatic cases are not the ones in which there is widest agreement, but those in which people with practical wisdom agree.

In any event, whatever the different forms adopted by the casuistic procedure may be, the ones already mentioned or others which give priority to the comparison of cases (Carson Strong), or to attention to the interests in conflict (Baruch Brody), basic and unavoidable tasks of casuistry continue to be: (1) the identification of 'paradigmatic cases' and (2) the ability to discover analogies between paradigms and similar cases (assimilable to such paradigms).

The appeal of this casuistic approach stems partly from the failure of the great ethical theories in the attempt to solve particular problems in specific situations, because to reply to the questions posed by each case and manage conflicts, casuistic reasoning proves more methodologically appropriate (the theory is not independent of the cases, which is the reason for the importance of paradigmatic cases) and also provides greater encouragement to furthering agreements and increased consensus.

But this casuistic particularism should not be equated with positivism, but rather with a certain pragmatism, given that casuistry starts from a presupposition that is incompatible with positivism: the relationship between facts and values, through assuming that the moral courses of action (values) can be laid down by analysing the circumstances of a case (the facts). This is a presupposition highly appreciated by tradition and by contemporary Aristotelianism in its different versions (in either the communitarian variety or in the so-called 'ethics of virtue') (Kucewski 1998; see also Oakley 2001) for it cannot go unnoticed that all casuistic approaches continue to resort to the Aristotelian notion of 'practical wisdom'. However, as I see it, this repeated resorting to Aristotle can and should be reinterpreted and incorporated in the framework of a hermeneutic-experiential reason, because the meaning of this new casuistry would be better covered by a hermeneutical paradigm than in a merely pragmatic one, since mere justification by the results which it achieves by applying its method to obtain agreement forces one to ask whether a time may not come around when this approach is reduced to an acritical pragmatism.

This revitalised form of casuistry has been called '*casuistry 2*' by John D. Arras, to differentiate this from traditional casuistry, which he calls '*casuistry 1*' (Gracia 1991, specially Ch. 7). The new casuistry takes into account the circumstances in each concrete situation and the interests of all those involved (a sort of 'moral triangulation'?). This seems to be connected, according to Diego Gracia, with a type of rationality surpassing the canons of mere formal logic and nurtured by historical and circumstantial components. In my opinion, this extension – rather than a mere comparison – of rationality is covered by the hermeneutical nature of applied ethics. Similarly many aspects of Aristotelian study of the dialectical and rhetorical dimension of the lógos (see Aristotle, *Topics* and *Rhetoric*; Gracia 1990) can be covered in a new hermeneutical context.

Applied ethics have no alternative other than to incorporate casuistic and pragmatic sense, and the major problem will be how to combine these with the also unrelinquishable meaning of so-called 'principlism', because mere casuistry is insufficient. Even the defenders of *casuistry 2* resort to 'explanatory ideals', 'paradigmatic cases', referential structures, that is, a series of 'presuppositions' without which the exercising of rationality lacks any significance. It is true that one needs to extend and go as deeply as possible into vital and historical experience and that reason is enriched by that experiential channel (Conill 1991; 2006). But the incorporation of the casuistic moment (that of the new '*casuistry 2*') in the formation of practical reason, particularly relevant in applied ethics, does not necessarily mean that this 'casuism' exhausts all the possibilities of the method proper to the new form of practising ethical reason. As Diego Gracia pointed out years ago, one has to go beyond *casuistries 1* and 2, and propose new foundations for a sort of '*casuistry 3*' (Gracia 1991, 109). The new intellectual concept provided by the so-called 'critical hermeneutics' comes in response to this integrating and also enhancing intention.

The procedure of new casuistry from Jonsen and Toulmin gives rise to 'serious questions' about such basic matters as 'moral truth' and the role of ethical theory in moral reasoning, as it attempts to implement a sort of casuistry that does without moral theories and avoids what it calls the 'tyranny of principles', as if 'consuetudinary and historical arguments' were enough to settle the moral conflicts that we come up against in the diverse spheres of social life, as if this channel really enabled us to reach the social and institutional agreements required for guiding action, as if we were not subject even more often to the tyranny of contexts and trapped by so many factical coercions.

This casuistic channel alone does not seem likely to be enough to let us overcome the contradictions arising in practical considerations, or to solve conflicts and even less channel the defence of personal beliefs and ideals as publicly defendable options, when on many occasions they prove irreconcilable. Casuistry does not guarantee the solution of conflicts, nor fulfils the intended mission of achieving consensus, nor even constitutes the best channel for forging a common will.

We consequently have to consider other possible paths to go further in the direction of mutual understanding and manage to share certain ideals or recognise certain contrafactical presuppositions in the exercise of applied ethics. In this respect, one step forward can be made in virtue of the deliberative approach provided by the proposal for 'deliberative democracy' that is explained below.

Deliberationism

Our aim in this section is to find out the virtualities provided for practising applied ethics by the deliberative approach. This takes a midway position between the homogenous unity put forward by communitarianisms and conflictualism (Coser 1976) (for which conflict unites more than prior agreement on substantive principles) and proposes dealing preferentially with deliberation processes, through which we not only manage the disagreements in social life but also form a deliberating community.

There have been – and still are indeed – diverse ways of understanding deliberation, from Aristotle to discursive ethics and Rawlsian political liberalism, and there has in recent times been increasing insistence on the need to open up spaces for deliberation in our companies and institutions, and not only in the political sphere (as in the renewed republican tradition of political philosophy) but also more specifically from applied ethics, such as our own Diego Gracia in bioethics.[4]

But we are not now going to go back to Aristotle and analyse his specific model of deliberation, because the practice of Aristotelian practical *lógos* takes place in a highly determined context of thought, that of architectural foundations of a natural (*physis*) and communitarian (*koinonía*) nature, thus alien to the present situation marked by the whole range of processes moulding modern life. In any event, when we resort to Aristotle, this will have to be filtered as far as possible – and as far as it should be – specifically in our proposal, through his hermeneutical updating (Gadamer 1975, Ch. 10).

Neither will we tarry to examine the position of discursive ethics, insofar as its contributions to the subject of deliberation are covered in critical hermeneutics through its internal correlation with the transcendental or universal pragmatics of Apel and Habermas, as well as in the reformulations in our own research team (Cortina 1985; 1990; García-Marzá 1992; Siurana 2003; see also the significant contributions in this field of Muguerza 1990).

4 At the Bioethics Institute at the Health Sciences Foundation in June 2001, directed by Diego Gracia, the 5th *Ateneo de Bioética* was devoted to the subject of deliberation in bioethics, with the significant involvement of A. Gutmann (from the liberal standpoint) and E. Emanuel (from the communitarian stance).

The present focus of our attention is going to be the methodological proposal of Amy Gutmann and Dennis Thompson (Gutmann and Thompson 1996), as it seems to provide a peculiar approach for dealing with conflicts, based on an initially political concept of 'deliberative democracy'. Its effectiveness can nevertheless be extended since, when highly controversial matters and problems have to be resolved in contemporary societies, there is – apart from the means provided by political power and juridical authorities – a model of deliberation which could function, as well or better in the diverse social and institutional spheres of applied ethics.

In my opinion, these authors, Gutmann and Thompson, have a conception which puts forward a peculiar pragmatic model of deliberation, quite unlike the Aristotelian one and the utilitarian approach, but which cannot be confused with the model of critical hermeneutics proposed by us either. Its *deliberative principles* are of a Rawlsian nature: they depend on the context, are developed and defended by means of reflection on cases, which is why the context plays a highly important role in this conception and the cases have mainly two functions: (1) to illustrate problems and principles and (2) to act as a concrete expression of pondered judgements, so this deliberative Rawlsian type method is a movement between general principles and pondered judgements about particular circumstances.

The principle of deliberative reciprocity

Gutmann and Thompson's model of deliberative democracy, whose basic idea is the need to justify policies to all those who are bound by them, is ultimately sustained on a principle of *reciprocity* and appeals to certain public principles.

One major contribution of this proposal to the public exercise of applied ethics is that it helps to live with disagreements but with mutual respect, to reason together when faced with moral disagreements in democratic contexts. Its four most specific contributions to the deliberative institutions of our societies are as follows: (1) a greater legitimacy by means of a growing process of inclusive deliberation; (2) an exercise of moral reasoning about common good; (3) a certain reduction in moral disagreement; and (4) an extension of knowledge and mutual understanding.

This apparent move from the political realm to the civic-social and institutional sphere in general entails some difficulties, but may initially guide a new form of exercising applied ethics in their respective spheres, above all in an aspect that is crucial in our societies, that of giving proper treatment to the challenge of 'moral disagreement'.

The first question that we should bring up is that of knowing what *reciprocity* we are talking about. The idea is naturally not to start from an ideal reciprocity, but not from mere bargaining either, because, when citizens reason together, they are seeking fair terms of social cooperation for its own sake. This is a point that is, in my opinion, essential for the development of applied ethics, since it would seem to presuppose a reciprocity in non-ideal conditions, but able to sustain important disagreements without shattering mutual moral respect (in spite of manifest disagreement). This model of deliberative democracy thus presupposes that one has to be able to live in continuing disagreement but maintain mutual respect, because disagreement is inevitable. What is more, the channel of continuous deliberation produces a moral improvement, a moral betterment, in spite of any enduring disagreements, insofar as it helps citizens to go on treating each other with respect.

The foundation of this reciprocity lies – in the Rawlsian style – in the capacity to seek fair conditions for social cooperation in themselves (Rawls 1993), and what underlies this reciprocity principle is the belief in the dignity and value of human beings.[5] This moral basis is what enables making reciprocal demands and motivates seeking fair conditions of social cooperation. This is why the reciprocity that is presupposed in deliberation, according to the model of deliberative democracy that we are dealing with here, cannot be mistaken for the principle of 'prudence' (reducing deliberation to mere bargaining), nor to what these authors denominate the principle of 'impartiality'. Regardless of how successful their nomenclature and its interpretation (difficult to share)[6] may be, the important thing is to stress the position taken by this principle of reciprocity and what is attempted to be achieved by this in the use of public reason (unlike what is known as 'prudence' and 'impartiality') and the scope that this could have for exercising applied ethics.

Reciprocity here lies somewhere between 'prudence' and 'impartiality' as the principle regulating reasons in democracy (Gutmann and Thompson 1996, 53; see Graph 1 below). The principle of reciprocity constitutes a guide for living with basic moral disagreements, but without ceasing to practice mutual respect and even develop certain complementary accommodation principles. This is a 'deliberative reciprocity' unlike mere bargaining on one hand and also unlike the all-embracing nature of comprehensive visions insofar as it wishes to integrate as hybrids the moment of mutual exchange (proper to prudence) and a basic moral content (by which it comes closer to impartiality). This reciprocity requires a moral component, because when people deliberate they are seeking agreement on substantive moral principles which can be justified on the basis of mutually acceptable reasons, and if this is not achieved reciprocity endures, awakening new demands, one of these at least being accommodation based on mutual respect.

Principle	Justification	Motive	Process	Goal
PRUDENCE	Mutually advantageous	Self interest	Bargaining	Modus vivendi
RECIPROCITY	Mutually acceptable	Desire to justify to others	Deliberation	Deliberation Agreement/ Disagreement
IMPARTIALITY	Universally justifiable	Altruism	Demonstration	Comprehensive view

Graph 1 (taken from Gutmann and Thompson 1996)

5 According to Gutmann and Thompson, though the moral presupposition of all human beings having dignity and value is not something that can be subjected to empirical research, it proves consistent with a set of social practices which are essential to democracy.

6 Both notions, both that of 'prudence' (quite unlike the Aristotelian one) and that of 'impartiality' (definitively, the Rawlsian one) are as I see it highly questionable.

According to this proposal, deliberative reciprocity thus is clearly distinguished from the one given in the prudential method, as this is based on self-interest, on bargaining (replacing moral reasoning) on maximising one's own or group advantage and on the threat of confrontation rather than on cooperation. For in a bargaining conception citizens have no reason to promote others' welfare, and what is rather actually being sought is one's own advantage at the expense of others, whom it considers as 'adversaries' rather than 'cooperators'.

Reciprocity in the practice of applied ethics would be materialised through the capacity for critical reasoning. However, these authors stress the fact that the result of the deliberative process between conflicting moral perspectives does not tend to be agreement, but precisely 'deliberative disagreement' and in their opinion it is precisely this aspect which establishes a basis on which those with moral disagreements may cooperate.

Deliberative disagreement and/but mutual respect

Deliberative disagreement arises in conflicts in which moral reasons so deeply divide citizens that no solution seems possible in fair terms of cooperation, when citizens continue to differ on basic moral principles, even though they go on seeking a solution which is mutually justifiable. Disagreement is fundamental because they not only differ as to the correct solution but also about the reasons based on which the conflict must be solved.

The paradigmatic case of 'deliberative disagreement' which tends to be referred to is that of legalising abortion. These deliberative disagreements involve the peculiarity that there are mutually acceptable reasons which not only put in question our best judgement but also allow other citizens to reject our judgement and defend other opposing ones. These are thus respectable disagreements. For this reason the principle of reciprocity must be extended by means of 'accommodation' principles, which are ultimately based on what constitutes the core value of reciprocity and of deliberation in a democracy: '*mutual respect*' (Gutmann and Thompson 1996, 79). This is what enables cooperation in fair terms and constitutes a form of *agreeing to disagree*, because this means a favourable attitude towards others and a constructive interaction with other persons.

This ultimately consists of excellence of character, through being open to deliberation in conflicts, of a deliberative (not merely negotiatory) attitude, which proves so fruitful in the practice of applied ethics. This is why Gutmann and Thompson consider mutual respect as a 'political' virtue generating a moral community and new more accommodating solutions to conflicts and inevitable disagreements, but in my opinion, the deliberative attitude, inspiring a new sort of 'reciprocal democracy' (and not merely procedural democracy)[7] becomes a need for any sphere of social life – not only in the political realm! If moral deliberation is to be used not only to justify

7 The radicalisation of democracy, not merely in a 'political' but also a civic and social sense, by means of exercising deliberating reason – for example in the spheres proper to each of the applied ethics – revitalises the moral life of the company by the channels through which citizens' everyday energies flow.

the order of the foundations of democracy with moral arguments, but must also function in the sphere of everyday political processes, if democracy must be moral not only in its foundations but also in its everyday processes,[8] I feel one would have to add that the need for moral deliberation has to be defended not only in politics, but in all spheres of everyday life, on all levels on which citizens live. This is the reason for the at least potential importance of this model for applied ethics. Making everyday life more deliberative is tantamount to fostering a more respectful life, and improving it morally.

I think that a perspective that combines exercising applied ethics with deepening democratic implementation processes is more appropriate and fruitful for the moral enhancement of democracy, as this constitutes an essential channel in modern life for fostering deliberation down all institutional and professional capillaries (Cortina 1993); it otherwise proves impossible to revitalise democracy as Gutmann and Thompson intend, insofar as there is a lack of channels for the required moral deliberation that they call for.

Without deliberation democracy is impoverished, because the critical capacity, progress and social cooperation are reduced, since what prevails is a conception of democracy based on pure power devoid of moral reason or only used in the form of instrumental rationalisation in the search of power through interest and bargaining between powers.

Behind it all Gutmann and Thompson's aforementioned proposal smacks on one hand of excessive trust in politics, perhaps as a result of its idealisation, when actually political models – much more so factical ones – are inappropriate for guiding deliberative processes, as these have been outlined. So, just as one has to confront 'economism', it is also necessary to unmask 'politicism' (attempting to solve all problems from presumed political reason, understood as 'bargaining' rather than as 'deliberation' thus turned into an instrument of the most powerful individuals' and pressure groups' private interests). The political model is not a good model for rationalisation of the world of life and the exercising of applied ethics.

Apart from this, throughout its conception there seems to be a certain idealising pragmatism, probably 'without express regulatory ideas' of the sort so pleasing to the philosophical tradition of continental Europe, but with the acceptance of ideal and contrafactical, not empirical, presuppositions which are considered unwaivable, something which also occasionally happens to Rawls, and which comes closer to a certain version of the 'unconditioned', however insatisfactory this may seem to its reluctant practitioners.

The point is that deliberation, if this is not to run adrift, if it is not to come down to pragmatic criteria guided by bargaining, must have certain significant (unwaivable, unconditioned?) presuppositions for the meaning of action, which neither new casuistry, nor the deliberationism defended by the theory of 'deliberative democracy' have been able to relinquish in practice.

---

8 'A democratic theory that is to remain faithful to its moral premises and aspirations for justice must take seriously the need for moral argument within these processes and appreciate the moral potential of such deliberation' (Gutmann and Thompson 1996, 40).

Critical Hermeneutics as a Framework for Deliberation with Foundations

In my opinion one should start by distinguishing between two different types of hermeneutics: the sort that relinquishes foundations (Nietzsche, Heidegger, Rorty) and another form of hermeneutical thought which continues to maintain a foundational claim (Apel, Habermas, Ricoeur …). That is, a clear difference should be discerned between the hermeneutics which relinquish any normative criterion and the ones that believe that they have found some critical normative authority, meaning that we could talk of hermeneutics open to a normative level and hermeneutics of a non-normative nature, depending on whether they have an unconditioned moment or not.

And there is even a position like that of Gadamer, who maintains the universal and critical nature of hermeneutics via a channel that is to some extent intermediate, which could be called 'experiential', which partly seems to come closer to the first in the distinction established above between non-normative and normative hermeneutics, insofar as it seems to relinquish the claim of foundations and lack any normative authority. This is because it takes us along the path of experience and its temporal productivity, which seems to imply waiving the foundational nature of reason.

It is nevertheless important to realise how to find aspects, even in this Gadamerian modality of hermeneutics, which can be taken advantage of for a new form of 'reason-giving' superior to the reductionist approach proper to the epistemological school, for example by analysing the historical and linguistic nature of the facticity of understanding (of the 'conscience of effectual history').

In spite of the difficulties as regards the foundational order, hermeneutics has made many contributions to contemporary thought (as opposed to positivism, analytical-linguistic philosophy and 'critical Rationalism'), to which we could refer and which would deserve specific treatment, such as for example, the establishment of a new philosophical model (in which the positivist and utilitarian approaches are improved on), the critique of idealism and methodologism (which granted priority to the theory of knowledge and epistemology), the updating and incorporation of Aristotle's practical philosophy in the hermeneutical sphere (Gadamer 1975; Conill 2006) and the relevance of a 'critical hermeneutics' as a new methodical approach in 'applied ethics' (beyond the diverse forms of 'casuistry').

But in this context it is crucial not to degrade hermeneutical thought by turning this into a mere contextualist approach, even by instrumentalising Aristotle's practical philosophy, whose final outcome would only favour the pragmatism prevalent in theory and in practice.

Consequently, to overcome the insufficiencies of contextualist and pragmatist factualism the moment of the *unconditioned* has to be stressed, since for example, from the level of reflection of ethical theory, pragmatist and contextualist hermeneutics go no farther than an *êthos* factically given at a specific point in history and on many occasions is even mixed up with certain utilitarian formulas, meaning that it would not go beyond an 'ethics of motives' (Cortina 1991, Ch. 2).

But the ethical realm cannot be confused with nor reduced to an external (heteronymous) incentive, as occurs in the ethics of motives, in which these are incentives such as well-being, remuneration, social (contextual) pressure and other similar aspects, either in a mercantile version or in a specific institutional and functional version. In any event, this 'ethical' concept is insufficient, even if this is put forward in a hermeneutical wrapping dressed in a certain Aristotelian element.

In my view, the moment of the unconditioned needs to be revealed. This can be done if one applies the ethics of objective ends and of internal goods, the Kantian deontological-eleutheronomic universalism or by means of certain ethics of justice.[9] We will now look at certain forms of making the moment of the unconditioned present.

(1) First of all, in the typically eudemonist ethical moment, often expressed (though not always appropriately) in terms of happiness, there have to be objective ends, certain goods internal to action and consequently internal motives, such as 'excellence', self-realisation, vital or professional fulfilment, aspiration to perfection. This ethical dimension is lived with a communitarian and institutional sense and can go as far as to form a social or institutional 'ethical culture'. The meaning of good and bad, fair and unfair, which is what ultimately forms the 'community'[10] is shared in this. The important thing is now that this eudemonist moment of goods internal to action is inserted in a postconventional, universalist communitarianism, able to surpass mere contextualisms, as these alone simply produce diverse forms of exclusion.

(2) A second ethical moment is the 'eleutheronomic, deontological' one[11] in which the unconditioned is expressed in a pure and formal way, as a form of guaranteeing universality as far as possible. Take note that universalisation is a formal way of defending freedom understood as personal autonomy and behind it all, human dignity. Because one can only universalise with meaning if there is something which is worthy by itself categorically; only then is it possible to formulate on proper grounds a categorical and non-hypothetical imperative, that is, one not dependent on any other condition (unconditioned!). The discovery of this ethical dimension is the basis of genuine credibility, so longed for in general and so highly appreciated in all human relations. Without credibility there is no fruitful action. Without an incorruptible 'value' beyond all 'price' there will be no underlying security. 'Only the fool fails to distinguish between worth and price.' This axiological wisdom is extremely necessary in spite of the unease and many difficulties that it causes in the economicist, bureaucratic and juridicist mentality, because it is the most effective antidote against possible manipulation.

---

9 Primary goods (J. Rawls), decent minimum (N. Daniels), minimum capabilities (A. Sen), minimums contextualised in the diverse spheres of justice (M. Walzer), mutual recognition of communicative competence (K.-O. Apel, J. Habermas), minimum ethics of the person as valid interlocutor (A. Cortina).

10 '*Koinonía*' (Aristotle), '*Sittlichkeit*' (Hegel). See Aristotle's *Politics*, Hegel's *Grundlinien der Philosophie des Rechts*, Conill (2006).

11 This has here a fundamental '*eleutheronomic*' (referring to freedom) meaning and not the one used for professional deontologies, which already belong to the contextual sphere of applied ethics in each concrete profession.

(3) Also some theories of justice, like that of Rawls (Rawls 1971; 1993) and the one supplied by discursive ethics (Cortina 1986; 1990; García Marzá 1992; Muguerza 1990), attempt to offer some authority or criterion to specify the minimum amount of goods or conditions that a society has to guarantee for a person to be included as a cooperating member of a society. This involves determining – and assigning – certain 'primary goods' and a form of understanding the 'equality of opportunities' which makes one feel citizenship, which is rather more than the contractualism of methodological individualism. For example health (and where applicable, health care) is thus a derived good, but one that can be included in the list of social goods, insofar as it is useful to recover persons for them to go on forming part of a society as cooperating members. Hence, justice is an essential condition for generating 'civility', without which none of our social institutions has any meaning (Cortina 1997; 1998; 2003; 2007).

(4) The 'ethics of discourse' has insisted on a peculiar ethical dimension, on dialogue and rational consensus, whose relevance in applied ethics is already thoroughly vouched for (Apel 1988). Institutions have to act in a framework of justice integrating the interests of all those affected. But how is an order of priority to be set up between the different interests? The criterion which acts as basic guideline is that of reciprocal recognition as valid interlocutors and that of universalisation. This is how a dialogical intersubjectivity is created, to express claims of validity (what is right, fair) in communicative action, which now has a meaning of its own, an internal télos, beyond instrumental and strategic action. Only this way is there a guideline for harmonising conflicting interests, as a result of pluralism and rational freedom, in the context of an ethics of convinced responsibility (but keeping here too the moment of the unconditioned).

Consequently, *hermeneutic-critical conditions of deliberation* are discovered by means of reflection, since Aristotle does not contain merely a pragmatic (technical) deliberation, but also a structural sort for the exercise of reason (a natural and communitarian foundational framework). Neither should deliberation today be reduced to an acritical pragmatic exercise, having instead conditions without which deliberation would not have any meaning (nor existence), but would boil down to mere 'bargaining'. Only if this is connected with one of the forms of the moment of the unconditioned can one avoid reducing this to the level of negotiating between those who have greatest power in each context. But where are the rational framework and the *êthos* to come from? In Aristotle there was a structural framework for the exercise of practical reason ('*phrónesis*'). What is today's structural framework (if there is one)? In my opinion both the proposal of new casuistry and the deliberationism of 'deliberative democracy' (inspired in Rawls) fall short. This is why it is so useful to go on with the task of hermeneutic-critical reconstruction of practical reason, to the extent that this can enable us to better understand the meaning of human activities and propitiate the social effectiveness of applied ethics.

References

Apel, K.-O. (1988), *Diskurs und Verantwortung* (Suhrkamp: Frankfurt).

Beauchamp, T.L. and Childress, J.F. (1979), *Principles of Biomedical Ethics* (Oxford: Oxford University Press).

Chadwick, R. (ed.) (1998), *Encyclopedia of Applied Ethics*, 4 vols. (San Diego: Academic Press).

Conill, J. (1991), *El enigma del animal fantástico* (Madrid: Tecnos).

—— (1997), *El poder de la mentira. Nietzsche y la política de la transvaloración* (Madrid: Tecnos).

—— (2006), *Ética hermenéutica* (Madrid: Tecnos).

Cortina, A. (1985), *Razón comunicativa y responsabilidad solidaria* (Salamanca: Sígueme).

—— (1986), *Ética mínima* (Madrid: Tecnos).

—— (1990), *Ética sin moral* (Madrid: Tecnos).

—— (1993), *Ética aplicada y democracia radical* (Madrid: Tecnos).

—— (1997), *Ciudadanos del mundo* (Madrid: Alianza).

—— (1998), *Hasta un pueblo de demonios* (Madrid: Taurus).

—— (2003), *Covenant and contract* (Leuven: Peeters).

—— (2007), *Ética de la razón cordial* (Oviedo: Nobel).

Coser, L. (1976), *The Functions of Social Conflicts* (New York: Free Press).

Feito, L. (1999), *El sueño de lo posible* (Madrid: Universidad Pontificia de Comillas).

Gadamer, H.-G. (1975), *Wahrheit und Methode* (Tübingen: Mohr).

García-Marzá, D. (1992), *Ética de la justicia* (Madrid: Tecnos).

Gracia, D. (1989), *Fundamentos de bioética* (Madrid: EUDEMA).

—— (1990), *Primum non nocere* (Madrid: Instituto de España, Real Academia Nacional de Medicina).

—— (1991), *Procedimientos de decisión en ética clínica* (Madrid: EUDEMA).

Gutmann, A. and Thompson, D. (1996), *Democracy and Disagreement* (Cambridge: Harvard University Press).

Hortal, A. (1999), 'Sobre lo que viene llamándose ética aplicada', in Quinzá, X. and Alemany, J.J. (eds), pp. 77–90.

Jonas, H. (1979), *Das Prinzip Verantwortung* (Frankfurt: Insel).

Jonsen, A.R. and Toulmin, S. (1988), *The Abuse of Casuistry: A History of Moral Reasoning* (Berkeley: University of California Press).

Kucewski, M. (1998), 'Casuistri', in Chadwick, R. (ed.), Vol. 1, pp. 423–32.

Muguerza, J. (1990), *Desde la perplejidad* (Madrid: F.C.E.).

Oakley, J. and Cocking, D. (2001), *Virtue Ethics and Professional Roles* (Cambridge: University Press).

Quinzá, X. and Alemany, J.J. (eds) (1999), *Ciudad de los hombres, ciudad de Dios* (Madrid: Universidad Comillas).

Rawls, J. (1993), *Political Liberalism* (New York: Columbia University Press).

Siurana, J.C. (2003), *Una brújula para la vida moral* (Granada: Comares).

Ulrich, P. (2000), 'Integrative Wirtschaftsethik: Grundlagenreflexion der ökonomischen Vernunft', *Ethik und Sozialwissenschaften* 11:4, 555–67.

PART 3
Applied Ethics in the Light of Globalisation

Chapter 6

Three Dilemmas in Applied Ethics

Matthias Kettner[1]

Today, ethics or moral theory is the philosophical discipline that most frequently appears in public discussion. The concepts of moral theory, its thought models, considerations and ideas are currently enjoying particular favour. What is most surprising about this situation is the way it is reversing a prolonged tendency in philosophy to withdraw from the public sphere. Certainly, the prepositivist philosophy of the 'big substantial issues' was able, on occasions, to present itself, critically and affirmatively, as representative of society's cultural and moral values, which assured it a certain aura of general transcendence, perceived even by its detractors. But despite the fact that its analytical method became international and spread to the most disparate range of minds, the philosophy of the last century seemed to have lost, together with its metaphysical assumptions, its penetrating scrutiny of the structures of rationality in the real world, and appeared to be incapable of developing a convincing language with which to interpret important events in contemporary history. Public perception and its social relevance duly declined.

The spectacular boom of 'applied' or 'practical' ethics that we have witnessed over the last three decades, particularly in the United States and, with the usual time-lag, increasingly in the Old World, appears in this way as an attempt by a sub-discipline of philosophy – ethics – to compensate and remedy, through the perception of significant opportunities in the public conscience, what philosophy as a whole had lost on its way towards the nirvana of social irrelevance (see DeMarco 1986; Ruddick 1980, 735; Singer 1986, 2; Rachels 1981, 4ff.). In this way, we may say that the practical turn philosophical ethics has taken constitutes a rebirth, since applied ethics is not a recently invented philosophy genre, but rather a new attempt to keep its old promise to contribute to the rational organisation of the social praxis.

'Philosophy goes public.' William Ruddick describes the factors that, since the end of the sixties, have led to a previously unimaginable public commitment on the part of philosophers. In particular, he mentions the pressure of the politicisation that had its roots in the Vietnam war, the 'glut' of unemployed philosophers and the increasing abandoning of the paradigm of logical positivism within analytical philosophy. Not only the wide range of journals, of which *Philosophy and Public Affairs* was the first, and perhaps the most important to date, but also the long list of institutes that have been founded testify to the interest of the renegade apostles of Moore, Russell, Wittgenstein, Carnap and Quine in the re-encountered political-social world. 'Philosophers founded the Hastings Institute of Society, Ethics and the

1 University of Witten/Herdecke.

Life Sciences in 1969; the Center for Philosophy and Public Policy (in Washington) in 1976; the Center for Business Ethics (Waltham, Massachusetts) in 1976, and the Center for the Study of Values at the University of Delaware in 1977' (Ruddick 1980, 736).[2]

Since then, philosophers have discussed the dangers of nuclear technology, the moral aspects of the problem of world hunger, experiments on animals, the public health system, pornography, discrimination and so on, and all of this in televised interviews, newspaper articles, manifestos, panel discussions, working groups and civic meetings. Philosophers are to be found in government commissions on genetic technology and the evaluation of its consequences; contributing on ethics committees alongside doctors and theologians; advising engineers, jurists and other professionals on how to formulate ethical orientations. They work on curriculum design and organise personnel training for organisations ranging from nursing schools to military academies. They justify and criticise wars; cooperate with urban planners; with prison governors and prisoners; with the business community and executives; with ecologists, pacifists and generals. Specialised journals have appeared for each of the three main fields of applied ethics defined to date: bio-medical ethics, business ethics and environmental ethics. And the philosophy curricula in the education systems of English speaking countries regularly include applied ethics issues.[3]

Applied ethics appears as a uniform term for different approaches and streams. How it understands itself varies according to the understanding we have of 'ethics' in each case, and to the way the application is understood. Without doubt, polemical motives also come into this set of differences. For some perspectives, defining ethics as 'practical' may already be more than mere terminology, namely a positive offer of transference that a particular philosophical current makes to society. For others, it is easy to malign alternative conceptions to moral and applied theory as lacking in effectiveness and useless when the conception itself is defined as 'practical': seemingly negating the idea that any other connotations can be so. Other connotations of the difference between 'ethics' and 'applied ethics', which we cannot go into here, are for instance: *applied ethics* vs. *pure ethics* (Lieberson 1981, 71–2); *special or particular ethics* vs. *general ethics or ethics itself* (MacIntyre 1984, 498) *theoretical ethics* vs. *empirical ethics* (Meggle and Fehige 1989, 35–6) *traditional or academic ethics* vs. *critical ethics* (Kettner 1992a; 1992b). While both generic expressions 'applied ethics' and 'practical ethics' are generally used synonymously, in the rest of this article I will use the term 'applied ethics'.[4]

---

2 The list of milestones in the institutionalisation of applied ethics could be extended considerably. In the German context, see above all Meggle and Fehige 1989.

3 See Bynum (1975, 97–9) on the rapid spread of philosophy in study curricula in North American schools in the first half of the seventies. See Heister and Seidler (1989) on the diffusion of medical ethics curricula in German universities. Further pertinent information can also be found in *Zeitschrift für die Didaktik der Philosophie* (*Journal for the Didactics of Philosophy*).

4 Equally erroneous is the frequent comparison between applied ethics and applied utilitarian ethics, although most available analyses today act as utilitarian premises. See contributions in Leist (1990). Notable exceptions are found in English-speaking discussion

But this current presence and importance of applied ethics counts not only on defenders among its ranks. There are also those of the opinion that, for example, the amount of attempts at didactic and practical application that applied ethics has made with John Rawls's theory of justice or with Kohlberg's theory of moral development has contributed with the undesirable effect that established professions have broadened their political power at the expense of active, democratic participation and co-management. We now examine in what way this occurs.

In the political context, some suspect that Rawls's concept of reflective equilibrium works more to maintain power in the hands of established groups than to protect freedom (Esquith 1985). For its part, the enthusiasm of educational and social reform for applied ethics as *moral education*, following, among other things, Kohlberg's just community approach, has brought about a certain disillusionment (Oser et al. 1986). So much so that the diffusion of applied ethics in numerous curricula has even been judged as morally damaging, since applied ethics courses – so the argument goes – which, according to their educational objectives should improve their participants' capacity for moral judgement and action, in fact prejudice these objectives as a result of their simplification and their use of stereotypes.[5] Moreover, it has been said that it may also contribute to the formation of a self-appointed and questionable class of philosophers 'expert' in moral issues.

Going beyond these two examples, and in keeping with the current importance of applied ethics, a range of diverse self-critical reflections have emerged and important debate has been generated. This is a clear indication of the need to prevent the precipitated optimism surrounding the social implementation of philosophical ethics as 'application'. This chapter aims to cover some of these criticisms from the discourse ethics perspective. Against the moral theoretical programme of discourse ethics and the concept of 'practical discourse', reproaches are often heard of an 'apartness from the praxis' or the 'impossibility of application'. At the same time, criticisms refer to already existing models of applied ethics that seem to work and presumably have no problems. It is therefore fitting to raise some basic problems that, in the form of dilemmas, emerge in every attempt at applied ethics, and then go on to analyse how discourse ethics might face up to them.

I refer to structural dilemmas, although in fact we are dealing with neither strictly logical alternatives (contradictions), nor irresolvable conceptual problems (aporias). Rather, the idea is to highlight, from ideal types, contrary positions that give rise to problem-generating spaces. The most important dilemmas can essentially be synthesised into three types referring respectively, to *theoretical architectonics*, to the *problems of grounding* and to *ideological content* (see on this division: Meggle and Fehige 1989, 30; Young 1986, 37–8; Borchert and Stewart 1987, 11; Brody

---

in the series edited by Brenda Cohen and Anthony O'Hear, *Studies in Applied Philosophy* (London: Allen and Unwin).

5 See Young (1986). Young's argument that the traditional study of philosophical ethics – and this alone – can contribute to moral education is somewhat unconvincing. Young's reproaches have not gone unanswered; see Thompson (1987). Olafson (1982: esp. 542–5) offers a sceptical examination of ethics in training and educational contexts, within the framework of a critique of progress oriented by the 'Dialectic of Enlightenment'.

1988, 12; for a possible origin of medical ethics see Hargrove 1989, 2). We now examine the extremes in each one of these spaces.

The *first structural dilemma* of applied ethics refers to the relation between the grounding theory and the conception corresponding to the application.[6]

The extreme points of this relation are *autonomy* and *dependence*. This is a theoretical-architectonic type dilemma. While the conceptions oriented from the autonomy of applied ethics aim to replace the grounding theory (e.g., because it is considered to be 'apart from the praxis') or they regard it as a non-problematic and incompetent input, conceptions oriented from dependence regard applied ethics as simply the logical extension of the grounding theory towards given problematic cases that are open to moral analysis (Toulmin 1981).

The simplest conception of dependence assimilates the relation of application to the image of the deduction of singular judgements of general laws, or more precisely, of moral rules, norms and principles that have already been previously determined, that may be self-sufficiently grounded and that ignore special social determinations. These rules, norms and principles can (supposedly) be known, or at least it is possible (presumably) to be convinced of their validity, *without* the need for any special knowledge about people's different experiences of action in concrete situations. (Thus, validity cannot be affected by specific experiences, in the same way that the validity of the logical principle of non-contradiction cannot be altered by specific experiences.) The facts themselves (e.g. the specific assumptions of the action in military systems, science, law, health, etc.) are presented as additional premises and constitute the particularities relevant to the case in question, the moral problematic of which should be resolved by applying the theory (on these positions see Brody 1988, 6; and Devine 1988, 213).

The autonomous conceptions of the application are affected by misunderstandings in relation to the grounding theories or are unnecessarily exposed – as can be shown in the case of 'Practical Ethics' by Peter Singer – to the opportunistic use by interests outside philosophy. They are both too modest and too pretentious. They are *too modest* because the autonomous conceptions of practical ethics, pragmatic without exception, want, like any other culture of experts (engineers, scientists etc.) to offer resources for a 'better resolution of the problems'. Ethics' claim to autonomy therefore breaks down when faced with competition from others offering resources in the context of knowledge application, thereby renouncing the moral normativity of the necessary negotiation process and becoming a strategically exploitable resource, for example, to construct political acceptance (Kettner 1992b; 1992d). They are *too pretentious*, because the autonomous conceptions with their theoretical means – provenly insufficient – also want to resolve, with a pragmatic blow, the problems for which the grounding theories are specialised.

6 By 'grounding theory' I understand the two usual components of philosophical moral theories: normative ethics and meta-ethics. The latter should clarify important moral concepts, principles and propositions and take stock of the logical forms of moral argumentation, and also ground them as valid; in contrast, 'normative' ethics should discover, formulate, construct and ground in a universally linking way, specific moral points of view, normally abstract, and normative principles or other prescriptive content.

Dependent conceptions, on the other hand, sketch distorted images of the phenomenology of the real moral practical reflection (see MacIntyre 1984 on the criticism). They are unaware of the demonstrable differences between the grounding and application (of a norm); more precisely, they inadequately reduce the theoretical-discursive difference between, on the one hand, the type of reasons used to examine norms (or other prescriptive content) that have already been proposed or presented, and are apparently valid in terms of their rightness, in other words, in terms of the claim for their possible acceptance by all those affected as participants in a practical discourse; and, on the other hand, the type of reasons with which – in view of a practical problem – aspects that can be moralised are discovered, 'applicable norms are selected and characteristic features relevant to the problems are defined' (see Günther 1988, 11–82; Kettner 1992c). As for the rest, the conceptions of dependence cannot, by themselves, explain the tacitly existing possibility of innovative feedback of the experiences of application on the grounding theory.

What is the position of moral discourse theory (discourse ethics) on this dilemma? The grounding ethics-discourse theory postulates practical discourse as the most appropriate means for its application. Given that practical discourse on *specific problems* is incited by the *praxis of action* (individual or collective) and given that for all versions of applied ethics, the concern for *normative analysis of the specific problems of action* is essential, discourse ethics proposals on practical discourse are equivalent to proposals that in other conceptions of the application are regarded as 'applied ethics' proposals. Practical discourses are *autonomous* in so far as the postulate of the practical discourses among the affected or among their representatives displaces all the philosophy theorists' (the 'discourse ethics philosophers') privileges and all possible content becomes historical. They are *dependent* in so far as the carrying out of practical discourses or the production of the conditions necessary to open discourse on the problems of action constitute the *best* alternative from a rational point of view. This can only be affirmed if we have regulative ideas needing a definitive foundation in the context of philosophical discourses of foundation.[7]

The *second structural dilemma* of applied ethics I wish to highlight briefly is the *cynicism-relativism* dilemma that affects the theoretical grounding.

All concepts of application that are not separated from the grounding theory demand, as a normative task for the 'appliers', the *establishment of a determined normative moral theory*. However, basic unresolved theoretical differences exist within the framework of the grounding theory. Yet it would be a harmonious fallacy to deduce from the many cases that undoubtedly appear, where *de jure* different moral *theories* lead *de facto* to pragmatically convergent decisions or values, that applied ethics is not generally affected by fundamental theoretical differences.[8] In

7 For a critique of normative moral theories see Lieberson (1981, 71–2) and Meggle and Fehige (1989, 34).

8 See Beauchamp and Childress (1989, 45–6): 'the profound disagreements in the theory of moral justification do not necessarily lead to disagreement in practical moral deliberation'. R. Hare (1989, 2) considers this experience, generalised on the base of medical ethics, as realistic. On the other hand, however, 'on any issue that is at least contentious, there

fact, some applied conceptions play with the perspective of being able to exempt themselves from the tiresome demands of foundation or even of ultimate foundations. These refer to superficial consensuses that pragmatically work sufficiently well (for example Meggle and Fehige 1989, 34). But this perspective fails in a general condition of adequacy to the rational justification of a person's moral judgements. This condition holds that a person's moral judgement X is rationally justifiable when X (beyond recourse to descriptive contents, that is, to specific *facts*): (1) may at least be supported by a *moral principle* or refer to the *prescriptive content* of a moral principle (whether normatively or evaluatively), and (2) when this moral principle, for its part, can be rationally defended. Thus, a theoretical-grounding link emerges between applied ethics and the grounding theory: the normative authority of this is, in a certain way, borrowed from the grounding theory. If this is the case, we only have two possibilities.

Either the 'applier' must justify why he or she stands by this moral theory rather than any other, that is he or she must criticise alternative grounding theories, and at the same time respond to criticisms of his or her preferred grounding theory. In this way, the applier falls hopelessly into the trap of the grounding philosophical discourse, in which anyone who wants to take advantage of the empirical possibility of surface consensuses that work pragmatically does not wish to be involved.

Or, the 'applier' must accept the proliferation of different grounding positions of moral theory as a *pluralism*, accepting the convergence of moral theories as a mere desideratum (Nielsen 1982). It is even possible to find good reasons to defend the opinion that normative philosophical theories increase the already diverse multiplicity of fundamentally normative orientations that can be found in the lifeworld (*Lebenswelt*) (Baier 1985a, 209). Hence, surely, the ethics 'applier' is left only with a relativist pseudo liberal position: faced with specific problematic cases, she or he can then only explain how one should behave, for example, as a deontologist, a utilitarianist, as a contractualist or as a discourse ethics philosopher, etc. Deontologist, utilitarianism, contractualist or discourse ethics, etc., would be right. But this is a *cynical* attitude, since it neither corresponds to the demands of moral pedagogy, nor can it make convincing contributions to the formation of will in specific problems (Wachbroit 1983, 62).

Discourse ethics is reproached for its supposedly exaggerated ambitions of grounding from many viewpoints. This is not the place to examine this complex subject, as it requires a discussion of the ultimate pragmatic-transcendental justification. Here, it should suffice to indicate that discourse ethics dissolves the cynicism-relativism dilemma by itself as it demands – at least in its pragmatic-transcendental variant – an ultimate foundation, although in my opinion, penultimate reasons would be sufficient (Kettner 1992a).

Applied ethics finds itself within the tensions of a *third structural dilemma*: the ideological dilemma of *grandiosity-resignation*.

Applied ethics affirms what exists through the simple fact of trying to improve it. Clearly, applied ethics should not only make intellectual comments about today's

---

are neither common convictions nor consensuses that can be appealed to'. See also Nielsen (1982).

problems. Rather, in a formulation that is both widespread and uncommitted, it should lead us to a better position from which to deal with problems in a morally responsible way or, a much more ambitious proposal, to solve them (Wachbroit 1983, 62). Critical moral theory as a configuration of philosophical illustration may contribute, in a similar way to psycho-analytical supervision, under favourable conditions, to a credible communication through which to express a public discourse, or to help the discussion of contradictions, whatever their degree of consciousness, in modern societies. What it cannot do, precisely as a critical theory of society, is prescribe a particular way of life. Rather, the task of the broadest framework of discourse ethics, understood as *critical theory of ethics in society*, is to develop a normative theory on those criteria of social rationality that are determinant for a rational discourse on the rules by which people live together.[9]

Linked to the inflated trust 'in ethics' in vogue today, are the big philosophical moral theories and a wide range of expectations of which too much, in some ways, is demanded *from the outside*. From the distorted question of whether we 'need a new ethics', messianic tones are insinuated even where – very rarely – it is denied. Applied ethics also becomes an excessive demand on moral theory from within because of the grandiose overestimation in cases in which practical ethics philosophers identify themselves uncritically through applied ethics with utopias of social reform to improve the world, on considering this excessive demand as simply an attractive 'challenge' to satisfy, as far as possible, exaggerated expectations.

The understanding that moral theory has no power over the situation, but rather that it is part of the situation, should lead it to an appropriate modesty. However, if we want to avoid this resulting in a *false* self-moderation of practical resignation, the consequence of which would be that applied ethics would go back to simply interpreting the world, to subsequently deposit its interpretations in specialised journals, moral theory should explore in much greater depth than it likes, the areas of power 'apart from reason'.[10] Part of this task consists of recognising that the praxis of moral theory has an aspect for which moral theory itself is praxis of power. 'The intellectual's role is no longer to place himself "somewhat ahead and to the side" in order to express the stifled truth of the collectivity; rather, it is to struggle against the forms of power that transform him into its object and instrument in the sphere of knowledge, truth, consciousness, and discourse' (Foucault 1974, 130).

The secret alliance of practical ethics with the conservation of the social *status quo* also belongs to this false self-moderation. The more provocatively, unconventionally or vehemently it behaves, the more applied ethics accepts society as it is, since it seeks the right ways to act exclusively among the possibilities that are practical in the social conditions-framework, without including these proposals from reality in the discussion on the question (Young 1986, esp. 40). The scenarios of the 'prisoner's dilemma' and the 'lifeboat', the calculations in decisions on catastrophic situations of scarcity (triage), considered with an obsessive obstinacy in much of the current

9 Horkheimer and Adorno's critical theory of society can be described, as a whole, as a programme for the development of normative criteria of social rationality.

10 A differentiated discussion on decisionism in moral theory should be raised here (see Kettner 1992a).

applied ethics literature, only metaphorically repeat the prioritised assumptions that exist in society.

But it is not possible to oppose this structural conservatism by simply returning to a utopian stance. Rather, we should look for channels of reflection on the historically modifiable conditions-framework of ethics itself in society. For the discourse ethics perspective, we can neither *prioritise* substantial ideas about the 'good life' nor can we *assume* such ideas from the stock of optimistic social utopias. The discourse ethics principle criticises what exists in the light of *regulative ideas*. Its place in practical life is in consensual action. Regulative ideas are not the plans for the architects of a 'new world order', but rather, they are tools for guidance in the critical-melioristic task of determined negation.

This has clear consequences for the appreciation of the inevitable fact that the vast majority of the analyses made by applied ethics act as utilitarian normative premises: moral theories that, like utilitarian theories, elevate as a programme the general application of a moral principle analogous to commercial relationships, find themselves allied with the colonisation of the lifeworld through economy-based categories. However, for the same reason, such moral theories have good access to the real problems of many spheres of praxis, in other words, in a certain way they have a *fundamentum in re*. The colonisation of the lifeworld through economy-based categories is objectively under way as part of the thrust of the social processes of capitalist modernisation. No moral theory would be able to bring this to a halt.

But, at least, we should then ask whether applied ethics achieves (in the face of the economic colonisation of the lifeworld) reflective behaviour, or whether it simply intermingles with it. Here, the same is valid as for the analytical therapy: much can be done, but everything depends on the extent to which its existential meaning is understood.

References

Almond, B.A. (ed.) (1982), *Progress and its Discontents* (Berkeley: University of California Press).

Baier, A.C. (1985a), *Postures of the Mind. Essays on Mind and Morals* (Minneapolis: University of Minnesota Press).

Beauchamp, T.L. and Childress, J.F. (1989), *Principles of Biomedical Ethics* (Oxford: Oxford University Press).

Borchert, D.M. and Stewart, D. (1987), 'Theoretical and Applied Ethics', *Listening* 22, 5–11.

Bradie, M. et al. (eds) (1983), *The Applied Turn in Contemporary Philosophy* (Bowling Green, Ohio: Bowling Green State University).

Brody, B.A. (ed.) (1988), *Moral Theory and Moral Judgements in Medical Ethics* (Dordrecht: Kluwer).

Bynum, T.W. (1975), 'The Philosopher as Teacher. The Quiet Revolution in Philosophy', *Metaphilosophy* 6:1, 97–9.

Caplan, A.L. and Callahan, D. (eds) (1981), *Ethics in Hard Times* (New York: Plenum Press).

DeMarco, J.P. (1986), 'The Challenge of Applied Ethics', in DeMarco, J.P and Fox, R.M. (eds), pp. 1–18.

DeMarco, J.P. and Fox, R.M. (eds) (1986), *New Directions in Ethics* (New York: Routledge and Kegan Paul).

Devine, P.B. (1988), 'Theory and Practice in Ethics', in Brody, B.A. (1988), pp. 213–23.

Esquith, S.L. (1985), 'John Rawls and the Political Education of Applied Ethics', *Social Theory and Practice* 11:3, 307–54.

Fauser, P. et al. (eds) (1992), *Verantwortung* (Seelze: Friedrich).

Foucault, M. (1974), *Von der Subversion des Wissens* (Munich: Hanser).

Günther, K. (1988), *Der Sinn für Angemessenheit. Anwendungsdiskurse in Moral und Recht* (Frankfurt: Suhrkamp).

Hare, R. (1989), 'Why do Applied Ethics?', in *Essays in Ethical Theory* (Oxford: Clarendon Press), pp. 1–14.

Hargrove, E.C. (1989), *Foundations of Environmental Ethics* (Englewood Cliffs, NJ: Prentice Hall).

Hegselmann, R. and Merkel, R. (1991), *Zur Debatte über Euthanasie* (Frankfurt: Suhrkamp).

Heister, E. and Seidler, B. (1989), 'Ethik in der ärztlichen Ausbildung an den Hochschulen der Bundesrepublik Deutschland', *Ethik in der Medezin* I, 13–23.

Kettner, M. (1992a), 'Der Dezisionismus, mit dem rationale Moralbegründung leben kann', *Ethik und Sozialwissenschaften* 3:1, 35–9.

—— (1992b), 'Diskursethik und Verantwortung für zukünftige Generationen', in Fauser, P. et al. (ed.), pp. 124–7.

—— (1992c), *Anwendungsdiskurse. Zur Kritik am Anwendungsmodel von Klaus Günther*, Gottingen.

Leist, A. (ed.) (1990), *Um Leben und Tod. Moralische Probleme bei Abtreibung künstlicher Befruchtung, Euthanasie und Selbstmord* (Frankfurt: Suhrkamp).

Lieberson, J. (1981), 'Why Should we be Moral', in Caplan, A.L. and Callahan, D. (eds), pp. 47–90.

MacIntyre, A. (1984), 'Does Applied Ethics Rest on a Mistake?', *Monist* 67:4, 498–513.

Meggle, G. and Fehige, C. (1989), 'Praktische Ethik. Ein Plädoyer für die Errichtung eines Instituts für Praktische Ethik', *Information Philosophie* 3, 30–39.

Moser, P. (1990), 'Behinderte gegen Philosophen. Bericht über die Singer-Affäre', *Information Philosophie* 4, 18–32.

Nielsen, K. (1982), 'On Needing a Moral Theory: Rationality, Considered Judgements and the Grounding of Morality', *Metaphilosophy* 2, 97–116.

Olafson, F. (1982), 'The Idea of Progress: An Ethical Appraisal', in Almond, B.A. (ed.) (1982), 524–45.

Oser, O. et al. (eds) (1986), *Transformation und Entwicklung. Grundlagen der Moralerziehung* (Frankfurt: Suhrkamp).

Ruddick, W. (1980), 'Philosophy and Public Affairs', *Social Research* 47:4, 734–48.

Singer, P. (1986), 'Applied Ethics', in *Applied Ethics* (Oxford: Oxford University Press).

Thompson, W.K. (1987), 'A Response to James Young's "The Immorality of Applied Ethics"', *International Journal of Applied Philosophy* 3, 83–4.

Toulmin, E. (1981), 'The Tyranny of Principles', *The Hastings Center Report* 11:6, 31–2.

Wachbroit, R. (1983), 'Ethics and Professionalism', in Bradie, M. et al. (eds), pp. 59–72.

Young, J.O. (1986), 'The Immorality of Applied Ethics', *International Journal of Applied Philosophy* 3:2, 37–43.

Chapter 7

Responsibility for Praxis: Discourse Ethics as Applied Ethics

Domingo García-Marzá[1]

Introduction

The dawning of the new century has brought with it a major comeback of the social significance of philosophy, which has once again become involved in the problems affecting our plural and global societies. This is chiefly due to the impulse of ethics, and in particular, of applied ethics. I would even say that the strength and drive of what we now tend to call 'critical philosophy' depends to a great extent on the perspective of applied ethics.

A variety of good reasons can be found to explain this current social demand for applied ethics. These range from the loss of trust and the meaning of 'public' to the breakdown of consensus over what the bases for our democratic and social states are; from civic apathy and lack of participation to the excess legal interference in social life; from the predominance of the market as a criterion of social validity to the uncontrolled political power of the multinationals; from the role of technological development to our impotence before the consequences of research into nuclear science and genetics, to give just a few examples.

All these fields have a common denominator: the problem is not that we have to choose from a variety of solutions, nor even that there is often no solution. Rather, the essential problem is that we need new concepts that will enable us to reflect on these new realities, new ideas to help us understand what should be. Concepts and ideas always represent areas of experience and learning processes, and therefore they must extend their meaning when dealing with the structural changes of social reality. We need a new vocabulary with which to face the challenges of the new global arena, where experience can offer very little in the absence of a normative horizon on what we want and how we wish to bring it about.

What Habermas would call this opacity and impenetrability nowadays has a new characteristic. The reduction of complexity, uncertainty and risk is not being put on hold while we come up with solutions constructed from a position of the common will of those affected. Rather, conflicts are being solved by systemic solutions that fall outside the normative correction perspective. While accepting that these solutions are necessary, and absolutely essential in our functionally differentiated societies, the corresponding reduction in autonomy that they involve is clearly disquieting.

1 University Jaume I of Castellón, Spain.

We are faced with a zero-sum game: each solution 'imposed' from a position of economic power, or from a judicial-administrative logic represents a lessening of our ability to use the resources of *lebenswelt* to find consensual solutions to conflicts of action. What we eventually achieve in this way is to increment the meaninglessness of social life.

I believe this is the great challenge facing applied ethics today: to facilitate a normative orientation that enables us to find solutions to problems from the position of a common will. Although these solutions occur within a judicial framework, they cannot be reduced to nor identified with legal procedures. Applied ethics opens the way towards the moral capabilities that we possess as individuals and that enable us to take on responsible commitments in order to solve conflicts of action.

I follow this direction in the present chapter, which sets out to analyse the problems and potentialities of discourse ethics as a platform for the various applied ethics. To do this, firstly the status of discourse ethics as applied ethics is examined. I aim to show that the Habermasian conception of the application of the moral point of view is totally insufficient and does not justify the potentialities embraced in the discourse ethics approach. Secondly, in an attempt to broaden the margins of discourse ethics as applied ethics, a reconstructive analysis of civil society is undertaken to demonstrate the role of moral resources as basic mechanisms for the coordination of action. Finally, a methodological perspective is proposed for applied ethics of a discourse nature as a three-level progressive integration between theory and praxis. This enables us to operationalise criteria of moral validity without losing the normative, and thus critical, perspective, and also avoids any utopianism. The search for a horizon of action that works for the good of everyone must never be simply confined to theoretical justification.

Discourse Ethics as Applied Ethics

By the expression 'moral sphere' I mean the human capacity to deliberate and decide, and through this, account for what we do or leave undone, what we say or leave unsaid. This constant 'justifying' or 'adjusting' to reality enables interaction between individuals and the constitution of their organisations. When we ask the question 'What should I do?' from a moral point of view, it is because the need for orientation affects the interests of others and in this sense refers to the possible regulation of interpersonal conflicts of action resulting from opposing interests (on this delimitation of the moral sphere, see Habermas 1991; also Rehg 1997 and García-Marzá 1992; see Cortina 1986 for a proposal for the extension of these margins). From this approach the moral sphere refers to the claim to validity that accompanies interactions regulated by norms and to institutions in which these interactions might be structured. Ethics is concerned with justifying this moral sphere.

The basic task of moral theory consists of grounding what we call the moral point of view, understood as a principle from which to decide the moral validity of our actions, norms and institutions. It is widely known that discourse ethics engages in a programme of pragmatic-transcendental grounding that enables it to explain and justify this underlying rational foundation of our moral judgements. By taking as its base the normative content of our capacity to communicate, to establish dialogues and reach agreements, I believe that discourse ethics succeeds in defending an ethical universalism that does not break with the framework of our plural and democratic societies since it limits itself to the basic rules that govern the discourse-based resolution of conflict. This is a procedural ethic that defines moral validity from the agreement reached between all those affected on whether the corresponding practice responds to the interests of everyone in equal measure (Habermas 1999, 67).

Deliberative examination is possible thanks to the principle of universalisation, which in these discourses take on the role of a rule of argumentation. Through transcendental pragmatic justification we can guarantee the universalism of the moral principle and at the same time avoid suspicion that an ethnocentric fallacy is being committed, since we start from the base of the linguistic structures that all competent speakers use in communicative action and argumentation. Only this universalism can respond to the claims for validity of an increasingly globalised social order; in other words, respond to the possible solution of problems that go beyond the limits of a specific community (Habermas 2000, 16; see also Habermas 1985).

The discourse principle, the expression of the presumptions that we necessarily make in practical discourse, only shows us that the unlimited exchange of reasons, totally free from any pressure, amongst those affected is responsible for defining the morality of an action, norm or institution. In this way, the prospect is demonstrated of a consensual, impartial regulation of any type of action that affects or might affect the other interests. As a basic rule for moral argumentation we have an explanation of the claim to validity that accompanies the norms, and thus, of the actions and decisions, and also of the institutions that these norms make possible. We can therefore say that a norm is valid when it designates generalisable interests, or put another way, when it expresses 'what is good for everyone'. From this procedural interpretation of the principle of autonomy the moral resources that form part of every social interaction can be made explicit, as we shall see in the next section. No other definition of the moral point of view is compatible with pluralism, and even less so in the present global situation.

Nonetheless, this principle only tells us when a norm is valid, and therefore, what legitimate expectations are at stake, that is, what we are obliged to carry out and what we have the right to expect. It does not, however, tell us anything about whether we can apply it or how this can be done in a particular situation or context. In other words, we have no indication of when and how we can expect and/or demand behaviour that conforms to this moral validity. According to Habermas, it is one thing to define and ground a moral point of view, but another to establish criteria for its possible application. In avoiding the extremes of an ethics of conviction, he establishes that moral conviction can only be demanded in moral contexts that are already themselves rational, in the sense that moral action does not come into conflict with one's own interests (Habermas 2000, 144).

But from this position, it would seem we have to conclude that we will *never* apply this moral criterion, nor will we be able to act in consequence, since it is obvious that these situations do not arise precisely in cases in which a moral intervention is required. One issue is that we should bear in mind the consequences of an action, an aspect that is covered in the principle of universalisation. However, a very different issue is that we cannot act or even morally judge an action if we do not have a context that 'guarantees' that everyone else will act in the same way. This final question is simply impossible. Habermas attempts to respond to this apparent paradox by differentiating between a discourse of justification and a discourse of application.

Discourse ethics takes a major step when it differentiates between the general question 'What should I do?' and the question 'What should I do in specific circumstances, faced with a certain type of problem and under the pressure of different realities?' (see Apel 2001). The principle of universalisation serves to justify specific expectations of behaviour and plays its part when we examine their validity, that is, what the norms allow or prohibit, but it tells us nothing about the possibility of it being applied in a certain context. From this differentiation, the problems of justification would not totally exhaust the idea of impartiality, but rather would still fall short of responding to the question of whether a valid norm is also 'adequate' in a particular situation (Apel 2001, 148). In other words, the validity of a norm would not be sufficient to determine moral judgement on a specific action or institution; its suitability would also have to be justified. According to K. Günther, in applied ethics the question is not the validity of the norm for each particular individual and his or her interests, but rather whether it is appropriate for all the characteristics of a particular situation (Günther 1988, 55).

One and the same procedure is offered for both levels, practical discourse, but what now makes consensus possible is the principle of appropriateness. While grounding discourses establish the *prima facie* validity of a norm, discourses specialised in application enable agreement or consensus to be reached on the relevant data for the definition of the situation, and the 'evaluative' criteria to determine what is real. Agreement on the appropriateness of the norm is also required here, but the valid norms play the role of reasons within a dialogue that is no longer, and cannot be, decontextualised (see Rehg 1997, 191; Toulmin 1976). The case may arise in which we have various moral norms that can be applied, and even in which different *prima facie* valid norms are in conflict with each other. Thus, the discourses now required are those that address the question of which circumstances are the relevant ones, and what consequences should be taken into account; in sum, whether the rule is applicable.

The idea of impartiality taken up from the moral point of view would therefore be defined as the sum of the principles of universalisation and of appropriateness, thereby guaranteeing the possibility of a prudent application to praxis. Criteria of coherence, of compatibility between the grounded validity and the circumstances of the specific problematic are necessary for this appropriateness to occur. Thus, as I will propose below, appropriateness could be an intermediate stage between the idea and its practical realisation.

However, with this necessary differentiation, Habermas does not manage to escape the problems that arise out of the central question for applied ethics: to respond from 'the exactability of moral behaviours' that actually occur in different social praxis, whether we are sure of others' behaviour or not. To this reference to praxis we must also add the fact that discourse ethics presents a procedural concept of justice that must take the step to real discourses, since a discourse in our internal forum leaves out of the discussion the needs and interests from which we make judgements or evaluations. The moral point of view demands that real discourses take place that allow us to break the circle that every socialisation process involves. From this point of view the realisation of real discourses belongs to the same idea as the moral discourse. The coordination of all the perspectives for interpretation cannot be carried out from one single perspective. According to Habermas, a public argumentation is always required (Habermas 2000, 163).

However we once again find ourselves before the same paradoxical situation as before: we will never have situations that might be defined as 'free of coercion', as required by the moral principle. We will never have the perfect participating conditions of symmetry and equal opportunities, the only way that an agreement strictly based on reasons can be achieved. It would seem that the moral point of view makes impossible demands. Thus, one of two things could occur: either no action deserves to be qualified as moral and must therefore be demanded, or else we have such a criterion that is capable of legitimising everything that it is within our power to define. It therefore becomes obvious that the relation between a well-grounded theory and a consequent application do not altogether fit. In my opinion, at this point we must fully exploit all the potential of discourse ethics and try to go beyond Habermasian thought.

Habermas is aware of this situation and his solution is to limit himself to the application to the area of the law, precisely because this field guarantees certain procedural conditions: 'the problem of the exactability of moral mandates leads to the step from moral to legal' (Habermas 2000, 125). In his whole interpretation of possibilities for application, Habermas focuses on the individual formation of will and when he proposes the step from 'I' to 'us', seems to reduce all possibilities of applying moral validity, the obligatory characteristic of norms, to the legal terrain. Put another way, Habermas does not go beyond the possibilities of complementing the moral with the legal. I believe the excessive responsibility he places in the judicial mechanisms, or his distrust of the mechanisms of civil society leads to a lessening of all possibility of efficient implementation of practical discourse in the legal field or, as we will see below, to a rather ethereal concept of civil society. His position is that any rational moral made efficient only through socialisation and through individual conscience would have a restricted sphere of action, while through a closely linked legal system, the moral aspect would permeate all arenas of interaction that come under systematic control (Habermas 1998, 183).

It can clearly be seen from this that he ignores all the strengths of the communicative mechanisms for coordination of the action, what we call here moral resources, beyond the establishment of expectations through the law. All systemic arenas, which naturally include the economic and political arenas, fall outside this possible direct application of the moral. In these, we can refer to negotiations and compromises, that is, of pragmatic discourses that, although requiring a moral perspective, constitute a different type of discourse. Ethics is left with little chance to perform except to give a simple critical perspective. Habermas confirms this when he states that practical discourse can only carry out other functions, in addition to critical functions, when the issue to be regulated refers to interests that can be universalised; in any other case, we can only reach compromises.

That said, as we already know, compromises refer to individuals' interests and in fact only come into play when generalisable interests cannot be found. This is effectively the case in most conflicts, but even so a series of questions arises that cannot be answered by the self-limitations of the theory. For instance, how do we justify the difference between just and unjust compromises? Or, how can we explain the coordination mechanisms which actually exist within the systemic arenas and which share a role with strategic mechanisms? It is my opinion that if we want to clarify how civil society's resources actually work we need to answer these questions, and to do that, discourse ethics has to be taken a step forward. Once again, our own moral language can act as a pointer in this direction.

The same intuitive knowledge that Habermas continually uses, our moral intuition, belies this reduction of the moral to the legal. It is obvious that a legal and political discourse theory, which of course includes a moral nucleus, is the most important step to be taken in our societies to bring about the institutionalisation of discourse. Even as critical theory, discourse ethics must start off from a situation in which, as Habermas states, whenever the prevailing relations represent a mockery of the demands of a universalist moral, moral questions become questions of political ethics (Habermas 2000, 125). But within the framework of the rule of law in our democracies, we have a set of practices that are to one extent or another institutionalised, and all manner of organisations and associations that also claim validity in their actions and legitimacy as institutions. It is not enough to reduce these cases to the existence of compromises and negotiations, since conflicts also arise at the core of these organisations between universal interests and not only each individual's particular interests or group interests. The trust with which they are accepted is a clear example of this claim to validity.

If we transfer this idea to the case of the company, we find an institution where 'internal interest should be harmonised with outside interest', but this is done, in principle, under conditions of unequal power and with an asymmetrical distribution of burdens and benefits. This situation does not prevent generalisable interests, nor for the same reason, validity claims, from being at stake. In the business world, as in any other area of daily life, we tend to demand behaviour that goes beyond legal obligation, yet is not seen as sacrifice beyond the call of duty. This is the case, for example, of companies' environmental responsibility, which forms part of their legitimacy or social credibility whether or not it is wholly covered by corresponding legislation. Furthermore, legislation nowadays can do very little about problems such as pollution, which by definition go beyond legal state boundaries. To put it more clearly, validity is claimed for many actions that, although covered by legislation, cannot be justified from a moral point of view and quickly lead to the loss of legitimacy and social mistrust (García-Marzá 2004, 145).

To my mind, it is not that the problem of moral exactability, specifically of moral validity, leads us to law; but rather that it takes us *only* in that direction. Various arenas that make up civil society are found within the legal framework, each with their varying degrees of legal formalisation and structuring. In the case of Habermas, the absence of any specific moral treatment of the various organisations that constitute civil society may derive from the sharp division he makes between state and civil society. Civil society may be conceived of from the logic of communicative action, understanding and agreement, but this does not mean that it should exclude institutions that from their outset, use differentiated power structures. Trust also occurs and is reproduced in these organisations, as does the communicative coordination of actions, negotiations, compromises and agreements, all of which claim moral validity. This reduction to the legal, and specifically to the political, of possibilities for institutional action is, to my mind, the reason why Habermas does not consider applied ethics and why he masks it in critical sociology or in a radical theory of democracy.

The need for ethics applied to all scenarios does not only come from the basic fact that negotiations and the compromises reached within them may be just or unjust. Applied ethics attempts to justify universal interests, or those that can be generalised and that indeed circulate in all spheres of civil society and if they are not satisfied, may lead to clear situations of injustice that must necessarily be condemned. This whole arena cannot be left to a political ethic, but rather an economic and business or health or professional ethic is also needed that is able to mediate between moral validity and unequal participation structures, justified by its efficiency in achieving proposed objectives. A company, a hospital, a newspaper, etc., are organisations that claim validity for themselves, a social legitimacy, that is not solely based on economic benefits or on their complying with the law.

Without this application of ethics to the various arenas of civil society, whether it be the economic and business praxis, the medical or hospital-based praxis, the mass media, etc., it is impossible to explain the moral resources that are actually operating on a day to day basis in these institutions. We cannot explain the agreements reached, nor the mechanisms we find for consensual resolution of conflicts of action; we cannot even clarify the base of social legitimacy that all of them claim, and on which social trust is based. Strategic rationality, for its part, cannot justify the rational conviction that accompanies moral validity and which we use as actors in the various praxis (Höffe 1979, 163ff.). If we are able to show the internal meaning of these resources, then applied ethics may be constituted as a basic mechanism for the structuring of civil society, within what Adela Cortina calls a public ethics (for this structuration, see Cortina 1993; 1995; for the concept of public ethics, see Cortina 1998, 27ff.). The governing idea that defines the importance of applied ethics is that with it, we directly ask to begin to form an active part in the responsibility for the course of events (Bayertz 1991, 20). There is no reason whatsoever to limit this responsibility to the legal terrain. Rather, this limitation represents a dangerous reductionism as it confuses validity and *what is* with *what should be*, since it is not able to leave the conventional terrain of the law. In sum, it comes as a bad deal to all critical perspective.

The Moral Nucleus of Civil Society: Moral Resources and Civil Society

Discourse ethics is presented as a cognitivist ethic as it defends the idea that the validity claims which accompany our actions, norms and institutions have a rational content. This signifies that its meaning goes beyond the expression of preferences or subjective decisions and also surpasses the traditional concepts of what is good or just, setting itself in a rational justification, within the moral point of view of impartiality. In fact, this position takes on our moral language with regard to the norms and institutions that seek credibility or have lost their expectations of legitimacy. In this way, our language expresses the basic intuition that we can reason with and convince others that what we say and do, or what we say nothing or do nothing about, is correct, moral or just (Habermas 1999, 33).

This capacity is clearly not limited to the terrain of judicial institutionalisation. We also use this intuitive knowledge when we enter the doctor's surgery or as members of a university department or during the simple act of reading a newspaper. In all these cases, expectations exist that define the meaning of each one of these activities and institutions, and obligations that we should respond to in order to maintain this meaning. None of these cases has conditions of symmetry, but despite this they claim their pretensions to legitimacy or justice, social credibility and trust. An ethical theory that aims to justify this basic aspect of our language and the social facts that it makes possible, to turn validity into social fact, must make explicit and justify this rational foundation. I believe that by grounding itself in the normative content of our capacity for communication, to establish dialogues and reach agreements, discourse ethics provides us with an excellent platform to define a methodology suitable for the range of applied ethics.

In his later works, Habermas analyses the importance of these moral mechanisms within our democratic rule of law. Without going into the basic coordinates of this analysis here, in *Faktizität und Geltung* he clarifies, to my mind, the basic elements of the democratic process and analyses the role played by moral discourses within legal discourses. In order to do so, he starts from the implicit knowledge that we possess as participants in the democratic process; in other words, in the meaning of these democratic mechanisms for citizens themselves. His analysis takes the first person perspective and the methodology consists of the reconstruction of intuitive knowledge that he indeed possesses as an involved party. From this analysis he defines the democratic process as the sum of state and civil society, which allows us to conceive the bases of a radical democracy in which civil society and public opinion play an indisputable critical and normative role (see García-Marzá 1998).

This dual conception of democracy responds to the current context in which globalisation and the corresponding loss of power of the democratic rule of law have led to the forceful reappearance of the old concept of civil society to refer to the whole network of social structures that does not directly depend on the state (see Keane 1992). In this way, the public is no longer identified with the state and no democratic theory can now stand in the way of the decisive role of civil society mechanisms. These mechanisms contain motivational factors of an empirical and strategic nature, but also include the capacity we have to commit to others and to act consequentially. In other words, the capacity also exists to act and relate to others according to moral criteria, by following our own practical reasoning. Applied ethics should move towards this potential embraced within civil society.

The judicial-administrative mechanisms for coordinating and regulating action, although they have the moral reference of their legitimacy, obtain their support from external coercion, while moral mechanisms by definition are only supported by self-obligation, by each individual's conviction, by the search for consensual solutions that are reciprocally accepted. Both mechanisms have in fact worked together side by side, in a complementary fashion we might say. However, if we consider freedom and voluntariness as basic characteristics of civil society, we are clearly in the terrain of ethics, since it establishes autonomy and thus free acceptance, as the sole criterion for the construction of social relations. Therefore, civil society becomes the field of action for applied ethics.

An ethic applied to any social praxis should firstly clarify how this free acceptance or rational conviction is the primary base for legitimacy or social credibility. This explanation must be undertaken through the reconstruction of the meaning that this range of activities has for us as workers, clients, patients, readers, professionals and so on. The link between civil society and applied ethics clearly appears out of this methodological proposal. The error has been, and continues to be, as we will see in the case of Habermas, to limit any implementation of moral ideas only to the judicial terrain, leaving without conceptualisation, and therefore without orientation for action, the whole range of possibilities that unfold when civil society is conceptualised as the proper terrain for applied ethics.

Reconstructive methodology is ideally suited to help rectify this error. The basic idea consists of analysing the practical knowledge used by every member of civil society to establish relations in any of its spheres. In other words, to bring to light our competences not only as state citizens, but also as leading actors in civil society.[2] Although the mechanisms of inclusion and the boundaries of this sphere are not clearly defined, we are able to explain the intuitive knowledge that, as members and participants, we apply in the specific relations that make up civil society; concretely, the mechanisms that enable the cooperative search for solutions. In my opinion, discourse theory and, in its foundations, the theory of communicative action that supports it, also allow us to justify this implicit knowledge that is used in the trust mechanisms or mechanisms for reaching agreements that, although within a legal framework, enable them to be differentiated from strategic mechanisms.

In order to carry out this task, we must first attempt to go beyond the Habermasian conception of civil society. I believe that the concept of civil society introduced by Habermas is too closely linked to the effort to reconstruct the normative proposals that as participants, we carry out in the democratic practices of our rule of law. According to his definition, civil society would be a voluntary network of non-state, non-economic associations that anchor the communicative structures of public opinion in the social components of the *lebenswelt* (Habermas 1998, 443).

The only point I want to highlight now in this conception of civil society is the exclusion of the economic, market and company arena, of the political-administrative sphere, of political parties, the legal system and in general, the whole parliamentary network (see McCarthy 1992 and Cortina 1998b). With this concept of civil society, ethics is helpless to contribute any type of orientation for action other than the search for generalisable interests constituted and favoured by public opinion. If, in this way, Habermas succeeds in introducing a normative dimension and through it, the critical perspective, into the theory of democracy, he does so by sacrificing to the

2 Reconstruction in the way Habermas uses the term, not that used by Cohen and Arato. See Cohen and Arato 2000, 394.

'systemic' terrain the spheres of action in which the vast majority of social relations are established and where social power is produced and reproduced. The question is once again the same as in the possible application of ethics: is it not possible to establish the *channels* for a discourse-based formation of will in civil society itself that goes beyond the law?

Habermas continues to limit all possibilities for real intervention of communicative power generated by dialogue and possible consensus as a mechanism to solve problems, to its transformation, through law, into administrative power. In a global context, this inevitably clashes with the state boundaries of the law. This difficulty appears clearly in the works of Habermas himself whenever he broaches the subject of controlling the globalisation process and with it, the harmful consequences for the state and political autonomy that it facilitates, for instance when he demands the rebirth of politics in the markets with the creation of actors capable of acting internationally (Habermas 1999, 101).

That said, who are these actors, and how are they going to act in environments that by definition only admit a functional and strategic perspective? In the case of the economy, Habermas repeatedly refers to the capacity, or in this case incapacity, of nation states in all attempts to regulate and control the economy and therefore has no option but to recognise, in the absence of any cosmopolitan political order, the 'impossibility of intervention' in this way. In my opinion, the state is evidently, and must continue to be, the ultimate guarantee of rights, whether civil and political, economic, social or ecological. But is there still not any possibility for intervention in the economic praxis that does not come from law, from the judicial-administrative terrain? Does applied ethics not have a space beyond the spheres of public opinion or as normative theory of state and law?

The absence of communicative rationality that characterises the economy and the state does not quite tally with the need for meaning, in other words, for legitimacy, that all social praxis claim, however functionally differentiated they might be. Meaning (legitimacy) is a scarce resource and cannot be produced or provided, as Habermas never tires of repeating, through legal-administrative channels, as these also depend on the credibility or legitimacy that meaning offers. Meaning comes from *lebenswelt* and the relations of reciprocal recognition that it consists of. From this point of view, no concept of civil society can exclude the relation that actually exists between *lebenswelt* and the political and economic systems, however convenient it might be to separate them analytically. If, following Walzer, we recognise the central role of the state as an association of associations that delimits the frontiers of the other spheres, it obviously cannot remain on the sidelines of communicative rationality and of the structures of solidarity and trust that it facilitates (see Walzer 1993). Habermas recognises this essential character, if we might call it that, of the lifeworld when he assigns it, as Gramsci had already done, the basic function of creation of meaning, a function that cannot be carried out through legal regulation, administrative control or political steering (Habermas 1998, 434).

I consider Habermas's concept of civil society as being too narrow and unresponsive to the real workings of communicative power in the different social praxis. We must therefore expand the concept of civil society presented by discourse theory, in order that it might more beneficially deal with the reconstruction of the implicit knowledge that, as participants in each sphere of civil society, we use on a daily basis. All the potential offered by applied ethics may be turned to advantage if we start from a concept of civil society that includes all action coordination, strategic and functional mechanisms. Our proposal would come close to the classic definition of civil society as a sector of a voluntary nature, in which men and women can freely choose their own form of association, or, following Walzer a space for human association without coercion and the set of relations that fill that space, so long as the social and economic conditions that enable that freedom and voluntariness are also specified (for this possible extension of the concept of civil society, see Barber 2000 and Walzer 1995; see also Cortina 1997 for the concept of corresponding citizenship). Only in this way can we be sure to have a clear delimitation of the structures that make up the 'territory of operations' of applied ethics and of the mechanisms we use to make coordination of action possible.

The first step in this proposal for extension is to analyse the existing relation between the proposals for communicative action and the basic mechanisms of civil society. To this end, we can make use of the theories of social capital, whose function is to clarify the social phenomena related to the individual's capacity to associate and act conjointly (see Coleman 1990 on this theory; for an analysis of these theories, see Herreros and De Francisco 2001). Through this theory we can reconstruct the resources, mechanisms or means that social actors possess to undertake social relations and, within these, identify the moral dimension. Trust constitutes one of the most widely studied elements of social capital and a useful line to follow in this task.

From a functional point of view, trust is understood as the expectation placed in the future behaviour of a specific person or organisation. Trust always involves decisions being taken in risk situations; in other words, in situations in which the possibility that the other actors involved might act is wide open. To put it more clearly, we use this resource when we expect that the other actors will not act opportunistically, when we have reasons to think that they will behave according to what we expect. It is clear that the more flexible and changing a society is, the more open it is to contingencies, and that the more distant the relations produced, the greater the increase in its vulnerability will be and the greater importance these types of mechanisms will take on (Gambetta 1988, 213).

Trust as an action coordination mechanism is not a merely psychological element, nor can it be reduced to traditional, community or historical factors (see critique by Margaret Levi in Putnam 2000). Within this social capital we may find a rational motivation that enables us to identify a moral dimension within the set of reasons that lead us to trust. From this point of view, I speak of trust as a moral resource, to employ Hirschman's concept (García-Marzá 2004, 49). We are dealing with a moral resource because, firstly, it works in the opposite way to other resources: the more it is used, the more of it we have, and when it is not used it disappears; and secondly, because it is interwoven with a potential of reasons on which its validity, and therefore the expectations on which it is based, ultimately depend.

This latter aspect is clearly revealed when we move from personal to institutional trust, when we enquire about mechanisms for the production, maintenance and development of trust in situations where we cannot rely on shared experiences or community-based routines. We then find a cognitive element, a rational base on which these beliefs or predictions about others' future behaviour are grounded and which leads us to reciprocal expectations of behaviour, that is, norms. It is clear that norms bind and are maintained, they are socially efficient because of the sanctions they incorporate and because of the way they are internalised in the socialisation process. They also possess a dimension of validity that goes beyond this social reality and that refers to the possible reasons that, when the case arises, might justify the norm and defend it from criticism. In other words, they refer to the possible justification of the expectations raised.

This set of expectations defines the structure of trust. Expectations are no more than the meanings an actor attributes to him or herself and others, in other words, the needs and interests incorporated within the norm; in sum, that which members of a community can expect of each other under given circumstances and limitations. Of these meanings, we are interested in moral expectations, those referring to the rights, duties and obligations that are transmitted through the norm. In this sense, trust is also supported by the fact that we have good reasons to believe that others will fulfil the responsibilities derived from actions delimited by the norm. In fact, these shared schemata of intelligibility and responsibility are just as socially efficient as the strategic orientations of means and end might be (McCarthy 1993, 65).

This internal connection between norms and reasons allows us to explain the existing relation between the moral conviction that accompanies the norms' validity and the trust that underlies the inherent meaning of the different spheres of civil society. The reciprocal conviction derived from the common recognition of the validity claims in fact means that we are tacitly accepting the obligations relevant for the action. The pretension to validity with which a norm is presented, or the pretension to legitimacy with which an institution or social praxis is presented express a specific network of demands and compromises, of rules and power structures. When the justness of a norm or institution fails, these expectations of reciprocity that underlie them also fail, and with them, the trust placed in the possibilities of conviction that are currently not proven (Habermas 1988, Vol. 2, 257). The result is social criticism, mistrust or loss of credibility.

Trust therefore has a cognitive structure, from which we can speak of the motivating force of rational discourse. This force, although it may go no further than the weak motivation of 'good reasons', still has its 'potentialities for power' precisely as a rational base on which legitimacy is grounded (Habermas 1988, Vol. 2, 215). Moral knowledge does not oblige us to enter into discourse, nor to carry out the corresponding action although we may have good reasons to do so. Even in this way we cannot explain the capacity that civil society actually has for cooperation and the common search for shared interests without reference to this cognitive base. One of the basic tasks facing applied ethics is to convert this communicative power, this conviction to act according to norms that have not been imposed from outside by mechanisms of sanction, but have been freely accepted, into social power; in other words, into power that generates morally justified social relations.

This potential must not be limited to the validity of duty that accompanies actions and norms, but should also be applied to organisations as networks of norms, as cooperative actions for the search or achievement of a specific objective or social end. If, like Habermas, we understand moral conscience as the expression of the legitimate demands that the cooperating members of a social group may place on each other, then organisations also have a moral conscience. In this sense, we are speaking both of the *moral contract* that characterises every organisation and on which its social legitimacy depends, ultimately the trust placed in it, and of its *moral responsibility*, as an expression of the need to justify, to respond with reasons; of the differences in the distribution of power, burdens and benefits involved in every organisation.

To deny organisations responsibility, as in the case of the company, means denying the possible existence of decisions beyond the strictly individual decision, as though all organised praxis had no culture, values, its own way of acting and coping with reality, an expected normative behaviour, as though they did not presuppose any structures that limited or strengthened those individual decisions. Applied ethics is often, and must continue to be, the ethics of institutional actions (Lenk 1992, 101ff.).

Neither does, nor should, the economy lie outside civil society and the field of applied ethics. Civil society cannot be the equivalent of the market, but neither can it be understood without the logic of efficiency, of supply and demand; in sum, without the logic appertaining to the production and distribution of goods and services. In this sense, civil society should also include economic institutions, so long as they operate from the perspective of communicative action, that is, from the understanding of or agreement on the rules of the game that every institutionalised and legally differentiated social praxis implies. This does not mean there are no strategies and compromises, but rather that dialogue and free agreement are the criteria for validity and justice in each one of these institutions.

With this objective, applied ethics of a discourse nature must specify the proposal of civil society with which it is going to work, and attempt to structure it into various settings that allow us to measure the principle of dialogue with the conditions from the various praxis. We cannot remain at a strictly normative level, but rather we must describe the social structures in which the offered conceptualisation can be 'recognised', a task that goes far beyond the limits of the present work. Here, we can only note that the concept of interest, interpreted in its most general sense as a 'product of will', may provide a good hermeneutic cornerstone for this task. Interests are always a motive for action and hence, spaces of action that we want to conserve or expand (see Hirschman 1978; also Geuss 1981). When we say a person has an interest, we are giving a possible reason why it should be fulfilled and with this, when the circumstances arise, enabling a rational discourse to take place. From this vision of interests, there are associations and organisations that seek generalisable interests, but there are also intermediary organisations that aggregate interests where the objective of the interaction may be a particular individual's interest or that of a specific group. But even in these cases, we *always* find universal expectations, interests that *everyone* wants to see satisfied, and that involve obligations and rights for everybody else.

From this point of view, what characterises civil society would not only be its reduction to generalisable interests, but rather its configuration as a horizon for the satisfaction of the interests at stake and for the resolution of conflicts of action from free agreement, in other words, as a criterion of validity for practical discourse in which conflicting individual or group interests are resolved.

From Theory to Praxis: Applied Ethics as Integrative Ethics

The first step in the clarification of the status of applied ethics may be summarised in the 'justification' of the moral resources that civil society possesses, good examples of which are the trust and credibility required and claimed by the praxis and institutions that form it. These moral mechanisms are implicit in every praxis, from the workings of a football club to a visit to the doctor. If the various applied ethics are able to reconstruct the intuitive knowledge used in each social sphere, we can make significant progress towards a future ethical structuration of civil society.

However, we must still deal with a basic question for all moral philosophy directly committed to problem solving: its relation with praxis. So far we have been concerned with the reconstruction of implicit knowledge, but we must now take the opposite direction to consider that the status of applied ethics also depends on how we understand this application.

Without this dual movement, we would lay ourselves open to two well-known criticisms. Moral expectations are grounded in a powerful idealisation that presents a hurdle to the understanding of how they can be applied. When we attempt, through dialogue, to reach consensual resolution to a conflict of interests that has arisen, we assume that our discourse is aimed at absolutely all those affected and/or involved, both present and future, and that everyone is able to take part in the discourse without any coercion and under conditions of perfect symmetry and power in which to present their reasons and for them to be accepted. These idealisations may explain the preparation of a possible agreement through reasons, but they do not give much help in building orientations for action that go beyond the 'ideal speaking situation' or 'unlimited communication community' as defined by Apel. What happens in real civil society situations? Aren't we condemning any possibility of orientation to impotence or even worse, to sacrifice?

At the same time, any response offered by applied ethics cannot renounce the unconditional element on which its normativity is supported, at the risk of losing all critical perspective and being watered down to a mere social instrument or technology (see Werner 1999).

These difficulties disappear if we are able to understand that the relation between theory and praxis cannot take place from a dual perspective, as though we were thinking of ways to build bridges across a river. The essential characteristic of the social world with which we are dealing here is precisely that it is linguistically constructed from the ideas we believe to be just and correct, where the variety of learning processes constantly transform validity into social reality (Habermas 1988, Vol. 1, 163ff.). We cannot separate social reality from validity, as though we had society and its institutions on one side and ethical values on the other. The moral point of view is embedded in the very meaning of social reality. To continue with our example of the company, there is no example of the company on the one hand

and the just company on the other: all companies, like any other institution, are just or moral to a greater or lesser extent.

The concept of application seems to bring with it this dual conception of a link between two kingdoms. We must therefore avoid two modalities of relation between theory and praxis that can only lead to the self-dissolution of ethical reflection. We must avoid both a corrective approach (ethics as a 'recipe book') that deductively tells us what the external boundaries of each activity, praxis or institution are, as well as a functional approach (the 'washes whiter' ethic) that only regards ethics as a strategy or instrument to achieve the proposed objective (see Ulrich 1987, 264; 1997). The former fails when faced with the pluralism and complexity of our societies and can do no more than seek refuge in the privacy of our consciences or in the conventionalism of our beliefs. The latter is diluted in systemic logic and is incapable of explaining the moral validity of our actions and institutions, on which we must not forget, a great deal of their credibility or legitimacy depend.

The status of applied ethics must be based on the integrative character of social reality itself, in which facts and values cannot be separated. From a methodological perspective, integration must also take place between normative stances, and those that naïvely put themselves forward as descriptive or empirical positions (Donaldson and Dunfee 1999). In order to carry out this integration, I believe we have to differentiate three levels on the path that takes us from theory to praxis. Discourse ethics can once again help us to find a definition of the steps required to configure applied ethics as an integrative ethic.

Throughout the whole of his work, Habermas has always expressed a particular concern for the relation between theory and practice. All his writings maintain the role of philosophy as the 'guardian' of rationality, as the key aspect in justifying the normativity that derives from different validity claims. From this normative domain, he can criticise, for instance, the colonisation of the *lebenswelt* that is taking place due to pressure from science and technology, the market and capital as well as through the law and bureaucracy (Habermas 1999, 331). I consider this to be one of the key roles of applied ethics, and particularly of economic and business ethics.

Nonetheless, one of philosophy's vital concerns has always been how to connect with reality, how philosophy might become practical. In *Theorie und Praxis*, Habermas deals with the problems arising from the institutionalisation of discourse and specifically from issues of the organisation. In this text, he differentiates three essential steps in the mediation between theory and praxis, three methodologically different steps that hence respond to different criteria of validity, but that occur conjointly in every attempt to solve a conflict of action by consensus. Firstly, theoretical reconstruction, submitted to discussion amongst the various philosophical positions; secondly, proposals for organisation in every social praxis, and finally the choice of strategies, subject to the logic of responsibility and prudence (Habermas 1987, 41ff.).

In my view, this differentiation of levels, although designed for political ethics, may be generalised in order to delimit the structure of an applied ethic derived from discourse ethics and that may serve as a nucleus for the various ethics of civil society. The proposal consists of differentiating amongst the following types of analysis so as to bring theory closer to praxis.

Level of justification

One of the key contributions of discourse ethics as a base for applied ethics is precisely what we might call its critical perspective. The qualifier 'critical' is methodologically related to the reconstruction of the practical knowledge that we use in all social spheres. We are already aware that discourse ethics provides the unconditionality that allows us to speak of moral obligatoriness starting from reflection on the conditions of possibility of the argumentation, of the possibility for the rational agreement that underlies normative validity. The thesis presented by a discourse approach to applied ethics is that such a critical reflection is also possible for civil society in its widest sense. Participation, dialogue, and where appropriate, consensus or agreement constitute the basic criterion for a moral evaluation of the various spheres of civil society.

This principle of dialogue and subsequent agreement, essential for credibility and trust management, does not define a social contract, but rather what we might call a moral contract, since the 'no coercion' condition delimits a situation where complete and perfect equality of opportunity and participation exists. Habermas speaks of a practical discourse, that is, a discourse in which only the reasons brought forward can lead to agreement or consensus. Only in these conditions of symmetry and equality may a rationally motivated consensus come about, and not through strategy, force or violence. Put another way, not simply any dialogue would do to justify an agreement; the agreement may be considered just when it is reached under specific conditions. Borrowing from various of Habermas's texts, we can summarise these conditions in the following four principles:

Principle of sincerity When discourse is entered into, the interested parties have no wish to settle their conflicts through violence or compromise (strategy) but rather through dialogue, which implies accepting the obligations and rights of argumentation.

Principle of inclusion All potential present and future affected parties, or where appropriate, their representatives, must take part in the dialogue. Nobody who might make a relevant contribution may be excluded from participating.

Principle of reciprocity The participants must be able to dialogue in conditions that assure absolute equality of opportunity and total symmetry in the conditions of participation and in the way the interests at stake may be interpreted.

Principle of publicity All interests must be considered equally and must be open to revision through argument: symmetrical distribution of communicative freedoms. No one interest may be considered definitive and free from criticism.

This situation effectively represents a counterfactual, a set of conditions that we believe are met when we enter into discourse. We can never be sure that they are in fact met, nor the extent to which they might be met, but we 'have to' suppose that they are met if we wish to make and find sense in what we are doing. The situation is not particularly complicated to understand, since any social interaction, from traffic regulations to a complex commercial transaction all work in this way. Imagine whether we would dare to drive if we did not start off with the presumption that all the other drivers were going to stay in their lane. Can we be a hundred per cent sure that this will be the case?

These principles do not attempt to describe a real situation, but rather they reconstruct the presumptions that we 'in fact' think will occur when as participants, we express our agreement or disagreement with a decision, action or institution. Their counterfactual nature indicates that we are not dealing with an operative decision criterion, but rather a regulative idea whose operationality must always be subsequently carried out in practice. Yet even so, this idea defines our conviction that these conditions are adequately met. From this perspective, these principles define moral validity, the final evaluation horizon from which the reasons that support or criticise our decisions, actions, norms and institutions must be 'constructed'. In summary, not just any dialogue constitutes the moral objective, but only the search for dialogues under these conditions. Hence, these rules constitute the cognitive source from which are constructed what we have called here moral resources, and which define all critical perspective.

Level of appropriateness

Reconstructive methodology cannot simply stop at this initial focus on the philosophical reconstruction of our capacity to establish dialogues and reach agreements. Once the conditions that presuppose the consensual resolution of conflicts of action have been established, we must turn to the possibilities of using this knowledge in specific situations, in particular social praxis or concrete institutions. From the reconstruction of meaning that, as participants and/or affected parties, we effect in diverse applied ethics, we must now take a further step and tackle the operationalisation of the so-called moral principle, making advances into the interpretation of moral principles from different arenas. Although discourse ethics puts forward practical discourse as the most suitable medium for application, it must now define how dialogue can take place at the heart of civil society. At this second level, application means adaptation to reality.

In the case of business ethics, for instance, the target is to reconstruct the conditions that make the company's credibility or legitimacy possible: conditions or presumptions that define 'what should be' rather than what is. They do not tell us how the company behaves, but rather how it should behave in order not to lose credibility and with it, the trust placed in it by all participants, all interest groups (see Cortina et al. 1994).

In order to deal with what we might call this element of responsibility, we need go no further than the framework established by discourse ethics, although it must be given content. The principle of universalisation that serves as our moral criterion requires that real dialogues take place, where agreement depends on all the interests at stake being considered and on the calculation of the consequences. The objective is now to measure this principle in the various praxis in which communicative action has broken down and attempt to reach consensual solutions, or at least compromises or negotiations.

However, this requires a hermeneutic task capable of reconstructing the meaning and the internal logic of each activity (see Cortina 1996 on this process). We must discover the reasons that justify the asymmetrical power distributions and the unequal opportunities for participation as pragmatic reasons to achieve the proposed social objectives. We must be able to rely on this strategic rationality in order to be able to speak of a practical rationality that falls neither into the trap of utopianism nor into justifying injustice.

The discourse approach now calls for an interdisciplinary effort involving theories and proposals that help us to apply the principle of dialogue. Here, we are concerned with presenting possibilities for the institutionalisation of discourse in the company praxis, and with proposing maxims for action that help us to give visible form to moral resources, maxims that we must justify from the very principle of impartiality or reciprocity. At this level, discourse ethics can no longer work alone and needs to be complemented by other theories of a normative and empirical nature that help to operationalise the reconstructed ethical principles. These theories must 'fit' with a hermeneutic synthesis that enables us to apply the reconstructed moral principle. Two examples might help to illustrate this complementarity amongst theories.

Firstly, the Stakeholder or interest group approach complements the ideas put forward most favourably. It attempts to find methodological strategies that enable us to integrate moral ideas with specific realities and the use of this theory at all its levels, normative, strategic and instrumental, is a good way to approach the reality of the organisation, as long as we know how to 'fit' these approaches within the ethics framework established in the previous level. In this way, we meet two objectives at the same time: on one hand discourse ethics can offer Stakeholder theory a normative grounding in accordance with the plurality and universality of current contexts, which to date has not been achieved (on the current situation of this theory see works compiled in Clarkson 1998; the special number of *Business Ethics Quarterly* 10:1; see also on this aspect Gibson 2000; on the need for an ethics perspective within this approach González Esteban 2002). On the other hand, the diverse visions of Stakeholder theory can offer discourse ethics a methodological access to the various structures of civil society adapted to the reconstructed moral principle, thus providing the theory with a way out of the excessive abstraction by which it characterised.

The second proposal for complementarity derives from the need to reduce the excessive proceduralism characteristic of discourse ethics at the previous normative level. We must therefore make explicit not only the conditions that make practical discourse possible in the form of duties and obligations, but the values that enable the action to be oriented towards the cooperative search for consensus must also be shown (see Cortina 2001 on the need for a wider vision of discourse ethics). Here, we refer to providing the practical discourse with content, through an analysis of which values, aspirations and behaviour models best fit the reconstructed moral point of view. In this way, we can introduce cultural specificities and a variety of traditional forms within the deontological framework.

Level of resolution

The demand of dialogue as an action coordination mechanism prevents a monological anticipation of the outcome. To put it another way, it demands that real discourses be carried out, and through them, the mediation of this moral demand with the realities of each praxis and institution that make up civil society.

The principle of discourse ethics emphasises one basic aspect: the concrete answers must always, necessarily be in the hands of those affected. In contrast to the corrective approach, no single ethicist, economist or politician may individually or monologically decide on the moral validity of an action or institution. Of course they may put forward and specify proposals for discussion and subsequent acceptance by the assembly of all involved parties and/or their representatives. From this, the current importance of the ethics committee can be seen: true interdisciplinary teams that are able to act from a variety of social practices.

Therefore, an applied ethic should offer for deliberation orientations and possibilities for action and participation that will encourage the resolution of conflicts of action by consensus. It should make proposals and move towards the definition of the conditions in which moral resources may be applied, although always as a subject for free and public discussion amongst all affected parties. The last word must always go to those who have to suffer the consequences.

To conclude, the role of the various ethics in civil society is precisely the construction of a communicatively structured social power based on these premises. In contrast to specialised law in administrative power, applied ethics directly allows the orientation of action and through that, enables a social coordination grounded in the strength of conviction of good reasons. The network of applied ethics derived from discourse ethics offers as a common denominator practical discourse as a mechanism for this action coordination. In this sense, in the words of Barber, civil society constitutes the domain of dialogue and dialogue, in turn, 'the capability to create active trust through an appreciation of the integrity of the other' (Giddens 1996, 99).

References

Apel, K.-O. (2001), *Filosofia primera avui i ètica del discurs* (Girona: Eumo).
Barber, B. (1983), *The Logic and Limits of Trust* (New Jersey: Rugers).
—— (2000), *Un lugar para todos. Cómo fortalecer la democracia y la sociedad civil* (Barcelona: Paidós).
Bayertz, K. (1991), *Praktische Philosophie* (Hamburg: Rowoholts).
Beiner, R. (ed.) (1995), *Theorizing Citizenship* (New York: State University of New York).
Business Ethics Quarterly 10:1 (January 2000, 10th Anniversary Issue).
Clarkson, M.B.E. (ed.) (1998), *The Corporation and its Stakeholders. Classic and Contemporary Readings* (Toronto: University of Toronto Press).

Cohen, J.L. and Arato, A. (2000), *Sociedad civil y teoría política* (México: FCE).
Coleman, J.S. (1990), *Foundations of Social Theory* (Cambridge, MA: Harvard University Press).
Cortina, A. (1986), *Ética sin moral* (Madrid: Tecnos).
— (1993), *Ética aplicada y democracia radical* (Madrid: Tecnos).
— et al. (1994), *Ética de la empresa. Claves para una nueva cultura empresarial* (Madrid: Treaty).
— (1995), *Ética de la sociedad civil* (Madrid: Anaya).
— (1996), 'El estatuto de la ética aplicada. Hermenéutica crítica de las actividades humanas', *Isegoría* 13, 119–35.
— (1997), *Ciudadanos del mundo: hacia una teoría de la ciudadanía* (Madrid: Alianza Editorial).
— (ed.) (1998a), *10 palabras clave en filosofía política* (Estella: Verbo Divino).
— (1998b), 'Sociedad civil', in Cortina, A. (ed.) (1998a), pp. 353–88.
— (1998c), *Hasta un pueblo de demonios. Ética pública y sociedad* (Madrid: Taurus).
— (2001), *Alianza y contrato* (Madrid: Trotta).
Donaldson, T. and Dunfee, T.W. (1999), *Ties that Bind* (Boston, MA: Harvard Business School).
Gambetta, D. (1988), *Trust: Making and Breaking Cooperative Relations* (New York: Basil Blackwell).
García-Marzá, D. (1992), *Ética de la justicia. Habermas y la ética discursiva* (Madrid: Tecnos).
— (1998), 'Weltpolitik und Weltwirtschaft-Die Notwendigkeit einer kosmopolitischen Demokratie', in Maak, T. and Lunau, Y. (1998), pp. 123–39.
— (2004), *Ética Empresarial: Del Diálogo a la Confianza* (Madrid: Trotta).
Geuss, R. (1981), *The Idea of a Critical Theory* (New York: Cambridge University Press).
Gibson, K. (2000), 'The Moral Basis of Stakeholder Theory', *Journal of Business Ethics* 26:3, 245–57.
Giddens, A. (1996), *Más allá de la izquierda y la derecha* (Madrid: Cátedra).
González Esteban, E. (2002), 'Defining a Post-Conventional Corporate Moral Responsibility', *Journal of Business Ethics* 39:1–2, 101–8.
Günther, K. (1988), *Der Sinn der Angemessenheit* (Frankfurt: Suhrkamp).
Habermas, J. (1985), *Conciencia moral y acción comunicativa* (Barcelona: Península).
— (1987), *Teoría y praxis* (Madrid: Tecnos).
— (1988), *Teoría de la acción comunicativa*, 2 vols. (Madrid: Taurus).
— (1991), *Erläuterungen zur diskursethik* (Frankfurt: Suhrkamp).
— (1998), *Facticidad y validez* (Madrid: Trotta).
— (1999), *La inclusión del otro* (Barcelona: Paidós).
— (1999), *Wahrheit und Rechtfertigung* (Frankfurt: Suhrkamp).
— (2000), *Aclaraciones a la ética del dicurso* (Madrid: Trotta).
Herreros, F. and De Francisco, A. (coords.) (2001), 'Capital social', Monograph: *Zona Abierta* 94–5 (Madrid: Fundación Pablo Iglesias).

Hirschman, A. (1978), *Las pasiones y los intereses* (México: FCE).
Hirschman, A.O. (1986), 'Against Parsimony: Three Easy Ways of Complicating some Categories of Economic Discourse', in *Rival Views of Market Society and Other Recent Essays* (New York: Viking Penguin).
Höffe, A. (1979), *Estrategias de lo humano* (Buenos Aires: Alfa).
Keane, J. (1992), *Democracia y sociedad civil* (Madrid: Alianza).
Lenk, H. (1922), *Wissenschaft und Ethik* (Frankfurt: Suhrkamp).
Luhmann, N. (1979), *Trust and Power* (New York: Wiley).
Maak, T. and Lunau, Y. (1998), *Weltwirtschaftsethik* (Stuttgart: Haupt).
McCarthy, T. (1992), *Ideales e ilusiones* (Madrid: Tecnos).
Putnam, R.D. (2000), *Per a fer que la democracia funcioni. La importancia del capital social* (Barcelona: Proa).
Rehg, W. (1997), *Insight and Solidarity* (Berkeley: University of California Press).
Toulmin, E. (1976), *El puesto de la razón en la ética* (Madrid: Alianza).
Ulrich, P. (1987), *Transformation der ökonomischen Vernunft* (Stuttgart: Haupt).
—— (1997), *Integrative Wirtschaftsethik* (Stuttgart: Haupt).
Walzer, M. (1993), *Esferas de la justicia* (México: FCE).
—— (1995), 'Civil Society Argument', in Beiner, R. (ed.), pp. 153–74.
Werner, M.H. (1999), 'Anwendungsprobleme in der normativen Ethik', *Berichte des IWE* 85.

Chapter 8

Globalisation and the Need for Universal Ethics

Karl-Otto Apel[1]

Globalisation as a Challenge to Universal Ethics

Globalisation in our day has become a key word for a process that is primarily concerning an international expansion of economy, or more precisely, a systemic intertwining of financial capitalism and communication technology that seems to exceed any control by the nation state and hence by social policy so far. Now, even considered in this narrow sense, globalisation, I think, provides a novel and highly urgent challenge to a universally valid type of ethics, say in regard to social justice on a global scale. But, at a closer look, the presently discussed economic process of globalisation turns out to be only the most recent stage of a development that was a consequence of the European predominance in science, technology and political economy that may be traced back to the age of discovery and colonization. Since then, a continuous and growing process of globalisation has taken place with regard to vitally important parts of human civilization. The scope and bearings of this process are characteristically attested by the fact that many aspects of apparently counter-globalistic developments – for example liberation movements in the Third World, self-exclusion of non-European countries from the tendential globalisation of economy, politics and even culture, politico- religious 'fundamentalism', and, on the other hand, involuntary exclusion of parts of the world (for example, Africa) from the positive effects of the market economy – can and must also be considered as integral parts of the modern globalisation process. For these latter phenomena show that today all countries of the earth are at least virtually affected by this one historical process. This is most strikingly illustrated by the so-called ecological crisis which is, after all, a consequence of modern science, technology and economy, proving that in our time, all human individuals, nations and cultures are, so to speak, in one boat, whether they like it or not.

The globalisation process characterised so far, is irreversible. It is typically one of those developments of human history that have taken place ahead of our reflection and morally responsible control. But this means that the process characterized so far should only be considered a phenomenon of first-order globalisation. It is a challenge to the philosophical reflection and thereby to a mobilization of moral responsibility

1 University of Frankfurt am main, Germany.

for the establishment of a novel order of human interaction that could be called second-order globalisation. Only such an effort can cope with the problematic aspects of first-order globalisation. This suggestion may, in the present article, serve as an account of the need for a universal ethics in our time. But to elucidate this idea, I will allow myself to have recourse to some autobiographical retrospection.

The Need for Universal Ethics as a Planetarian Macro-ethics of Co-responsibility in the Age of Science and Technology (A Retrospection)

I have been working at the foundation as well as the implementation of a conception of global and hence universally valid ethics since the end of the 1960s (Apel 1973). At that time, there was a need for a planetary macro-ethics in the age of science to be distinguished from the traditional or conventional forms of ethics, namely micro- and meso-ethics, which were restricted to loyalty within small groups or obedience to law and order within the nation state. In contradistinction to these traditional types of ethics, in the 20th century for the first time in human history, our ethical responsibility had to cope with the planetary range and risk of the effects and side-effects of science and technology.

At that time, the philosophical challenge of the approach to universal ethics was primarily represented by the fact that, during the first half of the 20th century, the scientistic type of value-neutral rationality almost completely prejudiced the philosophical discussion of rationality in general. Hence, on this presupposition, a rational foundation of a universally valid ethics seemed to be impossible, in principle. To describe the situation in more provocative words, the very rationality of science and technology which had brought about the novel situation and its challenge to a planetary ethics of responsibility, being monopolised as universally valid, seemed also to block any possibility of a rational foundation of the universal ethics required. It was to this paradox that I tried to give an answer in my transcendental pragmatic conception of communication or discourse ethics, which I have elaborated since then, partly in collaboration with Jürgen Habermas (Apel 1973; 1998; 1996d; Habermas 1976; 1983; 1991).

The point was, briefly expressed, that the blockade of the possible validity of a universal ethics pertains only to the subject-object-relation of scientific and, analogously, of instrumental-technological rationality, whereas in the complementary dimension of inter-subjective or communicative rationality – for example, within the community of scientific investigations taken as an ideal argumentation community – a universally valid ethics is indeed presupposed and recognized even by the co-subjects of value-neutral science and technology. Therefore the task of ethics was to overcome the modern absolutisation of the subject-object-relation of science and the accompanying methodological solipsism of philosophical epistemology (from Descartes through Husserl) with the aid of the hermeneutic and linguistic turn of the 20th century's philosophy, in order to reach an ultimate foundation of ethics through strictly transcendental reflection on the necessary presuppositions of the rationality of argumentation.

In this article I want to show that this approach may also provide an answer to the need for universal ethics that is evoked by the present dramatization of the situation of globalisation. But I will try to reach this aim more or less indirectly, namely through a critical reconstruction of some paradigmatic trends of philosophical ethics during the last decades. (In this context, I will in particular refer to those positions that were brought forward at the last Unesco conference on universal ethics in Paris, on 27 March 1997).

The Development of Philosophical Ethics after John Rawls's *Theory of Justice*: The Impact of Historicism-Relativism and the Search for Common Values

Since the 1970s the situation of philosophical ethics has changed in so far as the need for global or universal ethics has been widely recognized. Thus the positivistic abstinence with regard to ethics has been given up, in particular since Rawls's publication of this *Theory of Justice* (1971), and it has even given way to a boom in political ethics, especially with regard to the international discussion of human rights and the universal acceptability of democracy. In this context, even an ethical enlargement of the discussion of universal rights to a discussion of universal duties or obligations of all human beings has taken place; and, on this line, an international declaration concerning the project of global ethics has been brought about (Küng and Kuschel 1993; 1996).

However, as a professional philosopher, I have to note as well that the situation with regard to the general assessment of the possibility, or rather impossibility, of a rational foundation of a universal ethics has not properly changed since the days of scientism-positivism. True, the spell of the value-free rationality of the subject-object-relation of science and technology has been broken, in a sense, through the (hermeneutic) recourse to community traditions of 'strong values', that is ethos-traditions as parts of 'comprehensive world-views' (Honneth 1993; Brumlik and Brunkhorst 1993; Apel 1993, 149–72). On this line of thought, there was a broad convergence of continental-post-Heideggerian hermeneutics and post-Wittgensteinian or post-Kuhnian communitarianism. But this turn or recourse to concrete ethos-traditions (to what Hegel called '*substantielle Sittlichkeit*', or substantial ethical life, of the 'objective spirit' could not really solve the post-conventional and post-traditional problem of a universally valid foundation of ethics in the age of scientific-technological-strategic rationality. It could not even strive for such a solution, since it did not try to surmount the scientistic-technological-strategic monopoly of rationality by revealing a deeper (communicative-discursive) type of rationality. It rather evaded this problem through the pragmatic-hermeneutic recourse to the customs of a given 'form of life' as a 'contingent basis of consent' (Rorty 1991).

Now, at this point, the other characteristic dilemma of the ethical challenge of our situation of globalisation becomes visible: whereas the universal rationality seems to be value-neutral and hence cannot provide a basis for ethics, the existing foundations of ethics seem to be culture-dependent and hence cannot provide a basis for a global or universal ethics (Apel 1997, 199–212; 1999, 145–63). This dilemma comes to the fore as soon as – for example, in the context of the discussion about human rights – the second great problem of our situation of globalisation has to be faced, which is determining the moral and juridical conditions of a multicultural society, which today has to be realised at least on the planetarian level, but also as a paradigm of coexistence cannot even be avoided in most of the constitutional states. It seems clear from the outset that a recourse to historistic relativism à la Rorty (see in particular Rorty 1991, 175–96, and, for a critical comment Apel 1988, 398ff.; 1999, 145–63) is not compatible with a solution of this problem, since not only the differences of the existing, culture- dependent ethos-traditions have to be recognised and respected, as our post-modernist philosophers emphasise, but also, at the same time, the equality of the rights to uniqueness of the different cultures also has to be recognised and respected. Furthermore, even the commitment of history-related co-responsibility (say, with regard to the planetary environment) has to be taken over by all cultural communities.

We are here confronted with a problem of universal ethics that, in my opinion, has to be solved not only by hermeneutic recourse to the different contingent ethos-traditions but also by recourse to (that is, by transcendental reflection on) the moral presuppositions of our post-traditional philosophical and multicultural discourse about the problem of multiculturalism (see Apel 1997; 1999). Such a recourse by transcendental reflection could show that our procedural discourse rationality is, from the outset, committed to an impartial point of view which can provide the basis for a complementaristic solution of the problem of multiculturalism. Thereby is understood a solution that presupposes a relationship of reciprocal acknowledgement as well as confinement between the different projects of life and hence of values of the different cultures, on the one hand, and the unitary and hence universally valid normative principles of inter-cultural justice and co-responsibility, on the other. But before trying to explain this approach in more detail, let us again have a look at the philosophical solutions that are in fact proposed in our times.

The approach of discourse ethics, at least in its transcendental pragmatic version, has not met much understanding on the level of recent discussions, which are under the sway of hermeneuticism and neopragmatism. In particular, it has not been recognised that the way of strict transcendental reflection on the procedural presuppositions of argumentation is not just one more recourse to a comprehensive doctrine of metaphysics (which would of course be culture-dependent) but, on the contrary, is the only possible way of avoiding metaphysics and thus culture-dependence. It is indeed not a recourse to empirical facts either, and thus far it is not a way of anthropological or sociological inquiry (which seems to be extremely difficult to understand for most people in our times), for it looks for those moral principles that in order to save the self-consistency of reason we must acknowledge even if or, respectively, when we consider all empirically given ethos-forms only as conventional facts from which no binding norms and hence no moral commitments can be derived. (This point will be revisited later.)

In fact, the mainstream of philosophical ethics in our time pursues another route, in order to reach a practically relevant solution of the problem of a universal ethics in the face of multiculturalism. It seems to have given up or obsoletised the whole problem of ensuring a rational foundation for a universally valid ethics; it rather replaces this problem by that of providing empirical and pragmatical support for a factual, politically relevant agreement about the elements of a global ethics, in a similar way as, since the UN declaration of 1948, the factual agreements about human rights have been prepared and, so to speak, negotiated.

A good example of this pragmatical tendency of current moral philosophy is already presented by the development of the position of Rawls (Rawls 1971; 1980; 1993a; 1995, 133ff.; Apel 1999, 145–63). At the beginning, the *Theory of Justice* could be considered as a complementaristic approach to the problem of – intercultural – justice, since the free-standing philosophical foundation of the principles of justice was to ensure the priority of the right – and thus far of a universally valid morality – over the good of the different, culture-dependent, 'comprehensive doctrines' of metaphysics and religion. But the later position of Rawls in *Political Liberalism* (Rawls 1993a) has changed in many respects. It has abandoned the claim to a free-standing philosophical, and thus far, moral foundation of the theory of justice (obviously under the impact of the communitarian thesis that all philosophical theories of morality must be dependent on comprehensive views of metaphysics). Rawls now restricts the claim of his theory of justice to that of a political (hypothetical) proposition that may hope to find support from most comprehensive doctrines of the good and thus can become the basis for an overlapping consensus in the political world.

With regard to this outcome, I will only remark at this point that, by abandoning a philosophical foundation of justice, Rawls also gives up the possibility of a genuine principle of universalisation of Kantian provenance, that is, a principle that, in the name of its own moral authority, may also be directed against those types of overlapping consensus that in fact can be reached in face of the actual constellation of comprehensive views in the political world. By contrast, the procedural consensus principle of discourse ethics, which, as pointed out above, may be considered as a transformation of Kant's universalisation principle, demands a possible consensus of all affected persons with regard to the probable effects of a universal obedience of the norms that could be proposed in a practical discourse. This procedural principle establishes a post-conventional authority of its own and hence may serve as a regulative idea even for changing the traditional-multicultural conditions of reaching a factual overlapping consensus in the political world. With this moral-philosophical proviso against the approach of the later Rawls, it cannot be denied that, in the political world, we need factual agreements that are based on an overlapping consensus of the existing metaphysical and/or religious positions. But in the face of the novel challenges of the age of globalisation – as for example, the ecological crisis and the demand for social justice on the level of a global order of economy – we need also a post-conventional and post-traditional response of moral philosophy that can represent the interests of those virtual discourse partners – such as the members of the next generations or the poor of the Third World – who may not be sufficiently represented by those positions that in the factual political discourses may constitute the basis for an overlapping consensus.

The problem regarding the possible methods of responding to the challenge of globalisation to universal ethics becomes even clearer, if one starts out from the position of those contemporary philosophers, such as the communitarians, who expressly deny that there is a possibility of a free-standing philosophical foundation of a deontological ethic that could supplement and restrict the culture-dependent ethos-traditions or comprehensive views. In this case the question arises whether these philosophers – as in the case of many 'communitarians' – nevertheless feel the practical need for a conception of universal ethics and wish to contribute to the solution of this problem.

An answer to this problem that suggests itself, especially in cases of international and inter-cultural conferences, obviously consists in looking – more or less by empirical investigation – for what is common to the different ethos-traditions, for instance in the existing world religions, in order to distil from the overlapping features a minimal basis for a global ethics. This way is followed, for example, by Sissela Bok, who in her book *Common Values* (1995) gives a comprehensive overview of those morally relevant needs and hence 'down-to-earth values' that may be found to be recognised in a similar way in all human social groups as preconditions of their survival. By this method she comes to distinguish between three categories of 'global values', that is, 'duties of mutual support and loyalty', 'a limited set of constraints on specific forms of violence and dishonesty', and, third, views that select a 'thin notion of procedural justice' (Bok 1995, 57).

Such a comparative inductive approach seems to be very useful, in fact indispensable, if a certain minimalistic interpretation of the data in light of a universally accepted principle of inter-cultural justice can already be presupposed. For in order to make possible the transition from ascertaining the data in the comparative study of cultures to a conception of a minimalist global ethics two preconditions must be ensured, as follows.

(1) The acknowledgement of a universal principle of justice has to be ensured; for it is by no means a matter of course that the many social groups that – as we know from anthropology – recognise and obey the norms of loyalty that are indispensable for their survival, would also be prepared to extrapolate from the conventional loyalty within the groups (perhaps within the nation state) to the post-conventional solidarity with the equal rights of all parts of humankind to survive. F.A. von Hayek, the founder of the neo-liberalistic philosophy of economics, expressly denied this as a moral obligation that would go beyond the 'honesty' of keeping contracts; for he declared, shortly before his death, that if some of the people of the Third World died of starvation, because they could not help themselves, we – that is, the inhabitants of the First World – would not be morally obliged to help them. On the other hand, the author of the important book *Das Prinzip Verantwortung (The Principle of Responsibility)*, Hans Jonas, wanted to supplement or replace Kant's categorical imperative with a principle that would take into account our responsibility for a continued existence of humankind in the future. But he forgot the function of Kant's principle of universalisation, when he formulated his three categorical imperatives as demands for ensuring the continuation of the human species. From his purely ontological perspective, he could not reflect on the fact that racists, or at least social Darwinists like von Hayek, could fulfil the demand of his categorical imperatives as well (Jonas 1973–84; Apel 1992, 219–60; 1996b, 219–49).

(2) The given values of the different cultures and even the principle of universalization which has to mediate the use of the common values in a minimalist global ethics, must be interpreted without having recourse to a particular comprehensive view or doctrine which would again be culture-dependent. Now, this possibility is denied in our day by most philosophers; and even Kant could not ground the validity of his categorical imperative without making use of a dualistic metaphysics of the two worlds (or realms) and a corresponding splitting of the human self into an 'intelligible' and an 'empirical part' (Apel 1996c, 326–59). But now, with regard to this point, transcendental pragmatic discourse ethic is in a different situation: it does not need to take recourse to metaphysical presuppositions, since it only appeals to any arguer's possible reflection on those presuppositions of arguing he or she cannot deny without committing a performative self-contradiction. (These presuppositions include the procedural norms of discourse ethics, as I have still to show.) Thus reason here is no longer hypostatized as a metaphysical entity but, so to speak, is operationalised by recourse to what every possible discourse participant can consistently practise, the transcendental criterion of a communicative but culture-independent type of rationality. On this account, the assumed common values of the different cultures may only then be transformed into binding norms of a universal ethics if they, being exposed to a practical discourse, can stand up to the test of the consensus principle of discourse ethics, according to which the probable consequences of their obedience must be acceptable to all who might possibly be affected by them.

What I have suggested so far concerning the complementary relationship of the search for common values and the approach of discourse ethics, I would also propose as my stand with regard to Hans Küng's *Projekt Weltethos (Project of a World Ethos)* (Küng 1990; 1997a), which he already succeeded in suggesting as a basis to several international conferences on global ethics (Küng and Kuschel 1993; 1996). Being accustomed to understand the term ethos as designating an existing comprehensive morality of a community (something like Hegel's '*substantielle Sittlichkeit*'), I was first inclined to reject the *Projekt Weltethos* as something illusory or even incompatible with the plurality of existing ethos-traditions. But this obviously was a misunderstanding, for Küng expressly denies that the search for a '*Weltethos*' (world ethos) should be a search for a 'super-structure' that would 'make the specific ethics of the different religions and philosophies superfluous'. It would only focus on an 'ethical minimum common to all religions, cultures, civilizations' or a 'necessary minimum of common values, standards and basic attitudes' (Küng 1997b, 3 and 5).

Thus far Küng obviously joins the position of those thinkers who, as I indicated, take their orientation towards a minimalistic ethic based on common values, and he indeed agrees with the thesis of the communitarian philosophers, such as Michael Walzer, that a free-standing rational foundation of universal ethics is impossible, because even those 'common values, standards and basic attitudes' that can constitute the basis of the *Weltethos*, would in the human subjects of 'ethos' remain dependent on the different comprehensive forms of religious or metaphysical ethics (Küng 1997a). For the Catholic theologian Küng this position seems to mean that he himself must be prepared to bracket the dogmatic presuppositions of his religious belief and that he can suppose that all religious and philosophical positions can and must do the same with all of their presuppositions.

This parallelisation with regard to theology and philosophy indeed looks very plausible to an external observer, for example, for a politician in the face of so-called *Weltamchauungen*, and it is today extremely difficult to make clear that this parallelisation must be limited, or in other words, that there are transcendental presuppositions of reason that nobody who wants to argue can bracket. This is because these transcendental presuppositions of reason do not have the character of metaphysical suppositions but of undeniable presuppositions of arguing. And it is even more difficult to show that these presuppositions have a necessary function in grounding universal ethics, namely as a complement to an inductive collection of common values within a practical discourse that strives for a consensus about universal ethics. But I will try to defend this complementaristic approach to universal ethics through an argument with Walzer, who in the most sophisticated way has proposed the position that ethical minimalism, and only in this sense, universalism, can and must only be understood and, indeed, defended as a 'thin' overlapping of the different 'thick' versions of ethical maximalism (Walzer 1983), and that so far ethical universalism can and needs only be a matter of occasional, practically relevant agreement.

Walzer's Approach to a Minimalist Version of Universal Ethics and the Alternative (or Complement) of Discourse Ethics

Since Walzer from the outset denies any possibility of an autonomous, rational foundation of universally valid norms of ethics, or to put it more precisely: since for him – as for so many philosophers today – there seems to be no difference between the genesis of values (which of course has to be traced to the context of some historically developed community tradition) and the justification of the validity of ethical norms, and since he therefore must explain all so-called universally valid fundamental norms as abstractions from comprehensive ethos-traditions, it is not easy for him to give meaning and even relevance to the idea of a 'thin' or 'minimalist' version of universal ethics. And one has to acknowledge, that he does not suggest more than what can indeed be justified under his empiricist premises.

Thus he rejects the standard philosophical view of moral minimalism, that there is a universally valid morality focused on the ideas of truth and justice that can be grounded rationally as being objective and free from subjective interest and cultural expression and that this 'core morality' may be 'elaborated' according to different local circumstances 'in different cultures' (Walzer 1983, 4ff.). Against this 'wrong intuition' he puts forward the thesis: 'Morality is thick from the beginning, culturally integrated, fully resonant, and it reveals itself thinly only on special occasions, when moral language is turned to specific purposes' (Walzer 1983, 4). Thus far Walzer obviously sticks to the communitarian position.

How then do we come to agreement on a 'thin' but 'universal' morality? Walzer's answer reads:

> Whatever the origins of the idea of justice, whatever the starting point of the argument in this or that society; people thinking and talking about justice will range over a mostly familiar terrain and will come upon similar issues – like political tyranny or the oppression of the poor. What they say about these issues will be part and parcel of what they say about everything else, but some aspects of it – its negativity perhaps, its rejection of brutality ('grinding the face') – will be immediately accessible to people who don't know anything about the other parts and parcels. Pretty much anybody looking on will see something here that they recognize. The sum of these recognitions is what I mean by minimal morality (Walzer 1983, 5ff.).

As an example of his conception of the relationship between 'thin' and 'thick' morality, Walzer offers the experience of the people marching in the streets of Prague in 1989, demonstrating – as their carried signs indicated – for 'truth' and 'justice'. His question is: how was it possible for him and most foreigners to mentally join this march of protest although they did not share the whole cultural background of the marchers? And he answers: 'What they [the Prague marchers] meant by "justice" inscribed on their signs ... was simple enough [for appealing to a minimal morality]: an end to arbitrary arrests, equal and impartial law enforcement, the abolition of the privileges and prerogatives of the party elite – common, garden variety justice' (Walzer 1983, 2).

Since minimalist meanings of morality for Walzer are 'embedded in the maximalist morality expressed in the same idiom, sharing the same (historical/cultural/religious/political) orientation', he claims:

> Minimalism is liberated from its embeddedness and appears independently, in varying degrees of thinness, only in the course of a personal or social crisis or a political confrontation – as in the Czech case, with communist tyranny. Because (most of) the rest of us have some sense of what tyranny is and why it is wrong, the words used by the demonstrators shed whatever particularist meanings they mar have in the Czech language; they become widely, perhaps universally accessible. Were there no common understanding of tyranny, access would fail.

But he adds: 'At the same time, the same words have further meaning for the marchers, which they will argue about among themselves and which we, looking on from far away, may well miss. They resonate differently in Prague than their translations resonate in, say, París or New York' (Walzer 1983, 3).

Therefore human beings, according to Walzer, can only share minimal universal morality as they can share mentally the Prague march of the Czechs, that is on the occasion, 'for a time; there is no reason to think that they are all heading in the same direction' (Walzer 1983, 9).

> Minimalism makes for a certain limited, though important and heartening, solidarity. It doesn't make for a full-blooded universal doctrine. So we march for a while together, and then return to our own parades. The idea of a moral minimum ... by its very thinness ... justifies us in returning to the thickness that is our own. The morality in which the moral minimum is embedded, and from which it can only temporarily be abstracted, is the only

> full-blooded morality we can ever have … We ought to join the marchers in Prague, but once we have done that, we are free to argue for whatever suits our larger moral understandings (Walzer 1983, 11).

What have we to say on this account of the possibility of universal ethics? On the one hand, I think that Walzer, on his actual empiricist and communitarian presuppositions, is right, by and large. And I would consider this statement important with regard to the assessment of all the other positions that are trying to solve the problem of universal ethics by recourse to experiences of inter-cultural sharing of a minimum of common values. But on the other hand I do not think that this whole answer is satisfactory. In other words, according to Walzer's presuppositions, a fully fledged moral-philosophical response to the challenge of globalisation cannot be provided. It could be surmised that Walzer's assessment of the positive relevance of his account of the possibility of universal ethics, taken for itself, is somewhat illusory; for on the basis of the occasional and temporarily restricted sharings of values by the different culture-dependent maximalistic forms of morality, no common responsible policy, so to speak, of a rationally ruled and history-related morality of humankind can be grounded. Even the *ad hoc* solidarisations in crisis situations may be exposed to tragic misunderstandings, although one must not deny that the different comprehensive views of morality, taken as sources of the genesis of morality, bear the potential of sharing common values.

The relevance of Walzer's approach – as the interpretation of each single experience of shared values, and hence of a minimal common morality – seems to depend on the possibility of a complementary approach in the spirit of an autonomous, free-standing, rational foundation of what must be the basis of universally valid moral norms. (Common values are not being spoken of here because it could be assumed that values indeed belong to the contexts of particular life-forms and ethos-traditions which alone can provide the teleological perspectives for valuing needs and goods. This does not exclude, of course, that the obedience to universally valid norms and commitments to realising the conditions for their implementation may become common values for all cultures.)

An approach that is complementary to the empirical-inductive searching for common values can be provided in our days, as has already been suggested, by appealing to a transcendental pragmatic reflection (that is, not an empirical-introspective reflection and not a recourse to a metaphysics of the 'intelligible I') on those moral presuppositions of our actual argumentation (for example, in a discussion about the possible approach to universal ethics) that cannot be denied without committing a performative self-contradiction (Apel 1996b, Chs. 2 and 4; Kuhlmann 1985), and by following up the procedural consequences of this transcendental ascertainment for the grounding of material norms in practical discourses. Walzer, in the text quoted above, briefly mentions discourse ethics as an example of the proceduralistic version of a minimalistic approach to universal ethics. But his characterisation of this approach, and consequentially his objections to it, do not address its point.

First, he supposes that for discourse ethics the 'small number of ideas that we share or should share with everyone in the world guides us to producing the complex cultures that we don't and needn't share', and that, 'as in Habermas's critical theory, these shared ideas require a democratic procedure, indeed ... a radical democracy of articulate agents, men and women who argue endlessly about, say, substantial questions of justice' (Walzer 1983, 12).

This passage contains two points that are misleading. First, it is a misunderstanding to think that through the 'practical discourses' of grounding material norms, which are indeed postulated by the normative principles (the 'regulative ideas') of discourse ethical proceduralism, we should be guided to 'producing the complex cultures that we don't and needn't share'. By this understanding, the proceduralism of discourse ethics is unnecessarily made a rival of Walzer's empirical-genetic account of the occasional meetings of the different cultures and the subsequent returnings of their members to the complexity of maximalism. But this view completely misses the complementary function of the proceduralism of discourse ethics. I would consider Walzer's own account as a correct anthropological explanation of the conventional way people behave and are guided by their culture-dependent ethos-traditions. But the approach of discourse ethics is not concerned with this problem, but with the question how people can and should be guided on the post-conventional level of communicative rationality (that is, discourse rationality).

This approach works, of course, with counterfactual postulates or regulative ideas. But it can, nevertheless, be illustrated by the thousand conferences and dialogues we already have in our days about almost all relevant international and even intercultural problems of the present situation of globalisation: as for example, the problems of birth control in face of the threat of overpopulation, the closely related question of human rights, especially the rights of women, the responsibilities for the exploitation of natural resources and the pollution of the environment in the face of the ecological crisis, the distribution of burdens, in this and other global contexts, in the rich and the poor countries, and the even more profound problem of a just order of the institutions and rules of the global market economy. These conferences and dialogues, as they are factually practised, are of course not ideal argumentative discourses about validity claims as they are postulated by discourse ethics; for strategic negotiations (bargainings) concerning the rival interests will always play a large part. But on the level of the 'reasoning public' (Kant), that is today, of the global media, almost all parties in our days seem already to have internalised the procedural norms of discourse ethics; for they at least pretend to propose arguments in favour of solutions where the consequences would be acceptable by all affected people. These public discourses must not only be an occasion for a critique of ideology and similar unmaskings; they are also reasons for continuing the post-conventional enterprise of striving for universally valid moral solutions to common problems of humankind. For these solutions have to be reached not only by occasional declarations of solidarity but also through the enduring efforts of argumentative discourse.

With regard to these efforts of men and women 'who argue endlessly about, say, substantive questions of justice', Walzer (1983, 12), in his characterizations of discourse ethics, makes the second point that is misleading. It is true that there exists an internal relationship, which is historically conditioned, between the paradigm of discourse ethics and the procedures of democracy; but this does not mean that the fundamental procedural rules that are presupposed in a serious argumentative discourse, which indeed include acknowledgement 'of each other's equality … the rights of free speech … and … tolerance and mutual respect' (Walzer 1983, 12), are to be equated with or, in their validity, based on Western democracy, and thus constitute a concrete 'way of life' in the sense of 'liberal or social democratic thickness' (Walzer 1983, 12). This popular suggestion[2] is again a consequence of the fallacy of confusing the genesis and the validity of moral principles. For the fundamental procedural rules of argumentative discourse can be ascertained, in principle, at any time by transcendental reflection (although this has to be learned and historically was prepared, not only by Western democratic procedures but also, for example, by Socratic dialogue). Thus far the validity of these rules is, on the one hand, independent of the contingency of Western democracy; yet precisely for this reason, it may serve as a strong philosophical reason for defending the legitimacy of at least some core principles of Western democracy in discourses with representatives of non-Western traditions (this is of course the counter-position to Rorty 1991, 175–96). In our days the possibility of a post-conventional foundation of universal ethics depends in a crucial way on both a critical attitude towards the danger of culture-centrism and on resistance to the current temptation of a capitulation of self-reflective philosophical reason to the suggestions of historicism-relativism. It has still to be added to Walzer's talk of the 'endless' argumentations demanded by discourse ethics that this feature of the ideal paradigm of argumentative discourse obviously cannot have an equivalent in democratic discourses, say, of legislation; although even these discourses under pressure of time should correspond to the paradigm of ideal discourse, in that their results should be open to revision. Thus the feature of the 'endlessness of discourse', which obviously corresponds to the principle of fallibilism and the principle of taking into account the interests of all affected people, shows again that the principles of discourse ethics are transcendentally grounded and hence post-conventional, so that they never can be equated with concrete (conventionalisable) ways of life.

In the corrections of Walzer's characterisation of the approach of discourse- ethical proceduralism arguments have already been given against his further objections to this approach. Thus the supposition that the minimalism of discourse ethics by its rules implies the claim that it precedes the maximalism of a fully fledged culture-dependent morality in Walzer's sense has already been disputed (Walzer 1983, 13). According to its transcendentally grounded rules, discourse ethics leaves free space for a plurality of individual and collective projects of the good life or of self-realisation which may be equated with Walzer's ways of maximalism. At the same time, though, the postulated procedure of solving all deontological questions of morality through practical discourses of all the affected people (or their advocates, if necessary) indeed imposes constraints upon all maximalistic positions. For if it comes to questions of

2 Walzer on this occasion appeals to Habermas (1990) and to Seyla Benhabib (1986, Ch. 8). Indeed both of them, I think, are not innocent of suggesting the popular – because anti-transcendentalist – equation of discourse ethics with a reconstruction of the life form of Western democracy, which sometimes even attracted Rorty's sympathy. See with regard to Habermas (1990) my critical essay 'Normatively Grounding "Critical Theory" through Recourse to the Life world? A Transcendental-pragmatical Attempt of Thinking with Habermas against Habermas', in A. Honneth et al. (1992, 125–70).

inter-personal or inter-cultural justice (or even of co-responsible cooperation in cases of global emergencies), all maximalistic positions have to subject their interests of self-realisation to the discursive test concerning their compatibility with the interests of all the other maximalistic positions (or with the interests of humankind). In this case, by the way, the empirical-inductive procedures of ascertaining the common values of all cultures may very well be taken into account, within the discourse, as supports of a possible criticism of certain maximalistic positions.

Thus it turns out that the whole conception of the relationship between 'thin' and 'thick' versions of morality in Walzer's sense does not really light the transcendental pragmatic conception of discourse ethics. For this latter, in a way, covers the areas of both 'thinness' and 'thickness', but not in Walzer's sense. It is extremely 'thin', so to speak, with regard to its transcendental principles, because these immediately refer only to the undeniable moral conditions of the possibility of argumentative discourse, whereas all other questions are delegated to the postulated practical discourses. But precisely this postulated delegation provides a transition to the always provisory solution of concrete moral problems, thus in a sense moving from 'thinness' to 'thickness'. But the whole conception, obviously, is incomparable with Walzer's account – and, for that matter, with all other empirical approaches to universal ethics as minimalist ethics. It is a post-conventional normative approach that, notwithstanding our historico-hermeneutic insights into the genesis of all human conceptions of morality within the context of cultural traditions, with regard to the foundation of its own validity, derives from the transcendental self-reflection of discourse-rationality (which itself is not circumventible for arguers). It indeed leaps from this transcendental-reflective point of view 'like Athena from the head of Zeus', to quote, and turns to the affirmative Walzer's verdict against the possibility of a free-standing foundation of ethics (Walzer 1983, 12).

To state it even more provocatively, whereas Walzer is completely right, by his account, to state that people after an occasional solidarisation and sharing of common values (say, in the case of the Prague protests) will not and need not 'head' in the same direction (Walzer 1983, 9), this is precisely postulated, in a sense, by the regulative procedural principles of discourse ethics. For according to the rule of these principles, people cannot simply return to their culture dependent maximalist views but are obliged – on the post-conventional level of discourse rationality – to cooperate in searching for universally acceptable solutions of common moral problems.

The procedures of this cooperation are prescribed not by rules that can be identified with particular conventions of the Western tradition of democracy, although certain prefigurations of the search for procedural norms may in fact be found in that tradition. But even these – more or less suggestive – prefigurations have to be re-examined in each case from the normative point of view that determines all procedural norms of an ideal practical discourse, namely the principle that all proposed solutions, including all their foreseeable effects and side-effects, ought to be exposed to thorough discussion, with the aim of proving their acceptability to all affected people.

This is what we have necessarily recognised and therefore cannot deny without committing a performative self-contradiction in a serious argumentative discourse.

And even those philosophers – for example, Heidegger, Gadamer, Wittgenstein and the communitarians, who have discovered and described the 'facticity' of the 'prestructure' of our understanding of the life-world, namely our sharing 'always already' the 'pre-understanding' of the world, and hence the 'strong values' (C. Taylor) of a community tradition – cannot avoid addressing, albeit without transcendental pragmatic reflection (see Apel 1998, for critical comments on Heidegger, Gadamer and Wittgenstein), their own universal validity claims to the judgement of all the members of an unlimited, ideal argumentation community. Hence they are implicitly bound to also acknowledge the counterfactual consensus principle of an ideal discourse and its moral presuppositions.

Thus a rational foundation of universal ethics can indeed be delivered, as Kant postulated, by recourse to the principle of 'self-consistency' ('*Selbsteinstimmigkeil*') of reason, and thus to the 'fact of reason' ('*Paktum der Vernunft*'). But the self-consistency of reason is not, as Kant suggested, identical with the logical principle of non-contradiction, which, as Hegel objected, is morally sterile, but it is a comprehension (integration) of all those normative presuppositions of discursive rationality that can be discovered through the reflective test of the negation's leading to a performative self-contradiction; and the 'fact of reason' is not something that may be ascertained by empirical research, but is a term for the 'a priori perfect' (Heidegger) of what we have always already acknowledged by reason in so far as it is self-consistent.

The transcendental point of the procedural principle of discourse ethics becomes especially visible when one reflects on the unpopular difficulties of its application. Thus it seems clear that, under empirical circumstances, it can only function as a regulative principle, which admits many pragmatical restrictions of its ideal postulates but, at the same time, demands recourse to special reasons in every case of a necessary restriction. Thus the representation of the interests and hence of the possible arguments of all affected persons in most cases can only be realised by relying on advocates or even on mentally internalised discourses. (This pertains in particular to the interests of future generations, say in connection with ecological problems: see Apel 1992, 219–60.) But it is clear that in real discourses even in conditions of fair cooperation, we cannot always, or even in most cases, reckon with reaching consensus. (The risk of dissent is especially high in cases of dialogues between different ethnic or religious community traditions, say about problems of human reproduction, the rights of the women, abortion etc., see Apel 1999, 145–63.) In these cases, the regulative principle of discourse ethics cannot simply be satisfied by juridically relevant compromises, although these are indeed necessary; but the pursuance of moral discourses aims at least at a consensus about the reasons for the dissent.

In a more radical reflection, one has to realise that each factually reached consensus in a practical as well as in a theoretical discourse is of course fallible and hence provisional, for example, with regard to the required consideration of the interests of all affected persons and with regard to the ascertaining of the effects and side-effects of the considered solutions. From this fact it follows that the consensus postulate of discourse ethics cannot be satisfied by, say, the postulate of reaching an overlapping consensus, as it was proposed by the later Rawls in his conception of political liberalism. For this pragmatico-political postulate, which may be useful and even necessary on the level of politics, makes itself dependent on reaching a factual consensus, say, of the parties involved in a conflict of interests. Thus it cannot function as a genuine universalisation principle of morality which, out of its own authority as a regulative principle, must also be capable of preventing those factual forms of consensus that are reached at the cost of affected but absent parties. Conceived of more radically, the regulative principle of striving for unrestricted consensus must even be capable of initiating and regulating a change of the political conditions of consensus- formation towards taking into account the interests of all affected parties, for example, the interests and possible arguments of the poor in the Third World who, up to now, to a large part have been excluded from all politically and economically relevant dialogues about their situation (Dussel 1990, 69–96; Apel 1996e, 13–44).

This last interpretation of the consensus-postulate of discourse ethics shows, by the way, that the transcendental pragmatic transformation of the Kantian principle of universalisation, taken as a regulative idea, implies a teleological and future-related dimension that is not at all taken into consideration by the usual meta-ethical distinction between formal deontological ethics of justice, on the one hand, and teleological ethics of the good life, on the other. The novel point of the non-Aristotelian teleology of discourse ethics, though, becomes only completely visible if the normal application of the ideal version of the discursive consensus-postulate becomes impossible, because the application would be irresponsible. This becomes relevant in all those cases where we cannot suppose (or expect) that our opponents in a conflict should be prepared to join the discursive procedures of consensus-formation and to abstain from strategic practices including even violence. This may happen especially in the areas of economy and politics, either within the limits of states, where a law cannot be put through against criminality and corruption, or in the international area of foreign politics, where the Hobbesian 'state of nature' has not even been surmounted in favour of the state of law.

In these cases, which are at the centre of Max Weber's conception of an 'ethics of responsibility' as against an 'ethics of pure intention' ('*Gesinnungsethik*'), for traditional deontological ethics the temptation was always great to completely disregard the unpleasant problems and to leave them to extra-ethical areas like law, the economy and, in particular, to so-called real politics (*Realpolitik*). This attitude of academic ethics, I think, does not only abandon the politician who wants to be moral and responsible but, furthermore, overlooks the 'fact (of reason)' that after all we are morally responsible for the shaping and reshaping of social institutions, that is for striving to shape those institutions that facilitate the social implementation of morality.

Now in this case the transcendental pragmatic version of discourse ethics finds it necessary to introduce a distinction between a 'part N' and a 'part B' of the very foundation of deontological ethics. For it is only under the reciprocity condition of part A, where we can suppose fair cooperation of the opponents of conflicts, that we can responsibly dispense with strategic practices in favour of only relying on the consensual-communicative rationality of interaction. By contrast, in part B, where we cannot responsibly reckon with fair cooperation among our opponents, we are still compelled for reasons of moral responsibility to apply 'strategic-counter-strategic' practices (Kettner 1992, 317–48), which, especially in the field of politics, cannot dispense with lying and killing.[3] But, as it were, in compensation for this tragic deviation from the procedural norms of discourse ethics, all strategic-counter-strategic practices are subject to the moral duty of not just fulfilling the function of crisis management but also of collaborating in attempts to shape the institutional conditions of the postulated implementation of part A of discourse ethics.

An example of such a commitment in our time, as in Kant's time, is the project of establishing a cosmopolitan order of law that can be put through by adequate sanctions (Apel 1996c, 91–124; 1997a, 79–112).

Résumé: Discourse Ethics as a Response of Universal Ethics to the Challenge of Globalisation

At this point, we come back to the problem initially raised in this article, which is that of providing a response to the globalisation process of our time by showing the need and the possibility of universal ethics. Through my arguments with the current proposals of conceiving of global ethics without an autonomous (free-standing) foundation of its principles, it may have become clear what I can consider to be a response of philosophical ethics that is on the same level of standards as are the present challenges of ethics through globalisation. It should be more than an empirical-inductive ascertainment of common values and an *ad hoc* agreement on this basis, although this would be very useful, if it could be interpreted and justified in the light of an autonomous rational foundation of universally valid ethics. But a conception of universal ethics as a response to the globalisation process should be more than just an agreement on a certain enumeration of words for values (or even norms) that can be made the subject of a declaration, although such a declaration could be very useful and even politically influential, as has been shown by the UN Declaration of Human Rights of 1948. Hence we should indeed have a similar declaration of moral duties or responsibilities, in order to provide a counterweight to the rights talk, which has been accused of being an expression of Western individualism and egotism. But should it not be possible, furthermore, to formulate the procedural principles of discourse ethics as a rational frame of possible agreement about any material proposals that can be made with regard to common duties and responsibilities in our time, keeping in mind that, in a vague form, these procedural principles are already acknowledged in our thousand public dialogues and conferences?

References

Apel, K.-O. (1973), 'Das Apriori der Kommunikationsgemeinschaft und die Grundlagen der Ethik', in *Transformation der Philosophie*, Vol. 2 (Frankfurt:

3 I cannot here follow the 'moral rigour' of Küng (1997a) in his argument with Kissinger, Richelieu and Bismarck, although his opponents are representatives of *Realpolitik* rather than of a political ethics of responsibility in the sense of part B of discourse ethics.

Suhrkamp), pp. 358–430. Eng. trans. in K.-O. Apel (1980), pp. 225–300 and (1996d), pp. 1–67.

—— (ed.) (1976), *Sprachpragmatik und Philosophie* (Frankfurt: Suhrkamp).

—— (1980), *Towards a Transformation of Philosophy* (London: Routledge and Kegan Paul).

—— (1988), *Diskurs und Verantwortung* (Frankfurt: Suhrkamp).

—— (1992), 'The Ecological Crisis as a Problem for Discourse Ethics', in Ofsti, A. (ed.), pp. 219–60.

—— and M. Kettner (eds) (1992), *Zur Anwendung der Diskursethik in Politik, Recht und Wissenschaft* (Frankfurt: Suhrkamp).

—— (1993), 'Das Anliegen des anglo-amerikanischen Kommunitarismus in der Sicht der Diskursethik', in Brumlik, M. and Brunkhorst, H. (eds), pp. 149–72.

—— (1996a) 'Diskursethik als Verantwortungsethik – eine postmetaphysische Transformation der Ethik Kants', in Schönrich, G. and Kato, Y. (eds), pp. 326–59.

—— (1996b), 'Macroethics, Responsibility for the Future and the Crisis of Technological Society: Reflections on Hans Jonas', in Apel, K.-O. (1996d), pp. 219–49.

—— (1996c), 'Kants Philosophischer Entwurf "Zum ewigen Frieden": eine geschichtsphilosophische Quasi-Prognose aus moralischer Pflicht', in Merkel, R. and Wittmann, R. (eds), pp. 91–124. Eng. trans. 'Kant's Toward Perpetual Peace as Historical Prognosis from the Point of View of Moral Duty', in Bohman, J. and Lutz-Bachmann, M. (eds), pp. 79–113.

—— (1996d), *Karl-Otto Apel: Selected Essays*, Vol. 2 (New York: Humanities Press).

—— (1996e), 'Das anliegen der Befreiungsethik als ein Anliegen des Teils B der Diskursethik', in Fornet-Betancourt, R. (ed.), pp. 13–44.

—— (1997), 'Plurality of the Good? The Problem of Affirmative Tolerance in a Multicultural Society from an Ethical Point of View', *Ratio Juris* 10:2, 199–212.

—— (1998), *Auseinandersetzungen. In Erprobung des tramzendentalpragmatischen Ansatzes* (Frankfurt: Suhrkamp).

—— (1999), 'The Problem of Justice in a Multicultural Society', in Kearney, R. and Dooley, M. (eds), pp. 145–63.

Benhabib, S. (1986), *Critique, Norm and Utopia: A Study of the Foundation of Critical Theory* (New York: Columbia University Press).

Bohman, J. and Lutz-Bachmann, M. (eds) (1997), *Perpetual Peace: Essays on Kant's Cosmopolitan Ideal* (Cambridge, MA: MFF Press).

Bok, S. (1995), *Common Values* (Missouri, MO: University of Missouri Press).

Brumlik, M. and Brunkhorst, H. (eds) (1993), *Gemeinschaft und Gerechtigkeit* (Frankfurt: Fischer).

Dussel, E. (1990), 'Die "Lebensgemeinschaft" und die "Interpellation des Armen". Die Praxis der Befreiung', in Fornet-Betancourt, R. (ed.), pp. 69–96.

Fornet-Betancourt, R. (ed.) (1996), *Armut-Ethik-Befreiung* (Aachen: Augustinus-Buchhandlung).

Habermas, J. (1976), 'Was heibt Universalpragmatik?', in Apel, K.-O. (ed.) (1976).

—— (1983), *Moralbewusstsein und kommunikatives Handeln* (Frankfurt: Suhrkamp). Eng. trans. (1996), *Moral Conciousness and Communicative Action* (Cambridge, MA: MIT Press).

—— (1991), *Erläuterungen zur Diskursethik* (Frankfurt: Suhrkamp).

—— (1995), 'Disputation with J. Rawls', *The Journal of Philosophy* 92:3, 109–80.

Honneth, A. (ed.) (1993), *Kommunitarismus* (Frankfurt: Suhrkamp).

Honneth, A. et al. (eds) (1992), *Philosophical Interventions in the Unfinished Project of Enlightenment* (Cambridge, MA: MIT Press).

Jonas, H. (1973), *Das Prinzip Verantwortung* (Frankfurt: Insel). Eng. trans. (1984), *The Imperative of Responsibility* (Chicago: University of Chicago Press).

Kearney, R. and Dooley, M. (eds) (1999), *Ethics in Question* (London: Routledge).

Kettner, M. (1992), 'Bereichspezifische Relevanz. Zur konkreten Allgemeinheit der Diskursethik', in Apel, K.-O. and Kettner, M. (eds) (1992), pp. 317–48.

Kuhlmann, W. (1985), *Reflexive Letztbegründung. Untersuchungen zur Transzendentalpragmatik* (Freiburg: Alber).

Küng, H. (1990), *Projekt Weltethos* (Munich: Piper).

—— (1997a), *Weltethos für Weltpolitik und Weltwirtschaft* (Munich: Piper).

—— (1997b), 'Towards a Universal Ethics', paper presented at Unesco conference, Paris.

Küng, H. and Kuschel, K.J. (eds) (1993), *A Global Ethic. The Declaration of the Parliament of World's Religions* (London: SCM).

—— (1996), *InterAction Council. In Search of Global Ethical Standards* (Vienna).

Merkel, R. and Wittmann, R. (1996), *200 Jahre 'Zum ewigen Frieden'* (Frankfurt: Suhrkamp).

Ofsti, A. (ed.), *Ecology and Ethics* (Trondheim: Nordland Akademi for Kunst og Vitenskap).

Rawls, J. (1971), *A Theory of Justice* (Cambridge, MA: Harvard University Press).

—— (1980), 'Kantian Constructivism in Moral Theory. The Dewey Lectures', *The Journal of Philosophy* 77:9, 515–72.

—— (1993a), *Political Liberalism* (New York: Columbia University Press).

—— (1993b), 'The Law of Peoples', in Shute, S. and Hurley, S. (eds), pp. 42–82.

—— (1995), 'Disputation with J. Habermas', *The Journal of Philosophy* 92:3, 109–78.

Rorty, R. (1991), 'The Priority of Democracy to Philosophy', in *Objectivity, Relativism and Truth* (Cambridge: Cambridge University Press).

Schönrich, G. and Kato, Y. (eds) (1996), *Kant in der Diskussion der Moderne* (Frankfurt: Suhrkamp).

Shute, S. and Hurley, S. (eds) (1993), *On Human Rights* (London: Harper Collins).

Walzer, M. (1983), *Thick and Thin: Moral Arguments at Home and Abroad* (New York: Basic Books).

PART 4
Public Reason and Applied Ethics: Political Views

Chapter 9

The Domination Complaint

Philip Pettit[1]

It is possible to conceptualise political freedom as the absence of domination, arguing that a person is free to the extent that others do not stand over them, able to interfere at will and with relative impunity in their affairs. And this, furthermore, is how political freedom appears to have been conceptualized in the long and broad republican tradition: the tradition that stretches from republican Rome to revolutionary America and France, encompassing figures as diverse as Cicero, Machiavelli, Harrington, Montesquieu, Rousseau and Madison. I have defended those two claims, respectively philosophical and historical, in earlier writings, as indeed have a number of other authors (see Pettit 1996; 1997; 2001; 2002; Skinner 1998; Viroli 1998).

In addition to defending those two claims, however, I have also argued that there is a good case for resuscitating the republican viewpoint as a political philosophy, on the grounds that it has many advantages in comparison with contemporary alternatives. I concentrate in the present chapter on this third claim, approaching it from a new angle. The chapter is in three sections. In the first . the main constraints that we should expect any candidate for a central or supreme political ideal to satisfy, distinguishing between constraints of feasibility and constraints of desirability is studied. And then in the second and third sections the argument is expounded that the ideal of non-domination does remarkably well in satisfying those feasibility and desirability constraints. The argument in these sections is inevitably somewhat sketchy, since it often recapitulates points that have been elaborated elsewhere.

Constraints on a Political Ideal

Ideals and complaints

Any political ideal that aspires to be a central or supreme political role has to provide a basis for assessing the way the polity is constituted and the way it behaves within the limits set by that constitution. The assessment of a polity turns in the last analysis on how well it serves its citizens or members, answering to interests they avow or are disposed to avow; the assessment of the polity for its effects on non-members is abstracted here. And this being so, we must therefore expect any would-be political ideal to try and articulate the importance of something that people clearly have an

1 Source: *Nomos* 46 (2005), 87–117.

avowed or readily avowable interest in: something whose absence in their lives will spontaneously lead them to make complaint.

This condition is satisfied by every half-plausible political ideal. Take ideals such as those provided by the elimination of poverty, the achievement of equality, the approximation of justice, the minimisation of interference in people's lives or the maximisation of happiness. In every case we may expect people to be ready to complain about the absence of the condition recommended under the ideal: that is, to complain about poverty or inequality, injustice, interference or unhappiness. And that is as it should be. For were people not ready to complain in this way, then the ideal could hardly claim to reflect an interest that they were readily disposed to avow.

So much for what is described as the basic condition on any would-be candidate for the role of political ideal. With that condition spelled out, we can explore the further constraints that we might want a political ideal to satisfy. These are all well cast as constraints on the sort of complaint that an attractive ideal ought to articulate and are distinguished into two bunches. So far as the first bunch is satisfied by the complaint, the corresponding ideal will be a feasible ideal for the state to track; so far as the second bunch is satisfied it will be an ideal that it is also desirable that it should track.

Constraints of feasibility

The constraints of feasibility are: first, that the state or polity should be able to do something about relieving or remedying the complaint in question; second, that it should be able to provide an effective remedy that does not introduce new problems in place of old; and third, that it should be able to provide an efficient as well as an effective remedy: that is, a remedy that involves lower costs overall than any alternative strategy. In a phrase, the complaint must be politically remediable and remediable in an effective and efficient manner.

That the complaint must be remediable means that it must amount to something more politically interesting than a complaint about the constraints of social life, or a complaint about the *anomie* or *ennui* of human existence, or a complaint about the inequalities of status that emerge among almost all groups of human beings. There is little or nothing that government can do about such matters, however sharply they may impinge on people's consciousness, and so there is no point in using them as a basis out of which to construct a political ideal.

But a complaint might be remediable without the state or polity being able to provide an effective remedy. It might be that state intervention would be counterproductive, for example, engendering on novel fronts precisely the sort of complaint that it is designed to relieve. Thus it might do more harm than good in its attempt to reduce the net level of a certain evil – say, interference or domination – in the society: it might perpetrate more interference or domination than it prevents.

Finally, to turn to the third constraint, the fact that the state is able to remedy a complaint, and do so effectively, does not mean that it represents the most efficient way of dealing with it. There may be non-political ways of relieving the complaint that achieve better results for the same or for lower costs. If the complaint is to underpin a feasible political ideal, then the state should be able to remedy the complaint efficiently as well as effectively.

These three constraints are hard to resist, yet many proposed ideals seem to fail them. The first constraint would rule out trying to construct a political ideal out of wholesale antipathy to power, for example, as sometimes appears to happen in the work of Michel Foucault (see Foucault 1980). In railing against the capillary power that runs through the smallest veins of the system, Foucault does sometimes direct attention to phenomena which we might hope to be able to rectify. But often he seems to be castigating a sort of influence that is as inescapable in the social world as gravity is in the natural.

The second, effectiveness constraint raises serious questions about the libertarian ideal of ensuring that certain allegedly natural rights are respected in social life, in particular the right that people are assumed to have against the coercive restriction of choice. For there is no way in which the state can act so as to achieve that ideal without itself offending against it by coercively restricting the choices of individuals. This is the problem that Robert Nozick acknowledges as a challenge for rights-based libertarianism, going on to make an attempt to resolve it that is ingenious, if not successful (see Nozick 1974). He argues that even if people were entirely respectful of one another's rights, rational self-interest would lead them – without violating those rights – to institute a state: specifically, an 'ultraminimal' state of the kind close to that which he himself favours.

The third, efficiency constraint explains why most of us agree that we should not require the state to concern itself with saving people's souls or elevating their minds: with their fidelity to any particular religion or their achievement of any personal ideal. Seventeenth- and 18th century defenders of tolerance like John Locke made the relevant point when they argued that the way to win people's souls to the practice of any worthwhile religion is by free consent, not state coercion (see Locke 1985). There are better ways – certainly more efficient ways – to tackle a supposed problem of unbelief that to have recourse to the power of the polity.

Constraints of desirability

The second bunch of constraints on the sort of complaint that a plausible political ideal should reflect relate to the desirability of the state's relieving the complaint, as distinct from the feasibility of its doing so. There are three constraints that I distinguish in this category. The first is that the complaint be discursively admissible: that is, admissible as a relevant consideration in any open discursive discussion of how things are and should be organized in a society. The other two constraints bear on the substantive character of the complaint itself rather than on such a structural aspect. The second is that it is a significant complaint that it is hard to dismiss or downplay. And the third is that it is a complaint that subsumes a variety of other significant complaints within it.

The first constraint would rule out of consideration any complaint that is irreducibly relativised to a particular group within the society. Take a complaint of the form 'This is bad for us', where the plural refers to a particular group, not to the society as a whole. This might be just a way of drawing attention to a more general, non-sectional complaint, of course. The background assumption might be that the arrangement leaves others no better off, so that rejecting it would be a Pareto improvement: good for some – the complaining group – bad for none. Or the assumption might be that the respect in which the arrangement is bad for the group is a respect – say, that of access to one's own culture – on which all can agree that no group ought to be disadvantaged (Kymlicka 1995). But suppose that the complaint, 'this is bad for us', does not reduce to a more neutral form of complaint. In that case it would not be discursively admissible, though it might be admissible in the context of mutual bargaining. The ordinary practice of discourse or conversation would rule it out as an irrelevant consideration to raise in an unforced, cooperative discussion about how things ought to be politically organised; it would represent a sort of special pleading and would be inconsistent with the assumptions built into such a discussion (see Habermas 1984/1989; Elster 1986; and Pettit 2000). The response that the complaint would invite is: 'that's not germane; the point is to discover what's best for all of us in the society, not just what's best for your group in particular'.

But a complaint can be discursively admissible without being particularly significant and so without satisfying the second constraint of desirability. It may be that while almost any of us can understand why a certain complaint should be made, none of us thinks that the complaint is of the greatest moment. While believing that someone has a just complaint in some matter, for example, we may feel that the complainant is lucky to have nothing more pressing to complain about. Clearly, any complaint out of which a plausible political ideal is to be constructed had better not be a complaint of this kind. It should be what I shall describe as a significant complaint.

The third constraint I mentioned is that any complaint out of which a political ideal is to be constructed should subsume a variety of other presumptively significant complaints within it. This constraint bears in particular on any ideal that aspires to a central or supreme place in politics. What it is designed to rule out is the sort of ideal whose satisfaction would still leave a variety of other presumptively significant complaints unsatisfied. The ideal of maximal non-interference fails rather dramatically on this front, for example, since a society might realise such an ideal and yet be one where inequality, domination and poverty prevail. If a complaint is to provide the stuff out of which a central or supreme political ideal is to be fashioned, then the measures taken for satisfying it should serve as far as possible to satisfy such other complaints as well. This constraint may be hard to meet but it clearly represents a plausible desideratum. To the extent that a complaint satisfies it, the corresponding ideal will have a claim to a central and perhaps even supreme place among political ideals.

There are other desiderata that we might want a political ideal to satisfy but I shall stick with those just rehearsed. The next section looks at how far the republican ideal of non-domination satisfies the feasibility constraints and the final section looks at how far it answers to the constraints of desirability. While it is necessary to make the points quickly and without much elaboration, it is hoped that the overview provided will help to show just how attractive the ideal is.

Non-domination and the Feasibility Constraints

The three questions to be asked about the complaint that republican theory privileges – the complaint, about being dominated – are whether this is something that the state can take steps to remedy; if so, whether the remedy it can offer is effective, not counterproductive; and if it is effective, whether the remedy provided is efficient, comparing well with alternative strategies.

Defining domination

Before tackling those questions, however, consideration must first be given to what domination involves. This will be brief, drawing on work done elsewhere (see Pettit 1997 and 2001b). An individual or a group agent dominates an individual to the extent that they are in a position to interfere arbitrarily in the affairs of that person: to the extent, that is to say, that such arbitrary interference is accessible and uncostly.

My understanding of interference is narrow, so far as I take it to require intentionality or at least negligence – quasi-intentionality – on the part of the agent; it does not materialize just by way of brute accident but is something for which the agent can be reasonably held responsible (see Miller 1984 and 1993). My understanding of interference is broad, on the other hand, so far as I take it to include, not just removing an option from the range of options otherwise available in some choice to the person interfered with, but raising the costs of taking an option or even denying the person knowledge of the options available or of the costs in prospect (see Steiner 1994 and Carter 1999). The intuition driving the account is that interference should be equated with any initiative that intentionally worsens an individual's choice situation – and this, even if it is for the person's overall good – where contextual conventions and expectations may be involved in determining whether a certain act counts as a way of worsening that situation. Thus, to illustrate the approach taken, an agent may interfere with someone's choice, not just by forcibly or manipulatively rigging the options available, but also by threatening them sincerely with a penalty if they take a certain option or by actually penalising them for taking it. And an agent may interfere in the person's affairs by misleading them, as in the insincere but credible threat of penalty or in the deliberate withholding of information (see Pettit 2003).

An agent is dominated to the extent that a group or individual is in a position to interfere arbitrarily in their affairs. What makes an act of interference arbitrary? Not the effect of that interference itself: not, for example, the fact that it is to the detriment of the victim involved. Rather the fact that in choosing to interfere, the dominating agent is not forced to track the avowed interests of the individual interfered with – or the interests the victim is readily disposed to avow – but can interfere more or less as their own will or judgement dictates. An act of interference will be arbitrary to the extent that it is not controlled by the avowable interests of the victim but, as arbitrary interference usually will be, is controlled by the *arbitrium* of the interferer, where *arbitrium* may refer to will or judgement. Thus an act of interference may be done for the good of the victim, and may be successful in achieving that good, and yet be arbitrary. That it is arbitrary is fixed by the controls to which it is subject, not the ends that it happens to effect.

There are three respects in which domination, by this account, comes in degrees. An agent may have a greater or lesser capacity to interfere arbitrarily in someone's affairs, for the option may be more or less accessible or uncostly. An agent may have a capacity to interfere more or less arbitrarily, for they may be more or less unburdened by constraints designed to force them to track the avowable interests of the victim. And an agent may have a capacity to interfere arbitrarily in a larger or smaller class of choices by the agent, or in choices that are intuitively of greater or lesser significance to the agent (Taylor 1985). Domination, then, is not an on-or-off condition but one to which a person may be subject at a higher or lower degree of intensity. This should always be kept in mind, even when convenience of presentation requires us to describe it as if it were an on-or-off matter.

First feasibility constraint

Is the complaint about being dominated by others one that the state is in a position, at least in principle, to do something about? Clearly, I think, yes. In the nature of things, the state claims a monopoly of legitimate force in its community – if other agencies exercise legitimate force that is through being allowed to do so by the state – and that claim must be more or less effectively implemented within any well-ordered polity. But if the state has access to the use of force, and to the threat of force – to coercion – then it is in a position to reduce the degree to which people suffer at least certain forms of domination.

One way in which it might do this is by redistributing resources and powers of interference across the population in a society. Where X was previously able with impunity to interfere arbitrarily in Y's affairs, a redistribution might ensure that Y is able to retaliate, so that the expected cost of X's interfering goes up and the domination X enjoys diminishes or disappears. Call this the strategy of armament. Another way in which the state might reduce domination is by disarmament: that is, by removing the extra resources and powers that enable some to dominate others. And yet another is by protection – by putting defenses in place for those who might otherwise be dominated.

The armament, disarmament and protection strategies might in turn be pursued by the state in a more or less direct or more or less indirect way. Those who are dominated may be armed or protected by virtue of explicit legal and political measures. Or they may be armed or protected so far as the state facilitates and sponsors developments in civil society that serve suitable purposes. They may be armed or protected, for example, so far as the state is able to encourage a civic culture of condemnation for various forms of arbitrary interference and a culture of coming to the aid of those who suffer such interference. Again those who dominate might be disarmed by explicit state action or by recourse to less formal methods. Take the case where a monopoly firm in a company town dominates those who depend on the firm for employment. This firm may be effectively disarmed by the state's explicitly limiting its power of dismissal, or by its ensuring relatively generous unemployment benefits, or by its providing incentives or facilities that attract other employers into the labour market. The possibilities are legion.

Second feasibility constraint

Let it be granted that the state can do something by way of remedying the complaint many people will have – whether or not they phrase it that way – of being dominated by others: the complaint is not one of those irremediable complaints that no one, or at least not the state, is able to do anything about. The next question is whether in seeking to provide a remedy for the complaint of domination, the state is likely to do more harm than good. In particular, is it likely to represent a new force of domination at the very moment that it seeks to relieve people of domination? Is it likely to be counterproductive?

Consider first, not the ideal of non-domination, but rather that of non-interference. It is commonly acknowledged among those who invoke this ideal – this conception of freedom – that as the state tries to reduce the interference that some agents practice in the lives of others, it will itself have to interfere in people's lives. In order to prevent violence and coercion, it will itself have to coerce people into paying taxes and obeying the laws and it will have to practice penal violence against convicted offenders, whether in levying fines, imprisoning them or even resorting to capital punishment. 'As against the coercion applicable by individual to individual, no liberty can be given to one man but in proportion as it is taken away from another. All coercive laws, therefore, and in particular all laws creative of liberty, are as far as they go abrogative of liberty' (Bentham 1962). This means that there is a risk of the state being an ineffective agency for promoting non-interference –it may do more harm than good – though it does not mean that the state will necessarily be ineffective: there may be good grounds for hoping that the level of interference it perpetrates is less than that the level of interference it prevents.

How do things stand with the state as an agency for promoting non-domination, as distinct from non-interference? They stand even better. For not only is there bound to be a hope, if the state dominates people in some measure, that it will perpetrate less domination than it prevents. There is also a hope that while it interferes in people's lives, it will still not dominate them, or will dominate them only in a relatively insignificant degree.

The reason for this higher hope is that while the state has to interfere with people, if only by way of coercing them to pay taxes and obey the law, it need not interfere with them arbitrarily. It will not interfere arbitrarily, according to the account given earlier, if it is in the ready-to-be-avowed, overall interest of each to have a state that interferes in their lives, and controls their affairs, according to a certain brief. And it is plausible that this will be in the ready-to-be-avowed interest of each, provided that the interference allowed to the state is subject to a controlling brief which helps to ensure that on every issue it has to track the common, readily avowable interests of citizens, and only such interests. I conceive of common interests as those interests whose collective promotion is supported by considerations that people admit as discursively relevant but others may wish to introduce a different conception at this point (Pettit 2000). Whatever conception of common, readily avowable interests is adopted, however, the really telling question is whether there is any prospect of constraining the state, once established, so that it acts only for the furtherance of such interests: in the traditional phrase, only for the promotion of the common good (Pettit 2004).

The republican tradition has given enormous, sometimes almost exclusive attention to this question in the long history that involves Cicero and Machiavelli, Montesquieu and Rousseau, Harrington and Madison. The notion of the blended or mixed constitution – the sort of constitution that Polybius celebrated in Rome – was developed for example in the attempt to work out the sorts of arrangements that would constrain the state suitably and effectively, forcing it to serve the common good. And many other notions, some of them implicated in this master idea, were elaborated and varied with a view to finding the best institutional design. They include proposals for dividing up sovereignty both between the legislature, the executive and the judiciary and – as in bicameral arrangements – within the legislature; for requiring public decisions to be matters of proper legislation, and for legislation to conform to the rule of law; for ensuring that decisions are made according to agreed reasons and for establishing associated possibilities of appeal, review and consultation; for devising methods of election and appointment to public office that further the prospect of common avowable interests – the common good – being tracked; and for constitutionally limiting the range of matters over which government can have influence as well as for limiting the sorts of decisions it can make.

The most interesting challenge for republican thought today – that is, for the sort of thinking that is orientated around the ideal of non-domination – bears on how to design political arrangements so that, as far as possible, the state really is forced to track all and only the common, ready-to-be-avowed interests of the citizenry. The challenge is to see how far government may operate so that while it can have the reduction of non-domination as a central or even principal aim, it need not itself represent an arbitrary and therefore dominating influence (see Pettit 2000 and 2001, Ch. 7). It cannot be said that any institutional design is going to remove domination fully, and meet the challenge with complete success. But there is at least a hope that state domination may be reduced to a tolerable minimum: a level that is clearly compensated for by the domination that the state prevents.

That this hope is rational is enough for our purposes here; we do not have to do any more by way of vindicating it. For the fact that it is rational to hope for an institutional design that will curb the dominating potential of the state means that we cannot dismiss the complaint about domination as one that no state could remedy effectively. To dismiss it in such a way would be to surrender preemptively to despair at ever finding the sort of institutional design required.

The position adopted here is not one of utopian idealism. It may be conceded, for example, that even if the state does not interfere in an arbitrary and dominating way in people's lives, still it is bound to do some harm to their enjoyment of non-dominated choice. It is bound to limit the range over which people may enjoy non-dominated choice, just as natural obstacles limit that range. Like the non-intentional obstruction that the natural world or the social system may impose, non-arbitrary but intentional interference will condition people's enjoyment of non-domination, even if it does not compromise it: even if it does not itself represent a form of domination (Pettit 1997, Ch. 2). It will restrict the number of choices in which people may take advantage of their not being dominated.

The fact that the state is bound to condition people's enjoyment of non-dominated choice in this way does not mean that it will be an ineffective agency for promoting non-domination. We may disagree about how exactly to weight the two, but the compromising of non-domination that the state can prevent is intuitively more important than the conditioning of non-domination that it is bound to impose. Still, there is an important lesson that follows from the fact that even the non-dominating state conditions people's enjoyment of non-domination. This is that as between two forms of state that do equally well in reducing domination, where one involves deeper-running legislation and coercion than the other, we ought to prefer to have the one that interferes less.

Finally, we have an objection. If the state espouses non-domination as a goal, won't it find itself shackled to a project that will demand more and more in the way of resources and interference; won't it be at the mercy of an essentially insatiable goal? The range of matters that the state is allowed to take under its purview will increase dramatically, so it may be said, as the baseline of non-domination rises. And so it is bound to give rise over time to counterproductive, dominating effects that will leave people worse off in terms of non-domination than they would have been under a more modest regime.

This challenge articulates a danger, however, not an inevitability. And the danger teaches us that if we are to devise a set of policies for the state to espouse in the attempt to remedy complaints of domination, then we should be on our guard against the sort of power creep envisaged. There is undoubtedly a lot of room, starting from the sort of society most of us live in today, for the state to explore new policies. Imagine, then, that we introduce those initiatives incrementally, with a view to seeing how well they do overall in coping with domination. As we increase the initiatives explored, thereby enlarging the reach of the state, we should be alert to the likelihood of there being a point where there is no net gain in evidence or in prospect. At that point the state itself will begin to condition people's enjoyment of undominated choice in such a measure, or will threaten to compromise people's undominated status in such a degree, that the lesson is: stop! From that point on the certain damage done by state activity, even as that is assessed in the ledger books of non-domination, will be too great to compensate for any likely benefit it may achieve (Braithwaite and Pettit 1990).

There will undoubtedly be differences between people on the question of whether at any point the state has done all that it can do without becoming counterproductive; espousing the ideal of non-domination does not mean having an automatic resolution of those differences. The point to notice here, however, is that no matter how great those differences are, it can be agreed on all sides that there is an end at some point to what the state can productively do. There will be agreement that the cause of remedying complaints of domination does not threaten to legitimate rampant, uncritical recourse to the state. And that there is bound to be agreement on that point means that the complaint about being dominated does not hold out the spectre of an insatiable political ideal.

Third feasibility constraint

We turn finally to the third question of feasibility. This is the issue of whether relying on the state promises to do better than any other likely strategy for reducing domination in a society; in particular, whether relying on a state that is designed to track all and only the readily avowable, common interests of citizens promises to beat alternatives. If it does not promise to do better than other instrumentalities, then that is going to mean that it does not represent an efficient agency on this front.

The salient alternative to introducing a state, and authorizing it to act against the domination of some by others, is to rely on the spontaneous measures of economic and civil society to give rise to high levels of non-domination all round. But there is little or no prospect of spontaneous interactions and formations supporting a regime of non-domination. The problem is that resources generally attract more resources, power more power: to them that have it shall be given. Thus if social life is left to evolve without any political shaping, it will tend to allow the emergence of relatively few positions of influence and to open the way for the domination of the many by the few who command those positions. This is a melancholy observation but one that is supported by common sense, historical experience and the testimony of many literary traditions.

As the state promises to be an effective agency in acting against domination, then, so it looks likely to represent the most efficient instrumentality available. The state will be able to achieve only very little, as the long republican tradition emphasises, if it cannot rely on a fund of civic virtue and commitment for ensuring a regime of non-domination: 'just as good morals, if they are to be maintained, have need of the laws, so the laws, if they are to be observed, have need of good morals' (Machiavelli 1965, 241). But without the state as a guiding presence, as indeed Machiavelli takes for granted, there is no hope of such virtue and commitment – such good morals – achieving anything.

Non-domination and the Desirability Constraints

First desirability constraint

The first constraint of desirability on a political ideal is that the complaint it articulates be one that can be raised as a relevant consideration in discourse among people as to how their social and political affairs can be best organised. Does the complaint about domination come across as a consideration admissible in presumptively cooperative discussion, and not just as a complaint of the self-seeking kind that will be deemed irrelevant – an instance of special pleading – in such exchange? Does it present itself as a complaint that all must countenance and take into account? I believe that it does present itself as a complaint of that kind, and for the deepest of reasons.

When a number of people engage in discourse, their aim being to determine what is so in some domain or how it is best for them to act as a whole, then they give exclusive privilege to a particular form of influence that they may have on one another: that which occurs by virtue of producing reasons relevant to the outcome to be resolved. Thus they eschew the ways in which people influence one another when they exercise violence, or coercion, or intimidation, or anything of that kind. They authorise one another as voices that are generally capable of providing reasons relevant by discursive criteria and as ears that are generally capable of recognising such reasons when they are once produced. From the point of view of the discourse that they essay, only properly reason-mediated influence is legitimate (see Pettit and Smith 1996; the full details for the other paper are Pettit 2001).

This being so, any party to discourse is certainly going to be able complain admissibly about the existence of a form of influence that reduces their capacity to exercise or undergo discursive influence proper. It will be absolutely reasonable for anyone to complain, for example, about being pressured or coerced by others to go along with a certain line; those who attempt such pressure or coercion do not honour the constitutive requirements of discourse: they are playing another game. But the existence of a relation of domination between one party and some other or others means that that party is subject to a form of influence that reduces their capacity to interact discursively – it reduces their capacity to influence and be influenced in a purely reason-mediated way – and so it is going to be perfectly admissible for someone to complain about domination of that kind.

Why is domination going to reduce a person's capacity to interact discursively with others? Because, as a long tradition of thought insists, the fact of being exposed to the possibility of arbitrary interference from another impacts in a serious way on the likelihood that a person will speak their mind (see Skinner 1998). It will put in place a powerful incentive to keep the dominating parties on side, however beneficent they may be: to keep them sweet both by positive measures of ingratiation and by negative measures of avoidance and self-censorship. There is an old ideal, celebrated for example in the Quaker tradition, of speaking truth to power. But speaking truth to power is an ideal, precisely because it is recognised on all sides to be difficult. The person who speaks truth to power, never flinching from the most unpalatable forms of advice or rebuke, or the most unwelcome expressions of opinion, is a saint or a hero, not someone of merely regular nerve.

Not only is domination likely to lead someone to warp their voice, tuning it to the expectations and tastes of potentially dangerous potentates. This being a matter of common recognition – as it always has been a matter of common recognition – domination will also lead others not to take seriously the words uttered by anyone in a position of subordination and dependency. How can people trust the remarks of the vulnerable person, especially when they are tailored to fit with the opinions of someone to relation to whom they suffer vulnerability? They may seek out their opinions, particularly when it is they who are in the position of power – it is always pleasing, after all, to have some reinforcement of one's own views – but they will have no reason to take the dominated person really seriously; they will have no reason to grant that person a real voice or give them a genuine hearing.

I hope that these remarks will make it plausible that the complaint of being dominated is well suited in respect of discursive admissibility to underpin a central political ideal. But is the complaint a truly significant one, in particular a complaint fit to engage the attentions of the polity? That is the next question to be considered.

Second desirability constraint

The feature that marks human beings off from other species is our capacity to enter discourse with each other, relying on a common language in which we authorise one another as generally competent speakers and listeners: as speakers who warrant and deserve a hearing and as listeners who can acknowledge our claim to a similar hearing in turn. Let someone be denied full access to discourse with their fellows, or a full presence there, and they are denied full enjoyment of the treatment – the authorisation or respect – that marks them off as persons among persons.

The primary reason why the complaint about being dominated is of the first significance is that domination almost invariably undermines a person's capacity to enjoy respect in this sense. Where one person dominates another, it almost bound to be a matter of common awareness among the people involved, and among other relevant parties, that that domination exists. The question as to whether someone is dominated by another is one that will interest all those involved, after all, and the answer to that question will be obvious in most cases from the sorts of resources they control relative to that other. Thus we may expect most people to recognise domination when they see it, and this in turn being obvious, to recognise that others will recognize it too, thereby giving rise to the usual hierarchy of common awareness; each will believe that the person is dominated, each will believe that each believes this, and so on (see Pettit 1997, Ch. 2). Once it is recognised as a matter of common awareness that someone is dominated, however, then that person will no longer be able to enjoy the basic respect that we think personhood entitles them to. They will no longer have the sort of voice that can be reliably forthright, or can be expected to be forthright. They will always be under suspicion of playing to the audience of the powerful and never having anything worthwhile to say in their own right.

Dominated subjects of this kind may not be ignored or dismissed outright: they may be treated magnanimously to the trappings of respect. But they will not command respect; they will receive it only in the manner of supplicants. They may be treated as if they had the status of persons, so we might put it, but they will not really have that status. Being a person is inseparable from earning and receiving respect as of right – as of effective, not just formal right – and in their case there will be no question of earning or receiving as of right. What they receive, they will receive only as a gift – only by grace of the powerful.

This line of thought is a familiar and recurrent one in republican thought. It is worth mentioning in connection with it that Kant, the great philosopher of respect and personhood, seems to have shaped many of his ideas on that subject in his reflections on Rousseau's *Social Contract*, itself a book that belongs at least among the apocrypha of the republican tradition. The point is emphasised by J.B. Schneewind, who quotes Kant as saying 'It is not all one under what title I get something. What properly belongs to me must not be accorded to me merely as something I ask for' (Schneewind 1992, 311). Schneewind comments. 'If nothing is properly mine except what someone graciously gives me, I am forever dependent on how the donor feels toward me. My independence as an autonomous being is threatened. Only if I can claim the others *have to* give me what is mine by right can this be avoided' (Schneewind 1992).

Given the connection between enjoying respect as a person and not being subject to domination, there is every reason to treat the complaint of being dominated as extremely significant. What more serious complaint could there be than one which draws attention to a relationship in virtue of which one's very standing as a person who can command the attention and respect of others is put in jeopardy? This is no mere trifle to do with having one's nose put out of joint, or one's feathers ruffled. It is a complaint of the first moment. Let someone be dominated and to that extent they will be put out of any community that involves those who dominate them. They may aspire to community with such others and their presence may even be tolerated among those others. But they will always cut somewhat sorry or comic figures, and will always invite only condescension or contempt. They will have no more standing, in a somewhat archaic image, than dogs that cower at their master's feet or that snuggle up to their mistress's skirts.

One word more on the significance of the complaint about being dominated. People don't reveal their minds just in the words they explicitly stand over in discursive settings. They also express their discursive minds in the actions they choose to perform, because they routinely acknowledge that they may be held answerable for their actions in discourse: they don't deny the relevance of discursive challenge as to the legitimacy of what they do. But if someone is dominated by another – and even if that other does not exercise the domination in attempts at pressure or coercion – then we may expect the relationship to warp the things they do as well as the things they say. We may expect people to take positive measures of self-ingratiation and negative measures of self-censorship that would not appeal to them in the absence of the domination. And that being so, the deleterious impact of domination will be obvious, even short of actual interference by the dominating person, in the deeds as well as in the words of the victim.

This observation is worth adding, because it shows that just as the dominated person cannot be taken to enjoy the freedom of thought that is necessary if someone is to be worth hearing, so they cannot be taken to enjoy freedom of choice either. Operating within the gravitational field that relationships of domination establish, people are deprived of a measure of discursive control that would otherwise be available. When they purport to speak their minds or to display their minds in action, therefore, there is a robust possibility, marked in everyday expectation, that they are not fully their own masters; they are not reflecting their own best opinion of what circumstances require but rather the opinion that materialises most comfortably at their particular place in the field of dominating force.

The significance of the complaint about being dominated is borne out in the rich idioms associated with the complaint and with the many changes that have been rung, and that continue to be rung, on them. This is cast in melancholy tones as a condition of servitude or subordination, subjection or subjugation – at the limit, a condition of slavery – in which one can do nothing but by the leave or permission of others, one lives under their thumb as those in the Roman circus lived under the thumb of the emperor, one has to fawn and toady and kow tow in their direction, one has to ingratiate oneself with them or at least placate and humour them, and one has to tug the forelock or tip the cap, acknowledging them as one's superiors and betters. The condition in which the complaint has no ground is cast, by contrast, as an ideal of being able to stand on one's own two feet, and to walk tall, having a standing on a par with others; an ideal of being able to look others in the eye, not showing fear or deference, and not seeking grace or favour; and an ideal of being one's own man or woman or master: an ideal in Roman terms of being *sui juris*.

These phrases have often been formed in relation to contexts that no longer obtain very commonly. But there are plenty of contexts in contemporary society where the message they convey – ultimately, the complaint they carry – still clearly applies. Think of the child of the emotionally volatile parent; the wife of the occasionally violent husband; or the pupil of the teacher who forms arbitrary likes and dislikes. Think of the employee whose security requires keeping the boss or manager sweet; the debtor whose fortunes depend on the caprice of money-lender or bank-manager; or the small business owner whose viability depends on the attitude taken by a bigger competitor or a union boss. Think of the welfare recipient whose fortunes turn on the mood of the counter-clerk; the immigrant or indigenous person whose standing is vulnerable to the whims that rule politics and talk-back radio; or the public employee whose future depends, not on performance, but on the political profile that an ambitious minister happens to find electorally most useful. Think of the older person who is vulnerable to the culturally and institutionally unrestrained gang of youths in his or her area. Or think indeed of the young offender whose level of punishment depends on how far politicians or newspapers choose to whip up a culture of vengeance.

In all of these cases someone lives at the mercy of others. That person is dominated by those others in the sense that even if they don't interfere in his or her life, they have a more or less arbitrary power of doing so on a greater or larger front and in a more or less substantive measure: there are few restraints or costs to inhibit them. If the dominated person escapes ill treatment in such a situation, that is by the grace or favour of the powerful, or perhaps by dint of a native cunning and deception. The price of liberty in such a world is not eternal vigilance but rather, in a phrase once used by Gore Vidal, eternal discretion. The person lives in the power or under the mastery of others: they occupy the position of a *dominus* in his or her life.

Third desirability constraint

That the complaint about being dominated not only passes the feasibility constraints but is admissible and significant already goes a long way to establishing that it ought to have a serious place in politics; in effect, that the ideal of non-domination ought to be targeted by the state. But the complaint might be all of these things and not connect in any substantial manner with other complaints that have traditionally been placed within the province of the polity's responsibility. We turn now to the question as to whether that is how things stand with the complaint about being dominated. Is it a more or less stand-alone complaint such that rectifying it leaves many other putatively relevant political complaints unaddressed? Or is it a complaint such that if the state takes serious steps to put it right then it will at the same time take steps that put many other complaints right? Is it a complaint that subsumes a range of other complaints in that sense? I argue that it is a characteristically subsumptive complaint, not one of the stand-alone variety.

The best way to support this point, at least in the short compass available, is to consider how far the rectification of complaints about domination in a society would go to establishing a sample of other ideals. I shall include in my sample liberty, equality, and community – the three ideals of the French revolution – as well as functioning capability, in Amartya Sen's phrase (Sen 1993), and a contractualist conception of justice.

Liberty

I have argued elsewhere that liberty or freedom was long conceptualized precisely as the absence of domination: not being under the thumb of a master (Pettit 1997). If that construal is accepted, then it follows that someone may be unfree in doing something, even though there is no natural obstacle that constrains them to do it and no one forces or coerces them to do it. This will happen so far as the person is inhibited or intimidated by the presence of a power that has to be kept sweet. But if the construal is accepted, then another perhaps more surprising result also follows: this is that someone is not necessarily rendered unfree by the fact of a natural obstacle removing an option or raising the costs of taking it, or by the fact of an intentional agency interfering in their affairs to a similar effect. The natural obstacle won't dominate the person so it can't make them unfree. And the interfering agency may not dominate the person – the agency may be forced to track the person's avowed interests – in which case it won't make them unfree either. How easy is it to live with this implication, while claiming that the relief of domination will advance the ideal of liberty?

It is quite easy, I suggest, to live with this conclusion so long as we recognise that without compromising the enjoyment of non-domination – without itself being dominating – a natural obstacle or an intentional agency may still have a negative effect on that enjoyment; it may condition it, as we saw earlier, by restricting the range over which – or indeed the ease with which – the person exercises undominated choice. Even if liberty is taken to require the absence of natural limitation or the absence of intentional interference, then, we can see that the systematic remedying of the complaint about domination is going to involve, so far as possible, the reduction of non-intentional obstacles, and of intentional but non-dominating obstacles, to people's choices; we already mentioned this point in the second section.

If non-domination is used to conceptualise liberty, therefore, then it leads us to distinguish between primary and secondary restrictions on liberty. The primary form of restriction is domination by another person or group: in this case the person or group has more or less ready access to more or less arbitrary interference across a more or less substantial range of choices. The secondary form of restriction is the limitation imposed by non-intentional forces and the interference practiced by intentional but non-arbitrary agencies. It seems right and intuitive to me that this distinction is made between these two different grades of restriction, since only the primary form is inimical to an agent's status as a person; one is not de-authorized or disrespected by non-intentional or non-arbitrary influences in one's life. But it is important that even if people worry about the secondary form of restriction, they will see that a state committed to advancing the enjoyment of non-domination will go a long way towards satisfying their concern (Pettit 2003).

Equality

What now of the ideal of equality? There are many interpretations of that ideal, as there are notoriously many ways in which people may or may not be equal with one another. But from our point of view a very significant aspect of the ideal is going to be equality of non-domination: in effect, equality of the kind that is provided when people equally command the attention and the respect of others. An obvious question, then, is whether the attempt by a state to redress the complaint that individuals may have about being dominated is likely to push towards equality of non-domination or whether it is likely to create or support large inequalities, with non-domination being maximised at a point where there are such inequalities between people. It is often said that the maximisation of people's subjective utility or happiness may require that some are very unhappy, and in particular much less happy than others; that is how the sums may come out. Is the same sort of thing likely with the maximisation of non-domination? Or is there a closer tie between promoting this ideal overall and ensuring that the distribution across people tends towards equality?

As it turns out, there is indeed a close tie between maximising and equalising the enjoyment of non-domination (see Pettit 1997, Ch. 4 and Lovett 2001). Whether a person is to enjoy a good measure of non-domination in relation to others depends, not on their absolute level of power – their power of interfering, retaliating, defending themselves, and so on – but on their level of power relative to the power of others. A level of power that would give me absolute supremacy in one society may leave me relatively badly off in another; in the land of the blind, the one-eyed man is king. This means that if the power of some people is increased with a view to increasing the non-domination they enjoy, then by that very token the degree of non-domination enjoyed by others falls; any positive move on one front is at the same time a negative move on another.

But not only is there going to be interaction between different fronts in this way. A second equally plausible observation suggests that it will always be better from the point of view of maximising the enjoyment of non-domination in a society to act on fronts that make for its equalisation among members of that society. As we increase the relative powers of people with a view to increasing their non-domination, there will tend to be a better result available so far as we focus on relatively powerless rather than on relatively powerful individuals. The more powerful people are, the smaller will be the gain in making them more impregnable to others – the extra resources may be redundant – and the larger the loss in making others more vulnerable to them: the extra resources will impact ever more significantly on the prospects of the weak.

If the level of people's non-domination is sensitive to their relative degrees of power, and if this sensitivity is greater for the weaker than for the stronger, then any attempt to maximise non-domination overall is bound to focus at every stage on improving the lot of the weaker, and it is bound thereby to push towards more and more equality. This represents a fundamental tie between the ideal of non-domination and the ideal of equality, and one indeed that was well recognised even in Roman times (see Wirszubski 1968). Any society where people's non-domination is at a maximum will be a society in which people enjoy a corresponding equality of status, with each doing as well as can be expected in commanding the respect of their fellows. This sort of equality does not entail equality in every other dimension; it is consistent, for example, with inequality in the subjective well-being that people enjoy and with at least a certain degree of inequality in the objective resources at their command: in their wealth. But it still represents a substantial kind of equality and it should encourage egalitarians who might otherwise have baulked at making non-domination into a central, even supreme, political ideal.

Community

As there is a tie between valuing non-domination and valuing equality, in particular equality of status, so there is also a tie between valuing non-domination and valuing community. There are three points to make about this connection. The first is that non-domination has been understood in the long republican tradition, and is understood here, in such a way that it cannot be enjoyed by the solitary individual. To enjoy non-domination it is necessary, first, that there be other people about with whom one interacts; and second, that one not be dominated by those people: that one enjoy standing in relation to them, being able to look them in the eye, commanding their attention and respect. It is not sufficient that there be no one in one's vicinity and so, *a fortiori*, that one not be dominated. One must enjoy the absence of domination in a context where it is a real possibility, not enjoy it as a mere byproduct of total isolation. This condition already ensures a connection between non-domination and community, for it means that the ideal of non-domination is an inherently social value, not an atomistic one.

The second point to make in underscoring the tie to community is that if people are secured against domination by the operation of the institutional instrumentalities available for the state to deploy – the institutions of armament, disarmament and protection – then the connection between being non-dominated and those institutions is constitutive and not merely causal. To be non-dominated is to be more or less immune to the possibility of arbitrary interference and that immunity will come into being simultaneously with the introduction of measures that realise it, not as a causal consequence of those measures being in place: a consequence that might take time to realise. The connection between immunity to arbitrary interference and the presence of those measures will be like the connection between immunity to a certain disease and the presence of suitable antibodies in the blood. The physical immunity will not materialise as a contingent consequence of the antibodies that takes a certain time to eventuate; it is present as soon as the antibodies are there, being realised by the antibodies. And similarly a person's immunity to arbitrary interference – a person's non-domination – will not materialise as a causal result of the institutional measures taken to realise it; rather it will be constituted by those measures, being present just as soon as they are present (Pettit 1997, Ch. 4).

The fact that non-domination requires a community of individuals, and that a person's non-domination will be constituted by the institutional measures that make him or her more or less secure against arbitrary interference by other members of the community, means that for the state to work at promoting non-domination is just for the state to work at ensuring that people enjoy a certain sort of community: a sort of community that is bound to have the aspect of an ideal. The third point to add further emphasises this connection between promoting the two ideals.

The value of non-domination is tied up with its being a matter of common awareness that one is not dominated, as we saw earlier. That means that if one is to enjoy non-domination properly then one has to be more or less secure against arbitrary interference oneself, being personally protected, or having access to personal resources of retaliation. But it also means, we should notice, that others in any salient class to which one belongs have got to be secure in the same way. Suppose that you are a black or a woman or an indigenous person in a society where people in those classes are generally dominated in certain ways. The fact that you have purely personal resources against domination, say because of being very wealthy, will not ensure that you enjoy non-domination properly. For membership in that vulnerability class will convey the message to many that you are dominated and will constantly put pressure on the discursive status that you can enjoy; you will have to vindicate your standing, case by case, time after time. Thus if you are to achieve the proper enjoyment of your non-domination, it had better be the case that all others in your vulnerability class escape domination too. You cannot enjoy freedom as non-domination without others in every salient class to which you belong – including, in the last analysis, others in the society as a whole – enjoying that sort of freedom as well.

Functioning capability

I said that there are two other ideals, apart from those associated with freedom, equality and community, that are subsumed in the ideal of non-domination. The first is functioning capability in Amartya Sen's sense, and the second is justice in the contractualist sense associated with John Rawls (1971) and T.M. Scanlon (1998).

To enjoy functioning capability is to be in a position where the things one can do and be in one's society mean that by local criteria one functions perfectly well: intuitively speaking, one is not poor or deprived, even if one is not particularly rich. Capability in this sense will require access to conditions such as being fed, being healthy, being housed, being linked with family or friends, communicating with others, following what happens in public life, and tracking the opportunities for work and related activities (see Nussbaum 1992 and Sen 1993).There are two grounds for thinking that the ideal of non-domination subsumes this ideal of functioning capability (see also Pettit 2001, Ch. 7). The first is that to the extent that a person lacks such capability, to that extent they will be vulnerable to all sorts of arbitrary interference on the part of others. And the second is that even if someone's poverty or lack of capability does not expose them to further domination, still it will limit the range or ease with which they can enjoy non-domination, so that there is reason why a state that wants to advance such enjoyment should want, costs allowing, to put such lack of capability right too.

Contractualist justice

Roughly speaking, an arrangement will be just in a contractualist sense so far as people cannot reject it on the grounds that it violates an unobjectionable principle for regulating relations between mutually respectful individuals, in particular for regulating them politically; that the principle is unobjectionable means that it would attract no reasonable objection: no objection, as we may understand it here, that would survive discursive interrogation. Will a regime in which non-domination is maximised be likely to count as just in this sense? I think so. The sort of person who may be expected to complain about its injustice is one who suffers some redistribution of resources towards the poorer or some diminution of native advantages of power. But it is hard to see how the complaint made by such a person could stand up in the contractualist court.

The person envisaged acquiesces in the need for a regulation of the relations between mutually respectful people; specifically, in the need for a political regulation of those relations; and more specifically still, in the need for their regulation by a state that is designed as well as possible to advance all and only the readily avowable, common interests of citizens. There would be no issue to be considered, were this not so. The question, then, is whether he or she could identify an unobjectionable principle on the basis of which to protest against the loss that they suffer as a result of a redistribution of relative powers, even when the redistribution is necessary for increasing the non-domination enjoyed by people under the polity: that is, is necessary for meeting the complaints of various others about being dominated.

The person cannot dismiss the complaints about being dominated as ones that there are no reason to heed in discourse about how the state should be organised; after all, it is an admissible and significant sort of complaint, by the argument provided above. The only grounds on which the person can protest the redistribution, therefore, must be that the pattern of benefits and burdens that it imposes is unfair. But those grounds are bound to look hollow. In seeking to remedy complaints of domination, the state is trying to advance a common interest that all are ready, so we may presume, to avow. The benefits to be gained for the interest of the weaker are great and the costs to the person complaining are not comparable; that person does not lose out substantially in terms of non-domination, after all, even if they suffer some financial loss or some loss of privilege. And so it is hard to see how the person envisaged can identify any unobjectionable principle on the basis of which to protest the redistribution. Any redistribution that advances that cause of non-domination looks likely to advance also the cause of justice in the contractualist sense.

Conclusion

I hope that these brisk remarks will help to establish the powerful case that can be made for putting the complaint of domination right at the centre of political concerns and for making the ideal of non-domination one of the central ideals in politics, if not the supreme political ideal. The state can do something about this complaint, and do something that provides both an effective and efficient remedy. And the complaint is admissible in any open discourse on the best form of the state, and directs us to a significant and subsumptive ideal. The performance of the complaint on these fronts gives it a serious claim on our attention in normative political thought and presumptively, as my passing comments have tried to indicate, a more serious claim than any of its rivals.

Earlier it was mentioned that there are other desiderata or constraints that we might expect a political ideal to satisfy, apart from those we have considered. In conclusion

I might mention that one of these is the desideratum of being a measurable ideal, on which many recent writers have focused (see Steiner 1994 and Carter 1999). The measurable ideal will enable us to determine how well individuals within a polity are doing in relation to that ideal and how well the polity does in comparisons across time or with other regimes. The ideal of non-domination does not count as a highly measurable ideal. First of all, domination and non-domination come in degrees along at least three separate, dimensions that are not easily weighted against each other: it may involve more or less easy access to more or less arbitrary interference across a more or less substantive range. And secondly, there are two respects, also not easily weighted against each other, in which we will want the state to do well by the ideal: one, by reducing domination itself – by reducing the influence of factors that compromise undominated choice – and two, by reducing the presence of non-dominating factors that condition such choice without compromising it.

In view of these complexities the ideal of non-domination is not going to lend itself to ready measurement; there will always be issues of weighting that need discussion in any instance where it is to be applied. We might try to resolve those weighting issues at the abstract level but I see little prospect of doing so in a way that is going to win general support. Still, however, I don't think we should lose heart. The important thing with any political ideal is that it be amenable to disciplined arbitration in the course of a conversation that involves all relevant sides; it is not a vague and nebulous notion that allows everyone to think what they will. And in this respect non-domination promises to do quite well. While people may not easily come to agreement on weightings to be assigned in the abstract to the different elements it involves, it will usually be clear how these elements should be weighted in the context of concrete issues. The ideal may not make the algorithmic adjudication of political arrangements possible but it does represent a yardstick that will not easily bend to the grain of individual interest or bias.

This chapter was presented at the University of Valencia in July 2001, the European University Institute in October 2001, and Chiba University March 2003, I am most grateful for the very helpful comments that I received in those discussions. This version appeared in English in *Nomos* Vol. 46, 2004, pp. 87–117.

References

Bentham, J. (1962), 'Anarachical Fallacies', in Bowring, J. (ed.).

Bowring, J. (ed.) (1962), *The Works of Jeremy Bentham* (New York: Russell and Russell).

Braithwaite, J. and Pettit, P. (1990), *Not Just Deserts: A Republican Theory of Criminal Justice* (New York: Oxford University Press).

Carter, I. (1999), *A Measure of Freedom* (Oxford: Oxford University Press).

Dowding, K., Goodin, R. and Pateman, C. (eds) (2004), *Justice and Democracy: Essays for Brian Barry* (Cambridge: Cambridge University Press).

Elster, J. (1986), 'The Market and the Forum: Three Varieties of Political Theory, in Elster, J. and Hillard, A. (eds).

—— and Hillard, A. (eds) (1986), *Foundations of Social Choice Theory* (Cambridge: Cambridge University Press).
Foucault, M. (1980), *Power/Knowledge: Selected Interviews and Other Writings, 1872–1977*. Ed. and Trans. Coling, G. (New York: Pantheon Books).
Guyer, P. (ed.) (1992), *The Cambridge Companion to Kant* (Cambridge: Cambridge University Press).
Habermas, J. (1984, 1989), *A Theory of Communicative Action*, Vols. 1 and 2 (Cambridge: Polity Press).
Kymlicka, W. (1995), *Multicultural Citizenship II* (Oxford: Oxford University Press).
Locke, J. (1985), *A Letter Concerning Toleration* (Indianapolis: Hackett Publishing).
Lovett, F.N. (2001), 'Domination: A Preliminary Analysis', *Monist* 84, 98–112.
Machiavelli, N. (1965), *The Complete Work and Others*. Ed. and Trans Gilber, A. (Durham, NC: Duke University Press).
Miller, D. (1984), 'Constraints of Freedom', *Ethics* 94, 66–86.
—— (ed.) (1993), *Liberty* (Oxford: Oxford University Press, 1993).
Nozick, R. (1974), *Anarchy, State, and Utopia* (New York: Basic Books).
Nussbaum, M. (1992), 'Human Functioning and Social Justice' *Political Theory* 20, 202–46.
—— and Sen, A. (eds) (1993), *The Quality of Life* (Oxford: Oxford University Press).
Pettit, P. (1996), 'Freedom and Antipower', *Ethics* 106, 576–604.
—— and Smith, M. (1996), 'Freedom in Belief and Desire', *Journal of Philosophy* 93, 429–49.
—— (1997), *Republicanism: A Theory of Freedom and Government* (Oxford: Oxford University Press).
—— (2000), 'Democracy, Electoral and Contestatory', *Nomos* 42, 105–44.
—— (2001), *A Theory of Freedom: From the Psychology to the Politics of Agency* (Cambridge and New York: Polity and Oxford University Press).
—— (2001b), 'Capability and Freedom: A Defense of Sen', *Economics and Philosophy* 17:1, 1–20.
—— (2002), 'Keeping Republican Freedom Simple: On a Difference with Quentin Skinner', *Political Theory* 339–56.
—— (2003), 'Agency-freedom and Option-freedom', *Journal of Theoretical Politics* 15:4, 387–403.
—— (2004), 'The Common Good', in Dowding, K., Goodin, R. and Pateman, C. (eds).
Rawls, J. (1971), *A Theory of Justice* (Oxford: Oxford University Press).
Scanlon, T.M. (1998), *What We Owe to Each Other* (Cambridge, Mass: Harvard University Press).
Schneewind, J.B. (1992), 'Autonomy, Obligation, and Virtue: An Overview of Kant's Moral Philosophy', in Guyer, P. (ed.).
Sen, A. (1993), 'Capability and Well-Being', in Nussbaum, M. and Sen, A. (eds).
Skinner, Q. (1998), *Liberty Before Liberalism* (Cambridge: Cambridge University Press).

Steiner, H. (1994), *An Essay on Rights* (Oxford: Blackwell Publishers).

Taylor, C. (1985), *Philosophy and the Human Sciences: Philosophical Papers 2* (Cambridge: Cambridge University Press).

Viroli, M. (1998), *Machiavelli* (Oxford: Oxford University Press).

Wirszubski, C. (1968), *Libertas as a Political Ideal at Rome* (Oxford: Oxford University Press).

Chapter 10

Public Reason and Order Ethics: A Critical Assessment

Christoph Luetge

The Problem Setting: Do We Need a Moral Surplus?

Many contemporary positions in social and political philosophy, such as those of J. Habermas, J. Rawls, D. Gauthier or K. Binmore (1994 and 1998), discuss – implicitly or explicitly – the following question: Granted that actors in modern societies strive for advantages and benefits, do we still need some kind of a *social glue* beyond this mere quest for advantages and benefits? I would like to call this kind of social glue a *moral surplus*.[1] In this chapter, I will concentrate on Habermas's position of discourse ethics, which is prominent for its reliance on *public reason* as a basis for justifying moral norms. (This has been discussed extensively by the other authors in this volume.)

Like Rawls (1971 and 1993) or Gauthier (1986), Habermas argues that modern societies do indeed require a moral surplus to prevent them from destabilising. I will focus here on the following question: Can the moral surplus in question *remain stable* in face of opposing incentives?

This question can be explicated in the following, rather simple, way: The prime situational model for interactions that concern drastically disadvantageous incentives to all actors is the prisoners' dilemma (PD).[2] In PD situations, actors are permanently faced with the possibility of being 'exploited' by others if behaving cooperatively, and therefore they stop cooperating themselves *pre-emptively*. This leads to a situation where rational, self-interested actors end up with a result that leaves all worse and no one better off. It will be argued here that the question whether the moral surplus can *remain stable* must be answered negatively.

Discourse Ethics

In arguing for the importance of discourses as grounds for normative theory, Habermas makes a fundamental assumption: The participants of a discourse must allow their behaviour – at least partially – to be motivated by a *rational motivation*.[3] With the

1 For a more elaborated account of moral surpluses, see Luetge (2005).

2 For conceptualisations of the prisoners' dilemma, see Axelrod (1984).

3 See Habermas 1981, Vol. 1, 50 and 54; Habermas 1983/1999, 68 and 119; Habermas 1992, 19.

help of this concept, Habermas explicates the difference between his two opposing types of actions: strategic and communicative. This difference represents a central antagonism in Habermas's theory. While strategic action ('strategisches Handeln') is affected by incentives and sanctions, communicative action ('kommunikatives Handeln') is led by rational motivation (see Habermas 1983/1999, 68). But what, then, *is* rational motivation and where does it come from?

It is difficult to find an answer to this question in Habermas's writings. In the *Theory of Communicative Action* (Habermas 1981), he simply postulates: 'If arguments are valid, the insight into the internal conditions of their validity can have rationally motivating force.'[4] And a few pages earlier, there is a footnote in which Habermas (1981, Vol. 1, 50, fn. 42) admits that the concept of a rational motivation has not yet been analysed satisfactorily.

In later works, the situation does not get much better. In 'Diskursethik: Notizen zu einem Begründungsprogramm' (Habermas 1983/1999), the necessity of a rational motivation is stressed several times,[5] but only in one instance a justification is given. Here Habermas (1983/1999, 68) relies on the illocutionary effects of a *speech act*. He assumes that speech acts can force actors to perform certain actions and refrain from others. The core of this assumption is the idea of a *performative contradiction*.[6] According to Habermas, a rationally motivated actor is led by the desire to avoid a performative contradiction.

It is doubtful whether it makes sense to assume such a binding force of a speech act. It seems as if Habermas recognises this problem himself: He invents a dialogue with a fictitious sceptic who doubts exactly this binding force of speech acts. However, Habermas responds that the sceptic may well stick to his position, but then has to 'be silent'. He cannot escape the 'Lebenswelt', which – according to Habermas – is formed by cultural tradition and socialisation which in turn work through rational motivation. If he tried to escape, he would end in 'schizophrenia and suicide' (Habermas 1983/1999, 112; my translation).

In the 1990s, Habermas's thought develops in new directions. The problem of the sceptic is taken on again in Habermas (1991). Here, Habermas at first seems to weaken the power of rational motivation by attributing to moral norms only 'the weak motivating power of good reasons' (Habermas 1991, 135; my translation). He goes as far as stating that 'the validity of moral norms is subject to the condition that they are observed as the basis of a general practice' (Habermas 1991, 136; my translation), thus implying that individuals might be allowed to behave 'immorally' when faced with possible exploitation by others. This would be the case in prisoners' dilemma situations. However, in the rest of this article, Habermas makes it clear that he does not consider this a problem of *ethics*. Rather, he writes, it can only be argued within the discourse of *law* that some norms might be valid but yet not reasonable ('zumutbar') because of their lack of general acceptance.

Consequently, this leads Habermas to include institutions in his conception, which were rather neglected in his earlier work. He recognises that the problem of

4 Habermas 1981, Vol. 1, 54, my translation; see also Habermas 1981, Vol. 1, 70.

5 See Habermas 1983/1999, 68, 82, 119.

6 For further explication, cf. Habermas 1983/1999, pp. 100f.

compliance to norms cannot be solved by postulates of rational motivation or by citing developmental psychology.[7] In *Between Facts and Norms* (Habermas 1992), he explicitly develops an account of law and institutions. However, even here it soon becomes clear that he does not rely on sanctions and incentives alone as a means for governing modern societies. Rather, the citizens must still have certain characteristics: They have to accept – not only the legal rules, but also – normative claims resulting in turn from the idealised discourse assumptions.[8] Habermas still assumes a 'coordination of plans of actions' (Habermas 1992, 34) *by language* – thus still assuming the existence of rational motivation working via speech acts. Thus Habermas' main claims are still intact in his second, institutional, phase.

Now the two questions mentioned above become relevant. I will focus on the second one: Can rational motivation remain stable in view of opposing incentives? Regarding Habermas's argument concerning speech acts, one problem is his reconstruction of the 'Lebenswelt'. In my view, there are alternative, and less harmonious, reconstructions of the Lebenswelt possible in which the binding force of speech acts is much weaker. One major example is the game-theoretic approach that reconstructs all human interactions as being 'riddled' with dilemma situations like the prisoners' dilemma. These situations can be either manifest (as in open market interactions with competition being obvious) or hidden. Hidden PD situations that have been overcome are exemplified prominently in all the institutions, like police and jurisdiction, that come into effect as a consequence of the social contract, which lets the actors escape from the natural state (that is, a PD situation).

In a phenomenalistic perspective that does not look beyond the surface, it looks as if the individuals have been moved by a rational motivation. However, in another perspective, the 'deeper' structures behind become visible – and it becomes clear that it is not just rational motivation, but rather (in this case, informal) incentives and possible sanctions that hold this social practice in place. This casts doubt on Habermas's claim to have found the only reconstruction of everyday practices.

Moreover, while Habermas – as I have shown – introduces institutions into his conception in later works, thus allowing for sanctioning by legal rules, he still relies on his original idea of rationally motivated individuals. Institutions are therefore assigned only a secondary place, while the original moral surplus survives intact.

Order Ethics

The idea behind the approach which I would like to sketch here – as an alternative – is to develop an account of norms as functional for social stability while weakening the assumptions on the actors' part, that is, minimising the necessary moral surplus. This alternative view is a conception of ethics that proceeds systematically not from the problem of justification, but from the problem of *implementation of norms*.[9]

7 In some (earlier) works (see Habermas 1983/1999), he makes extensive use of L. Kohlberg's developmental psychology.

8 See Habermas 1992, 34 and 678ff.

9 See Homann 2002, Homann and Luetge 2004, Luetge 2005.

Some philosophers believe that the *justification* of norms has always been the key problem of ethics. However, an informed view of economic and social history tells us that the questions of norm implementation *and* justification have generally been posed *together*, but this was not made explicit in former centuries. The implementation of norms that had already been justified was not regarded as particularly difficult, for two reasons: First, the modern pluralism of values and life styles had not yet developed, and second, social relations were not yet as anonymous as in modern times. In particular, commonly accepted norms could be enforced much more easily through face-to-face sanctions.

Since the beginning of modern times, however, this situation has changed dramatically. As especially N. Luhmann[10] has described, modern societies consist of functionally differentiated subsystems. The actors in modern societies must act in social subsystems under completely different governance mechanisms; with regard to ethics, this often leads to laments about loss of values. The question of how norms can be enforced becomes therefore much more pressing under modern conditions and must be put at the beginning of a conception of ethics for modern societies. I would like to call such a conception an *order ethics* or, in a different regard, an *ethics of advantages and incentives*. We must count on the fact that all actors look for their advantage (whereby the term 'advantage', of course, covers not only material advantages), and we have to set the right incentives in order to deal with this quest for advantages.

The basic problem of order ethics is this: Under conditions of competition, individuals cannot comply with moral norms in case this leads to higher costs which in turn leave them worse off than their competitors. Situations like this systematically lead to an erosion of compliance to moral norms. Via evolution, individuals behaving 'morally' will be singled out.

This problem is the starting point of order ethics, which fundamentally distinguishes between two different social situations: Modern and pre-modern societies. The basic concepts of ethics have been developed with reference to the conditions of pre-modern societies. These conditions included most notably zero-sum games. Pre-modern societies played zero-sum games in which people could only gain significantly at the expense of others.[11] Within ethics, this problem resulted in an 'ethics of temperance' which demanded not to strive for excessive gains and advantages, but to remain within the limits of 'moderate' profits. This was a natural consequence of a situation in which the available resources could not be increased. In this way, the Christian canonical prohibition against lending money at interest and the ethical condemnation of accumulation of capital were justified. In a zero sum society, ethics called for domesticating the striving for advantages.[12]

10 See, for example, Luhmann 1997.

11 Historical evidence can be found, for example, in the works of Christian Meier (1998) on ancient Athens or in Eric Jones's (1981) study of the causes of the 'European miracle'.

12 Many other conceptions of ethics – historical and contemporary – can be regarded as ethics of temperance, for example, Kantian approaches (like discourse ethics, see Habermas 1981 and 1992) and Aristotelian approaches (like virtue ethics, see Foot 1978) call – in one way or another – for *taming* the quest for advantages.

In modern times, however, the dominating model is a society differentiated in various functional systems (Luhmann 1997) and characterised by continuous growth. The modern market economy led to an enormous rise in wealth. The basis for this has been the modern competitive market economy which enables everyone to pursue his own interests *within a carefully devised institutional system*. In this system, positive sum games are played, which makes it in principle possible to improve the position of every individual at the same time.[13]

The structures of society have changed in modern times, but ethical concepts and categories have – at least to a large extent – *not* changed: Many ethical concepts are still based on the conditions of zero sum games of the pre-moderns. Most conceptions of ethics still require us to be moderate, to share, to redistribute, to sacrifice. They call for altruism, for the priority of common good and the like. The pursuit of self-interest, of individual advantages is often still ultimately seen as something like an evil drive that needs to be tamed.

In this situation, ethical concepts lag behind. Those concepts that were developed within the framework of pre-modern societies, are inadequate for fruitfully connecting the ideas of ethics and economics. These concepts fail to see the idea that the individual pursuit of advantages *within an adequate institutional system* does not necessarily imply exploitation of others, but can lead to mutual improvements. Traditional ethics cannot understand that the individual pursuit of advantages can – very effectively – *promote* the traditional ideal of solidarity. It cannot understand that competition can become an efficient form of charity, whereby charity is distributed not via the benevolence of people, but via the usual processes of market exchange. It is visible in the form of innovative products at good value for money, of jobs, of income, or of taxes. So, within the positive sum games of modern societies, the individual pursuit of advantages is in principle compatible with traditional ethical ideas like the solidarity of all.

There is a second important distinction, namely the distinction between *actions* and *conditions of actions*.[14] Traditional ethics concentrates on actions. Its norms require individuals to change those parameters they are able to control through their actions. The conditions of these actions, however, have been taken as 'given', as they have remained stable for centuries. These conditions include laws, constitutions, social structures, the market order, and also ethical norms.

Since the beginning of modern times, this situation has changed dramatically. We have increasingly become able to control and fine-tune the conditions of our actions, like constitutions, the market order and others. A great deal of what Aristotle and many others thought to be the unchangeable *conditio humana* can now effectively be changed.

Adam Smith recognised this: He introduced systematically the difference between actions and conditions of actions in order to link competition and morality together (see Smith 1776/1982): Morality can be found on the level of the conditions, the *rules*. Only then can competition be made productive – by making the individuals'

13 Of course, distributive aspects have to be addressed here, too.

14 This mirrors James M. Buchanan's distinction between *choices within rules* and *choices of rules* (see Brennan and Buchanan 1985 and Buchanan 1975).

moves moral-free *in principle*. With the aid of rules, of adequate conditions of actions, competition is directed at realising advantages for all people involved. In this way, moral behaviour of individuals cannot be exploited by others, as rules are the same for everybody.

Thus, an ethics under modern conditions has to be conceptualised on two different levels, as an ethics of actions and as an ethics of conditions of actions, most notably of rules or institutions – of the order framework.[15] This latter is called order ethics.

It is most important not to let the two levels get in opposition to each other. We can expect ethical behaviour on the level of actions only if it is not punished on the level of institutions. The relevant model here is, again, the prisoners' dilemma: In their individual actions, the prisoners cannot compensate for the lack of a co-ordinating institution and thus end up with an inferior outcome.

But according to which criteria are rules evaluated and selected? This is especially important, insofar as we can no longer count on *common values* as a foundation for those criteria. In the age of globalisation, the pre-modern consensus on values has forever gone.

The only criterion left that does not rely on prior normativity in the form of common values and the like is the criterion of mutual advantages and benefits. This has been the core of social contract theory from Hobbes (1651/1991) and Spinoza to Rawls. Interests and advantages are seen as prior to morality: ethical norms are established in order to fulfil the citizens' interests, indeed, the interests of each single citizen. This is the idea of Kantian autonomy under modern conditions: people constrain themselves – autonomously, but collectively – by rules, for the sake of greater benefits. The condition for this is the consent of all others. They have to accept the rules as well and will do so only if they can themselves expect to profit from them.

To be sure: Advantages are not meant simply as monetary, or financial, or even material advantages. Conforming with modern economics, advantages are characterised as everything that people take to be advantages (for example also health, reputation, or the Aristotelian good life).

The problem of justification can now be seen as justification in terms of (mutual) advantages. But the problem of implementation remains: Why should people adhere to ethical norms if these norms require them – according, at least, to traditional Western ethics – to abstain from seeking advantages?

Order ethics addresses this question by making a difference between an individual action and a sequence of actions. People abstain from taking 'immoral' advantages only if adherence to ethical norms yields greater benefits over the planned *sequence* of actions than defection in the single case. Thus 'abstaining' is not abstaining in the long run, it is rather an investment in expectations of long-term benefits. By adhering to ethical norms, I become a reliable partner for interactions. The norms do indeed constrain my actions, but they simultaneously expand my options in *inter*actions.

---

15 This is not self-evident. The vast majority of modern ethics literature – from Habermas to Analytic Ethics – does either not recognise this distinction or does not regard it as central. See Homann 2002.

This implies that morality does *not* require us to *abandon* the calculation of our (individual) advantages. It does, however, ask us to *improve* our calculations. We should – first – calculate in the long run rather than in the short run, and we should – second – take into account the interests of our fellows, as we depend on their acceptance for reaching an optimal level of well-being, especially in a globalised world full of interdependence. In this globalised economy, we also have to recognise that it is in our interest to include the billions of people in a global social contract that are excluded today.

If only an ethics based on expectations of mutual advantages can solve the problem of implementation, likewise all conceptions of ethics must fail that do not justify ethical norms in terms of (mutual) advantages or benefits. Jürgen Habermas, for example, openly admits not to know how to deal with this problem. He states explicitly that there is no direct linkage from ethical insight to action ('von der diskursiv gewonnenen Einsicht gibt es keinen *gesicherten* Transfer zum Handeln', Habermas 1996, 51; his italics). This position is a consequence of an ethical conception among whose – implicit – premises still rank the conditions of pre-modern societies. And under these conditions such a conception would be fully workable. But it is not adequate for modern societies.

The problem of implementation can now be placed at the beginning of a conception of modern ethics, justified with reference to the conditions of modern societies. Under the conditions of pre-modern societies an ethics of temperance had evolved that posed simultaneously the problems of implementation and justification. The implementation of well justified norms or standards could then be regarded as unproblematic, because the social structures allowed for a direct face-to-face enforcement of norms. Pre-modern societies not only favoured an ethics of temperance, they also had the instrument of face-to-face-sanctions within their smaller and non-anonymous communities.[16] This instrument is no longer functional in modern anonymous societies (see Luhmann 1989), and so we have to face up to the problem of implementation right at the start of our ethical conception.

To put it in another way: Order ethics might also be characterised as an 'ethics of advantages and incentives' (see Homann 2002). We must count on the fact that all actors look for their (not just material) advantages, and we have to set the right incentives in order to deal with this quest for advantages. Order ethics therefore relies on the implementation of sanctions for enforcing *incentive-compatible rules*. In modern societies, rules and institutions, to a large extent, must fulfil the tasks that were, in pre-modern times, fulfilled by moral standards. This means that rules move into the centre of attention, supplying information about how others should behave and how they will – provided, the rules are sufficiently well enforced. Only if mutual expectations about behaviour develop and stabilise, prosperity and social progress can be hoped for.

16 See Meier 1998 for how this instrument was used in ancient Athens. Meier clearly shows that Athens was not a democratic state in the modern sense, mainly as public and political participation was required *and enforced* in quite other ways than today.

Incomplete Contracts

However, there is still room for an *ethics of actions*, even if morality is already implemented on the level of rules. My remarks were based on the assumption that interactions (and their outcomes) are *completely determined* by rules and contracts. This would mean that all elements of contracts were completely fixed in terms of quality, date, or content, for any possible circumstances in the future, and despite any difficulties in enforcing these contracts. This is, of course, quite an unrealistic assumption, especially under conditions of globalisation.

This is where the economic theory of *incomplete contracts* comes in. Incomplete contracts are contracts, in which one or several of the following conditions apply:[17]

(1) The obligations of each party resulting from the contract are not specified exactly, in view of changing conditions such as flexible prices of raw goods.

(2) It is difficult and/or expensive to determine whether the contracts have been fulfilled. External consultants have to be employed.

(3) The enforcement of the contract is very difficult, very expensive, or even downright impossible, due to insufficient systems of law in certain countries.

This means that especially those contracts are incomplete which extend over a longer time, or which deal with complex issues. But these are the very contracts most prominent in the globalised economy, such as work contracts, long-run cooperation contracts, insurance contracts, and so on. Within these contracts, there is much room for interpretation. Rights and obligations resulting from such contracts must be continuously redefined.

The main problem regarding incomplete contracts is the kind of interdependence resulting from such contracts. Even if partner A is honest and completely fulfils his part of the contract, he cannot be sure whether partner B does the same. B may point to gaps within the contract, he may propose differing interpretations, and it may even be too expensive to enforce A's claims.

So in the face of incomplete contracts, what can a rational actor do? Basically, he could just not sign such contracts for fear of being exploited. But is there any other way?

One answer would be to make incomplete contracts complete. The obligations of each party would have to be specified exactly, for every single possible case, and enforcement would have to be guaranteed. For several reasons, this is no sensible way to go. First, it is very expensive to make contracts 'watertight'. Second, listing all possible cases and all possible ways of exploitation might destroy the trust necessary for such contracts. Third, and probably most important: The incompleteness of contracts is not just a bad thing, but instead *necessary and productive*, as the partners can react quickly to new situations. We cannot know every possible situation in advance, and so we cannot know possible *chances and opportunities* in advance.

17 For incomplete contracts, see Hart 1987 and Hart and Holmström 1987.

Thus it would not be rational to try to rule out incompleteness, as it enables partners to seize opportunities when they are there.

A second way, and this is my proposal for dealing with incomplete contracts, is to rely on ethics. We need trust, fairness, integrity, and good will for carrying out contracts in the globalised economy. If contracts are becoming increasingly incomplete, we need both an ethics for the interior relations of the company (workers and management) as well as an ethics for the exterior relations to customers, banks, suppliers, and the public. It is rational for a company to *invest* in these ethical categories, as it contributes to the company's success.

So this could be regarded as the justification for an *ethics of actions*: If rules (in the sense of *formal* rules, see under 'Order Ethics') are lacking or if they are incomplete – for good reasons! – then substitutes for formal rules can be provided by actors (in this case, companies) committing themselves to certain policies, to mechanisms of trust and fairness, for example. This commitment has to be made credible through organisational measures and must be signalled to others. In this way, actors create by themselves the very reliability that would normally be expected from formal rules. They create a *reputation*, which especially under conditions of globalisation is a necessary prerequisite for success in the long run.

So the idea here is that we may now systematically *combine* order ethics and an ethics of actions in the following way: The general problem is how to create reliability in the globalised economy. Reliability can be provided in two ways: First, by way of *collective self-constraint* (formal rules and legal enforcement), and second, by way of *individual self-constraint* of a company committing themselves to specific values or ethical standards of behaviour. This commitment must be signalled, and thus becomes an asset for the company. In this way, complete formal contracts and rules, with guaranteed enforcement, on the one hand, and incomplete contracts, with enforcement by soft factors like ethics and reputation, on the other hand, are both important. They depend on each other, but to some extent they can also be substituted by each other. At the moment, we probably face a situation in which we gradually shift to a greater role of incomplete contracts.

From a philosophical viewpoint, an important problem now remains: Do companies not implement ethics by just acting from self-interest, from 'profit maximisation'? Yes, they do, but, as Adam Smith (1776/1982) already observed, the immediate motive of self-interest does not preclude anything for the ethical judgement. Yes, companies act ethically, for example by not seizing advantages in singular cases, *from self-interest*. Thus the pursuit of advantages remains their main motive. So what does this have to do with ethics? I will turn to this question now.

Is Order Ethics Compatible with the (Western) Tradition of Ethics?

As I have remarked, the conception laid out here makes changes in ethical categories necessary. Instead of calling for temperance and sacrificing, ethics should promote investing. Instead of demanding redistribution, it should favour exchange. Self-interest should not be 'domesticated', but unleashed. What does this have to do with ethics?

Looking back at the (Western) ethical tradition, neither the Golden Rule, which has sometimes been regarded as the common core of all conceptions of ethics across cultures, nor Kant's categorical imperative deny the legitimacy of the individual pursuit of advantages. They indeed take it for granted, and then aim at constraining it. The new element within the conception of institutional ethics advocated here is just that these constraints are themselves justified by the expectation of greater benefits across a sequence of actions.

Many ethical conceptions do not recognise this, but rather derive the constraints from some form of 'higher' morality, from 'reason' or from the 'human condition'. The most prominent one of these, Kantian ethics, is commonly seen as being directly opposed to an ethics based on the pursuit of individual advantages. But some elements of Kant's original conception are commonly overlooked. In his *Groundwork of the Metaphysics of Morals*, Kant states: ' … denn dieses Sollen ist eigentlich ein Wollen' ('… for this properly an "I ought" is properly an "I would"', Kant 1785/1974: BA 102). Even for Kant, the core of normativity is made of 'wants', of interests, namely the interests of perfectly rational beings. We – as beings that are not perfectly rational, but that are also affected by 'springs' ('Triebfedern') of a different kind – we may sometimes get astray. But this 'getting astray' can in my view only be interpreted as the impossibility for people to escape from social dilemma situations. In these situations, individual rationality indeed leads us to act against our own interests. Therefore, we have to establish rules for overcoming these situations. But these rules are themselves legitimated by our (long-term) interests.

Getting back to Kant: I maintain that, for Kant, interests are the legitimate basis of norms. But these interests must pass two filters – according to the categorical imperative: (a) They have to be pursued within a *long-run* perspective (based on a 'maxim' (Maxime), not on a single opinion), and (b) we have to take into account the vital interests of others, as we need their (at least implicit) agreement or toleration (maxim as a basis for a general law ('Maxime des Willes zugleich als Prinzip einer allgemeinen Gesetzgebung'). So even for Kant, ethics does not require us to abstain from seeking advantages, but rather to improve our calculation of advantages by taking a long-run rather than a short-run perspective and by taking a social or cooperative rather than individual view. Again: Abstaining is not really 'abstaining', but investment in the stability and further development of the social order.

Conclusion

This chapter began by discussing the problem of moral surpluses with a particular focus on Habermas's discourse ethics. I have contrasted discourse ethics with the conception of order ethics, which relies on a two-dimensional normativity of actions and rules. A modern society that wants to profit from deep specialisation and competition has to switch to a system of governance by rules. With the use of pre-modern governance mechanisms, the benefits of modern societies cannot be appropriated. Within this framework, an ethics of actions fits in according to the theory of incomplete contracts. Incomplete contracts leave room for ethical behaviour of individuals and companies. Finally, the argument has been made that pursuing self-interest is compatible with important (if not all) traditions of ethics.

An order ethics requires actors only to (a) comply with the rules, and (b) engage – from their own interest – in the further development of these rules in mutually benefiting ways. Such further development can only come into effect if the individuals affected agree to it. In view of PD situations, it is systematically not enforceable against the wishes of these individuals.

However, there is a role for what I would like to call *heuristics*. These heuristics are values and ideas from philosophical, religious, scientific, literary, artistic or other traditions. They can point the actors in new directions where new gains of cooperation may be found. But they are conceived here in a very different way than the moral surpluses. Most important, they do not erode in PD situations. By contrast, the moral surplus that Habermas argues for is conceptualised *in opposition to* interests, advantages or incentives.

In an order ethics, moral surpluses might be made productive. They might be seen as part of an heuristics which asks anyone to calculate his/her advantage better in a better, more sophisticated way: In short, this heuristics calls for *investing*. Eventually, this could turn out to be the heuristics not only of occidental, but of many traditions of ethics.

References

Aaken, A. van, List, C. and Luetge, C. (eds) (2004), *Deliberation and Decision: Economics, Constitutional Theory, and Deliberative Democracy* (Aldershot: Ashgate Publishing).

Axelrod, R. (1984), *The Evolution of Cooperation* (New York: Basic Books).

Bewley, T.F. (ed.) (1987), *Advances in Economic Theory* (Cambridge: Cambridge University Press).

Binmore, K. (1994), *Game Theory and the Social Contract. Vol. 1: Playing Fair* (Cambridge, Mass.: MIT Press).

—— (1998), *Game Theory and the Social Contract. Vol. 2: Just Playing* (Cambridge, Mass.: MIT Press).

Brennan, G. and Buchanan, J.M. (1985), *The Reason of Rules: Constitutional Political Economy* (Cambridge: Cambridge University Press).

Buchanan, J.M. (1975), *The Limits of Liberty: Between Anarchy and Leviathan* (Chicago: University of Chicago Press).

Eatwell, J. et al. (eds) (1987), *The New Palgrave: A Dictionary of Economics* (London and New York: Macmillan and Stockton).

Foot, P. (1978), *Virtues and Vices* (Oxford: Blackwell).

Gauthier, D. (1986), *Morals by Agreement* (Oxford: Clarendon).

Habermas, J. (1981), *Theorie des kommunikativen Handelns*, 2 vols. (Frankfurt: Suhrkamp), Engl. Trans. (1984), *Theory of Communicative Action* (Boston: Beacon).

—— (1983/1999), 'Diskursethik: Notizen zu einem Begründungsprogramm', in *Moralbewußtsein und kommunikatives Handeln* (Frankfurt: Suhrkamp), pp. 53–125.

— (1991), *Erläuterungen zur Diskursethik* (Frankfurt: Suhrkamp).

— (1992), *Faktizität und Geltung: Beiträge zur Diskurstheorie des Rechts und des demokratischen Rechtsstaats* (Frankfurt: Suhrkamp), Engl. Trans. (1996), *Between Facts and Norms: Contributions to a Discourse Theory of Law and Democracy* (Cambridge, Mass: MIT Press).

— (1996), *Die Einbeziehung des Anderen: Studien zur politischen Theorie* (Frankfurt: Suhrkamp), Engl. Trans. Cronin, C. and De Greiff, P. (eds) (1998), *The Inclusion of the Other: Studies in Political Theory* (Cambridge, Mass: MIT Press).

Hart, O.D. (1987), 'Incomplete Contracts', in Eatwell, J. et al. (eds), Vol. 2, pp. 752–9.

Hart, O.D. and Holmström, B.R. (1987), 'The Theory of Contracts', in Bewley, T.F. (ed.), Ch. 3.

Hobbes, T. (1651/1991), *Leviathan*, edited by Tuck, R. (Cambridge: Cambridge University Press).

Homann, K. (2002), *Vorteile und Anreize: Zur Grundlegung einer Ethik der Zukunft*, edited by Luetge, C. (Tübingen: Mohr Siebeck).

Homann, K. and Luetge, C. (2004), *Einführung in die Wirtschaftsethik* (Münster: LIT).

Jones, E.L. (1981), *The European Miracle: Environments, Economies, and Geopolitics in the History of Europe and Asia* (Cambridge: Cambridge University Press).

Kant, I. (1785/1974), *Grundlegung zur Metaphysik der Sitten* (Frankfurt: Suhrkamp). Engl., *Groundwork of the Metaphysics of Morals*.

Luetge, C. (2005), 'Economics Ethics, Business Ethics, and the Idea of Mutual Advantages', *Business Ethics: A European Review* 14:2, 108–18.

— (2007), *Was hält eine Gesellschaft zusammen? Ethik im Zeitalter der Globalisierung* (Tübingen: Mohr Siebeck).

Luhmann, N. (1989), 'Ethik als Reflexionstheorie der Moral', in *Gesellschaftsstruktur und Semantik*, Vol. 3 (Frankfurt: Suhrkamp), pp. 358–447.

— (1997), *Die Gesellschaft der Gesellschaft*, 2 vols. (Frankfurt: Suhrkamp).

Meier, C. (1998), *Athens: A Portrait of the City in its Golden Age* (New York: Metropolitan).

North, D.C. (1990), *Institutions, Institutional Change and Economic Performance* (Cambridge: Cambridge University Press).

Rawls, J. (1971), *A Theory of Justice* (Cambridge, Mass.: Harvard University Press).

— (1993), *Political Liberalism* (New York: Columbia University Press).

Smith, A. (1776/1982), *An Inquiry into the Nature and Causes of the Wealth of Nations* (Harmondsworth: Penguin).

Index

Wherever possible in the case of topics with many references, these have either been divided into sub-topics or the most significant discussions of the topic are indicated by page numbers in bold

For Product Safety Concerns and Information please contact our EU
representative GPSR@taylorandfrancis.com
Taylor & Francis Verlag GmbH, Kaufingerstraße 24, 80331 München, Germany

www.ingramcontent.com/pod-product-compliance
Ingram Content Group UK Ltd.
Pitfield, Milton Keynes, MK11 3LW, UK
UKHW022126190926
475702UK00013B/1679
* 9 7 8 1 1 3 8 2 6 6 2 9 2 *